A Regional Study of Yorkshire Schools 1500-1820

Front Cover:

Batley Church and Grammar School, 1830.

A REGIONAL STUDY OF YORKSHIRE SCHOOLS 1500-1820

John Roach

Mellen Studies in Education
Volume 39

The Edwin Mellen Press
Lewiston•Queenston•Lampeter

Library of Congress Cataloging-in-Publication Data

Roach, John, 1920-
  A regional study of Yorkshire schools 1500-1820 / John Roach.
    p. cm. -- (Mellen studies in education ; v. 39)
  Includes bibliographical references (p.   ) and index.
  ISBN 0-7734-8250-4
  1. Education--England--Yorkshire--History.   I. Title.
  II. Series.
  LA638.Y6R6   1998
  371' .0009428' 1--dc21   98-30871
                                                 CIP

This is volume 39 in the continuing series
Mellen Studies in Education
Volume 39 ISBN 0-7734-8250-4✓
MSE Series ISBN 0-88946-935-0

A CIP catalog record for this book is available from the British Library.

Edited and typeset by Wordwise Edit, Hope, Derbyshire.

All rights reserved. For information contact

<table>
<tr><td>The Edwin Mellen Press
Box 450
Lewiston, New York
USA 14092-0450</td><td>The Edwin Mellen Press
Box 67
Queenston, Ontario
CANADA L0S 1L0</td></tr>
</table>

The Edwin Mellen Press, Ltd.
Lampeter, Ceredigion, Wales
UNITED KINGDOM SA48 8LT

Printed in the United States of America

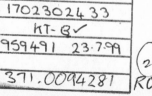

To the historians and antiquaries of Yorkshire without whose labours this book could not have been written

Contents

Acknowledgments

Permission to make use of manuscript material has been given by:

Professor D.A. Cressy, Dr C.J. Kitching, Dr J.E. Stephens (PhD theses)

Rev. Peter Facer (MA thesis)

Borthwick Institute of Historical Research, University of York

President and Fellows of Corpus Christi College, Oxford

Sheffield Archives (Director of Leisure Services and Head
   of Libraries, City of Sheffield and S.W. Fraser Esq.)

Society for Promoting Christian Knowledge, London

West Yorkshire Archive Service, Leeds

Yorkshire Archaeological Society, Leeds

York Minster Library and Archives (Dean and Chapter of York)

Preface

Professor John Roach has made a major contribution to our understanding of the history of English education. He is particularly well known for his two volumes, *A History of Secondary Education in England 1800–1870* (1986) and *Secondary Education in England 1870–1902* (1991). He and others have established the general outlines of the subject at a national level.

At the local level, thousands of histories of individual schools have been published, often to celebrate a centenary or some other event, but very few historians have attempted to integrate this material in a meaningful way. In other branches of history the approach of the local and regional historian now has a respectable pedigree. The study of agricultural history, industrial history, vernacular architecture and even of political history has been enriched enormously by detailed enquiries that often challenge conclusions arrived at through the 'broad brush' approach. The new national histories that have had to be written are much fuller than their predecessors and represent more accurately the diverse experience of different parts of the country. National histories provide the broad framework, local and regional histories deal with the reality on the ground.

The study of the history of education will surely benefit from a comparative approach whereby the subject is viewed from a variety of regional standpoints. This pioneering book has little comparative material to draw upon from other parts of England, but it suggests areas where the experiences of other regions might resemble that of Yorkshire and others where they might differ. Even within a single county the educational opportunities that were available differed from one local landscape and economy to another. The historic county of Yorkshire has districts as different in physical appearance and the nature of the available work as Swaledale and Holderness. Of course, all the various districts of England responded to ideas and fashions that spread throughout the country and to parliamentary decisions, but they did not always respond in the same way or at the same pace. Some of the best ideas started not in the capital but in the provinces. The regional approach brings out the rich variety of English experience and also highlights the contribution of particular initiatives, as at Giggleswick or Acaster Selby.

This history of Yorkshire schools over more than three centuries will appeal to readers with an interest in the county, but it has a wider purpose in advocating an approach that, hopefully, others will follow elsewhere. In so doing, they will deepen our understanding of the educational history of the entire country.

David Hey

Professor of Local and Family History, The University of Sheffield

Foreword

This study of Yorkshire schools grew out of my earlier work on secondary education in the 19th century which produced two books, published in 1986 and 1991. In writing these I did a good deal of research in local libraries and archive collections in many parts of the country, which introduced me to the great wealth of information on schools and schooling which is available in such sources and which has been little used by scholars. During the last few years I have also studied various aspects of the history of Sheffield, and from these varied sources, I gained a growing conviction that a regional approach, combining both local history and the history of education, offered an important area of investigation. A few scholars have attempted something of the sort, for example Margaret Bryant in *The London Experience of Secondary Education* (1986). However there is still much to do, and, once the idea had germinated in my mind, the county of Yorkshire, with its historic distinctiveness, its internal variety and contrasts and its rich collection of libraries and archives, offered itself as an obvious candidate for such treatment, particularly since I live in the county and have the resources at hand for the work.

When I began in 1991, I was myself starting on a voyage of discovery with not very much idea what I was likely to find on the way. I had to learn a great deal before I could make effective progress, and it was quite a long time before the final shape of the book emerged in my mind. I was clear from the beginning that I wanted to start around 1500, but my original intention had been to carry the story down to the Education Act of 1902 and the emergence of a coherent state system of education. I soon decided that it would not be possible to include the 19th century partly because this would have made the book very lengthy, but even more so because a real break appeared around 1820–30 when the historical focus changed radically. I have tried in the following pages to explain my reasons for coming to this judgment. Put very simply, my argument would be that after about 1830 the dominant themes are national whereas before that date they had been primarily local and regional. Consequently the regional approach is much less valuable for the later period.

I have concentrated in this book on schools and schooling rather than on the wider cultural and intellectual background, though large formal institutions play a much smaller part in the story than they would do in more recent times. Most schools were small and many teachers taught outside them. I have tried to say something about schools of many different types and I have given much attention to the activities of the various religious bodies which profoundly influenced the whole story. I have not attempted any treatment of higher education beyond a few references to scholarships and exhibitions available to Yorkshire boys at Oxford and Cambridge. I have tried to provide some vignettes of individual people and to say something about the wider aspects of learning and culture even though my primary concern is with institutions. Information can be found about individuals of widely differing social ranks, though inevitably more is known about the aristocracy and gentry than about their more humble contemporaries, and much more about men than about women. Finally it is important to stress that schools and schoolmasters existed in particular communities, and the story broadens out into wider themes of local history. To put education firmly into its local context has ranked high among my objectives.

I have to thank in particular Professor David Hey, who made valuable comments on my first draft and who has written a preface, as well as Dr Clyde Binfield and Professor Richard Aldrich. I have had much help from many libraries, in particular those of the universities of Sheffield and of Cambridge. A list of those institutions and individuals who have given permission for the use of manuscript material is to be found on page vii. To all of them I offer my sincere gratitude.

John Roach

List of abbreviations

ALB	Abstract Letter Books, Society for Promoting Christian Knowledge
AR	Butler, L.A.S. (ed.), 1986/1990. *The Archdeaconry of Richmond in the eighteenth century. Bishop Gastrell's 'Notitia', The Yorkshire Parishes 1714–25*
BIY	Borthwick Institute of Historical Research, University of York
EYS	Leach, A.F., 1898, 1903. *Early Yorkshire Schools*, vols I, II
ER	East Riding of Yorkshire
GBM	General Board Minutes, Society for Promoting Christian Knowledge
Herring Returns	Ollard, S.L. and Walker, P.C., 1927–31. *Archbishop Herring's Visitation Returns*, 5 vols
LM	*Leeds Mercury*
Nom SM	Schoolmasters' Nominations, Borthwick Institute of Historical Research, University of York
NR	North Riding of Yorkshire
par.	parish
PP	*Parliamentary Papers*

SA	Sheffield Archives
SPCK	Society for Promoting Christian Knowledge
VCH	*Victoria County History*
WR	West Riding of Yorkshire
WYAS	West Yorkshire Archive Service, Leeds
YML	York Minster Library
YAS	Yorkshire Archaeological Society

Part One

The sixteenth and seventeenth centuries

CHAPTER 1

The Schools before 1540

Until the 19th century much of English history was regional history. Though central
power was strong, men and women lived in communities very much driven by their
local concerns which might reflect ideas rather different from those coming out of
London. England has enjoyed for centuries, perhaps as a reflection of this situation,
a strong tradition of local history, concentrating on the church and the parish, the
borough and the county. In recent years there has been a recrudescence of interest
in such studies, exemplified by a series like *A Regional History of England*, edited
by Barry Cunliffe and David Hey, which Longman began to publish in the mid-80s.
Some parts of the country fall much more naturally into a 'regional' pattern than
others, and this difficulty can clearly be seen in some of the volumes of the Regional
History series which have already been published. Yorkshire, the largest of the
ancient English counties, has always formed a strong natural unit. Though its
different sections differ a good deal from one another, as is shown by the division
into three ridings, all the parts share a strong common identity of tradition, speech
and legend. York has always been the county capital and the ecclesiastical centre,
not only of the diocese but of the whole northern province. Yorkshiremen have
always considered themselves to be a slightly superior race, entitled to look down
on the lesser breeds without; for example, no one, until very recent times, could
play cricket for the county who had not been born within its bounds.

The regional idea has not been much applied to the history of education. In that field studies have been either national, covering periods of time or selected themes, or specifically local in the histories of individual schools. Hundreds of such histories exist, and more are added every year as some particular foundation reaches a special landmark – a centenary, the celebration of four hundred years, or whatever it may be. Such works are always the fruit of piety in the proper sense of that word, and they vary in value enormously as pieces of historical writing. After saying that, it is also necessary to say that without such books more extensive work at the local level would be much more difficult. Between such school histories and the national studies there is a broad gap, and there is a strong case for bridging this by regional studies of education, especially in those parts of the country where the idea of the region has a natural validity. It has already been argued that Englishmen before the 19th century lived in highly localized communities, a fact which has been recognized in many studies both of economic and of political history. Similar forces can be seen at work in the growth of the schools. If this growth is examined on a regional basis, it becomes possible to inter-relate national movements with local conditions so that each throws light upon the other, and in so doing enriches our understanding of both.

It has already been claimed that Yorkshire forms a strong candidate for such a regional treatment. Though the county is large and diverse, it has a strong underlying unity going back to Anglo-Scandinavian times. On the other hand, its very size and complexity bring up general issues and social differences which might not show themselves so clearly against a smaller canvas. If the general argument for such a study be accepted, the next question to consider is how it should be undertaken. The period of time selected here is the three centuries between 1500 and 1815/20. By the first date a basic pattern of school provision was coming into existence. By the second the county was on the verge of major political and social changes which produced a new pattern of education.

Within this wide time-span of three hundred years the treatment must be selective if the whole study is not to become of inordinate length. What will be attempted here is a concentration on certain themes rather than a comprehensive coverage of facts and events. Some of these themes, like the pressures to achieve political and religious uniformity under the Tudors and early Stuarts, are national in scope, but in the Yorkshire example there were stronger Recusant and Puritan pressures than in some other parts of England. There was throughout the whole country a keen interest in founding schools in the Elizabethan and early Stuart period, but it seems that in Yorkshire local initiatives and local pressures to cooperate for pious and charitable ends were particularly strong. When after 1660 Anglican orthodoxy gradually broke down and the control of the Established Church over education was slowly relaxed, Yorkshire saw important initiatives by both Dissenters and Roman Catholics. In other ways, of course, like the decline of the grammar schools and the development of education of a more 'modern' type, developments in Yorkshire mirror those in England as a whole.

Recent historians like W.K. Jordan, Joan Simon and Lawrence Stone argued that there was an educational revolution in Elizabethan and Jacobean England. While this was certainly a period when many schools were founded and when large endowments were devoted to education, it is also true that many schools had been founded in the Middle Ages. A.F. Leach wrote long ago: 'It may be said broadly that wherever there was a cluster of houses which could be dignified with the name of town, there was a grammar school in the midst of it'.[1] Leach's conclusions have been broadly supported by contemporary scholars like Nicholas Orme, for the country in general, and Jo Ann Hoeppner Moran, writing on the pre-Reformation diocese of York.[2] Medieval schools and teachers seem much more important in the 1990s than they did 20 years ago when attention was concentrated very much on post-Reformation developments. Orme argues that the most important of the medieval schools were both public and secular – that is, that they were open to all who could afford to attend them, and that their teachers and pupils were secular

5

priests and laypeople and not members of religious orders.[3] Such schools fell into two groups

> Some were elementary in character and taught 'reading' (the Latin alphabet and the ability to recognise Latin words) and 'song' (the reading and singing of the ecclesiastical psalms, hymns and antiphons). Others were grammar schools and taught, often alongside the elementary subjects, the ability to understand the Latin language, to speak and write it fluently in prose and in verse, and to read some of its easier authors.[4]

Both the teachers themselves and the subjects which they taught will be considered in a later part of this study. In the later Middle Ages their work became centred to an increasing extent in formalized and endowed institutions, but it is a mistake to think of medieval education entirely or primarily in such terms. Many schools were ephemeral; the fact that a school can be identified in a town or village at a certain date, and that there is a similar reference at a later date does not necessarily imply that the institutions existed continuously from one date to the other. Much depended on the presence or absence of an individual teacher at a particular time, and this must have been especially the case in the more remote communities and in the teaching of the elementary subjects. There is an interesting Yorkshire example of this in the case of that major educational benefactor, Archbishop Thomas Rotherham, who described in his will that he had laid the foundation of his college on 12 March 1483 in his birthplace. When he was a boy, the archbishop says, a grammar master had come to the town of Rotherham

> coming I know not by what luck, but I believe he came by the grace of God, taught me and other youth, whence others with me came to greater things.

The master was a private tutor or he kept a private school apparently in the house of Rotherham's father.[5]

6

This reference to the future archbishop's schooling is explicit, but in many cases it is very difficult to track down references to such individual teachers, and it is a reasonable guess, particularly in the case of the elementary subjects, that a good deal more was being offered than it is now possible to document. J.A.H. Moran, in her study of York diocese, makes extensive use of evidence from wills which often mention small bequests to children who sing or read lessons at funerals or who are named simply as 'scholars' or 'boy-clerks'. She argues that such references are evidence that an education in reading or song was available at the time in the place named, though she considers that these are 'tentative descriptions' only.[6] Once again the evidence can be handled in too hard and definite a fashion, and references to children who can read or sing does not mean that they learned those skills in schools in the formalized modern sense of that word. But someone must have taught them, and though in some cases they may have learned their lessons within the family circle, in many others they will have been taught by a professional teacher. This evidence from wills is interesting too because it throws some light on elementary education, a topic far more difficult to investigate that the studies of the grammar school.

There was a close connection between medieval education and religion, and a large number of teachers were priests or clerics of some kind and, in the case of the elementary schools, parish clerks. Yet the medieval church interfered very little with the schools, and the close control later exercised by both church and state was a product of the Reformation and of the need for an embattled government to control the agencies – school, press, pulpit – through which opinion was formed. One important religious institution of the later medieval world which had a particularly close connection with education was the chantry, an endowment for a priest or priests to say masses for the souls of the founder, his family, and often for more general purposes like the welfare of the king and the royal family.[7] Chantries existed in large numbers throughout the country, they were comparatively inexpensive to set up, and they made a strong appeal to the gentry, to the wealthier clergy and to the prosperous townspeople of the day. The chantry priests, once they had said their daily masses, often had time on their hands, and were glad to earn a little additional money to supplement their salaries. Many of them acted as assistant curates in the parishes. Some were required by their foundation deeds to teach, but many more made a personal choice to do this and devoted to this work time they had to spare after they had fulfilled their other duties. However, many chantry priests never taught at all, and it is a mistake to think that a chantry foundation necessarily involved a school as part of its functions.

Up to 1440 the number of new chantry schools was small, but it grew towards the end of the century.[8] During that century the foundation of endowed schools became common, and there was a growing interest in education generally. Some of those involved in the movement were clerics like Thomas Rotherham, who has already been mentioned, but an increasing share was being taken by the gentry and the richer townspeople. Not only did these people make bequests; they took a share in the management of them, and they increasingly sent their own sons to the grammar schools. The pressure to establish more schools had built up throughout England at least a generation before the Reformation era of Henry VIII and Edward VI, and the 'educational revolution' of Elizabethan and Jacobean England had important earlier antecedents.

At all times the development of education has been deeply influenced by the general course of historical events. In the 14th century, Yorkshire, like the rest of England, had suffered from natural disasters and from plague and pestilence. The years 1315–22, according to David Hey, 'witnessed a series of harvest failures and livestock disasters almost without parallel in the history of English agriculture'.[9] The Black Death reached the county in spring 1349, and similar infections returned on later occasions. As a result the population fell. This meant, on the one hand, that more land became available and that many people were better off. On the other hand, many villages were deserted by their inhabitants, and in the 15th century towns like York and Hull, Beverley and Ripon decayed. In the mid 16th century the population of York was one third less than it had been at its early 15th century peak. However the picture is not entirely gloomy, for it was at this time that the cloth industry developed in the Pennine foothills, and that there was a steady growth of industry and wealth in the district stretching from Wakefield and Leeds to Halifax and Bradford. In 1515 Yorkshire stood twelfth among English counties in the amount of tax paid and in 1524–5 eleventh.[10]

In the county as a whole the great families like the Percies, the Nevilles and the Cliffords long retained their power, providing a tradition of local independence which counterbalanced the authority of central government in London. There had been active fighting in Yorkshire during the Wars of the Roses, and the county remained restive and turbulent under Tudor rule. The Pilgrimage of Grace of 1535–7 elicited widespread support, some of it fuelled by religious, some by economic, grievances. In 1569–70 the North Riding was affected by the rising of the Northern Earls, though this gained less popular support than the Pilgrimage of Grace had done. After the rebellion of the earls had been suppressed there was no more open trouble, but Roman Catholicism was strong in the north, and Elizabeth and her ministers were always zealous to enforce uniformity in church and state. It should be remembered that 20 Roman Catholics were martyred at York between 1582 and 1589.[11]

Despite this rather turbulent religious and political background there was a steady growth in the number of schools in 15th and early 16th century Yorkshire, and the county seems to have kept abreast of what was happening in other and more economically favoured parts of the country. One particular feature of the story is the way in which in many places schools came into existence because a number of local people, many of them individually not rich, worked together to set them up. Better schooling was, so to speak, a favoured community enterprise.

No precise figures can be given for the number of schools in Yorkshire at the time of the Reformation, but several scholars have made estimates which give a fairly clear general picture. A.F. Leach in 1896 printed a chronological list of

9

schools mentioned in the chantry certificates and the continuance/re-foundation warrants (c. 1548–50). There are 33 Yorkshire schools, all founded before 1548, in this list, and 5 of them are noted as elementary.[12] In 1956 P.J. Wallis and W.E. Tate printed a register of old Yorkshire grammar schools. [13] This is specifically a list of grammar schools, though it is not confined to endowed schools, and the authors point out that the status of a school might change from time to time. They are careful too to warn against a 'hasty and uncritical simple totalling of the entries in the various columns'. If that caution be remembered, their lists show a total, excluding schools in the city of York, of 45 schools (West Riding 28, North Riding 9, East Riding 8) mentioned before 1545. The figures form at least what engineers call an 'order of magnitude', though they do not provide a precise statistic.

The increased attention given by scholars in recent years to medieval education has produced further such estimates. Nicholas Orme (1973) gave a 'list of medieval English schools 1066–1530'.[14] Of those listed 36 were in Yorkshire (excluding the city of York), that is 18 in the West Riding, 10 in the North and 8 in the East Ridings. Most of these are grammar schools, though there are song and reading schools listed as well. Orme himself says that he has perhaps erred on the side of caution, and H.M. Jewell (1982) and J.A.H. Moran (1985) have given considerably larger totals. In both cases York city is again excluded. Jewell lists 'places (in the north of England) offering secular educational facilities before 1550'.[15] In 59 Yorkshire examples grammar schools are noted (West Riding 39, North Riding 10, East Riding 10), and in 9 of these writing, song and reading schools are mentioned as well. In addition there are ten places where the type of school is unspecified or is given as a song or reading school. Moran's figures go up to 1548 and like Jewell's are based on places.[16] 68 refer to definitely established schools of all types (West Riding 39, North Riding 17, East Riding 12). 94 are largely references in wills to scholars who read or sing (West Riding 23, North Riding 34, East Riding 37). These certainly suggest some kind of education but not necessarily the existence of an organized or continuing school. It must be

10

emphasized that this division into two groups is my own interpretation of the evidence provided by Moran, but this seems a logical division to make, and it can to some extent be checked against Orme's figures for established schools. In York the minster grammar school (St Peter's) probably went back to the 8th century. There was also a grammar school connected with St Leonard's Hospital until it was dissolved in 1539, and there were reading and song schools in several parishes. Some boys were housed and educated by the cathedral dignitaries and the city clergy,[17] though no attempt is made here to examine private education of this kind.

Moran's research relates to the diocese of York which, until the 19th century, included Nottinghamshire, and, until the creation of the diocese of Chester in 1541, north Lancashire and part of Westmorland, as well as the geographical county of Yorkshire. However the numbers of schools, estimated from Moran's lists, relate to the county only. She argues that, though the number of grammar schools increased in the late 15th/early 16th centuries, there was a particular increase in the number of elementary schools.

> By 1500 the elementary institutions were three times more numerous than the grammar schools, and even with the development of grammar education after 1500 the elementary schools still outnumbered grammar institutions by nearly two to one in 1548.[18]

She identified, in the period up to 1548, 161 reading schools as confirmed or probable and 13 as possible, together with 84 song schools. These are figures for the whole diocese and should be compared with the estimates already made on the basis of her material for the county itself. Within such a large area the distribution of schools was uneven. There was a large group on the line between Doncaster and York and in the southern parts of the West Riding. In the northern and western parts of the North Riding, where population was scant, there were very few.[19]

In this kind of discussion it is impossible to be precise, but the evidence is sufficient to suggest that schools – alongside more informal methods of learning –

were widely available throughout Yorkshire before the Reformation took place. The grammar schools are simple to identify because so many of them have left a continuing record, but the comparatively widespread provision of elementary education is surprising and indeed unexpected, since it was rarely enshrined in institutional forms and is difficult to trace. The number of clergy in the diocese increased after 1460, a change which may have been connected with the better provision of schools, while in turn the growing number of clerics meant that teachers became easier to obtain. It has already been argued that the number of educated laymen grew, but this did not affect the primacy of the clergy in the skills of learning and literacy in the years before the Reformation. Moran estimates that in 1530 there was a lay literacy rate in northern England of 13% to 14%.[20] It should be noted that almost all the founders of pre-Reformation schools in Yorkshire were clerics. The most scholarly Yorkshire layman of that time, Roger Ascham, author of *The Scholemaster*, born in 1515/16 at Kirby Wiske, near Northallerton in the North Riding, was educated out of the county in the household of Sir Humphrey Wingfield in Suffolk until he went up to St John's College, Cambridge, in 1530.[21]

Lay influences were growing in strength, but in Yorkshire change seems to have taken place very slowly. One sign of the strength of traditional ideas – and a feature closely linked with education – is the enduring popularity of chantry foundations, which shows the strength of the belief in purgatory and in the value of intercessory masses for the dead. In the West Riding there were almost ten times as many intercessory institutions per parish as in Suffolk; nearly 60% of parishes contained an institution capable of supporting a priest. Over the whole county with 490 parishes 223 of them, or 45.5%, contained such institutions.[22] Many of the cantarists were not well educated enough to be able to teach very much, and it has already been argued that the closeness of the connection between chantries and schools can be exaggerated. Nevertheless it is important to note that chantries were so numerous in Yorkshire. Their dissolution in 1548 must have left an enormous gap in the religious and social life of many, if not most, of the communities in the county. And the educational effect of the changes must not be forgotten.

Much of our information about the most ancient schools in the county still derives from the work of A.F. Leach,[23] though he has been criticized for attempting to push the history of schools too far back and for neglecting the non-classical schools.[24] At York, as we have seen, the minster school was one of the most ancient in England, and a number of other schools are recorded as well. There is a reference, for example, to the appointment of a master of the Minster Song School in 1531.[25] It has been suggested in the case of another of the secular cathedrals (Exeter) that the cathedral was an important 'educational agency' which provided local boys with 'educational amenities and opportunities: maintenance, schooling, practice in the liturgy and the use of books',[26] and this may have been true of York as well. St Mary's Abbey, until it was dissolved in 1539, had kept a boarding house for 50 scholars attending the minster school, 30 of them maintained by the convent and 20 supported from the left-overs from the common table. The loss of this large group of boys must have damaged the minster school.[27]

There were other schools in the county which at the Reformation already had a long history, such as Beverley, Pontefract, and the two schools, Howden and Northallerton, situated in peculiars of the see of Durham and under the authority of the prior of that cathedral. At Ripon, like Beverley a kind of sub-cathedral of the great diocese of York, there are references to the schoolmaster in the 14th and 15th centuries, and 'one scolemaster of gramer' is recorded when the collegiate body was dissolved under Edward VI.[28] In the West Riding a school is mentioned at Doncaster in the 14th century,[29] and at Penistone Thomas Clarel, lord of Penistone, granted a piece of land in 1392 which became the site of the school.[30] The Commissioners of Charitable Uses referred to it in 1604 as an ancient foundation.[31] In the North Riding there are references to a school at Richmond in both the 14th and the 15th centuries.[32]

Sometimes a school was patronized by the leading members of an urban community because it provided services like instruction in Latin which such a community needed. The best example of such a development in Yorkshire is at Hull where in the 15th century the school was maintained by the mayor and aldermen, while the schoolmaster largely supported himself by the fees which he charged. In 1479 John Alcock, bishop of Worcester and later of Ely and himself a Hull man, founded a chantry in Holy Trinity Church, the main duty of the chantry priest being, it seems, in addition to saying his masses, to teach the boys in the existing grammar school. Alcock's endowment provided both an income for the master and free education for the pupils, while the school kept its close connections with the town government through all the upheavals of the Reformation and beyond. The school's modern historian writes

> In sum, the evidence shows that the school the chantry priest had to teach
> was the school previously maintained by the town, that it continued in the
> old building, and eventually after the Bishop's death came under the
> town's patronage, but was made free and financially independent with an
> existence permanently guaranteed by an endowment.[33]

It should also be noted that Alcock's schoolmaster was to pay 40 shillings a year to the parish clerk ' to teach children to sing', which was possibly an attempt to endow an already existing song school.[34]

All the schools which have already been mentioned had come into existence to serve the needs of their own communities in ways and at times which to us are unknown. No one can be certain that they enjoyed a continuous life in the intervals between mentions in the records. With Bishop Alcock, who died in 1500, we reach the line of founders who set up and endowed schools, many of which were to have a continuous history. Alcock was only one of a group of Yorkshire school founders, active in the three-quarters of a century before the Reformation. Two of these men, like Alcock, were bishops, Robert Stillington, bishop of Bath and Wells, a York man by origin who died in 1491, and Thomas Rotherham, archbishop of York from

1480 to 1500. Stillington founded a college for a provost and three priest/fellows 'to praye for the soweles of Kynge Edwarde the IIIIth, the Queene his wyffe, the prince his sonne, the Founder, and all Cristen sowles'.[35] The college was situated at Acaster Selby in the parish of Stillingfleet, and one of the fellows was to be grammar schoolmaster. The college perished with the dissolution of the chantries, but the grammar school survived, and the master, William Gegoltson (also called Jelletson and Gelatson), who was there at the dissolution, was still there in 1570. A list of masters survives up to the time of the Civil War.[36] The school also appears in the York Schoolmasters' Nominations at the end of the 17th century.[37] However Acaster Selby was too small and remote a place to be a good site for a flourishing grammar school.

Thomas Rotherham's College of Jesus, founded in his native town in 1483, was a more important institution, established on a carefully considered plan. The statutes established a college of a provost and three fellows. The provost was to be a preacher and theologian, appointed by the regent and non-regent masters of the university of Cambridge. One fellow, with the largest salary of the three, was to be the grammar schoolmaster. The second was to teach the song school so that divine service might be more fittingly celebrated. The third was to teach writing and accounts because there were many able boys in the district who did not wish to be priests, but who might learn the mechanical arts. There were to be six scholar-choristers, who might be maintained up to the age of 18, and accommodation was to be provided for the chantry priests of the town so that they might be encouraged to devote themselves to music and study. In his will the archbishop recounted the story of the arrival of a grammar teacher in Rotherham during his own boyhood which has already been mentioned;[38] he had been anxious that he might not appear ungrateful for having received such benefits.[39]

The next three schools to be considered were all closely linked with chantries and were founded by clerics who, like Rotherham, had strong local connections. The first two were located in the remote and hilly western reaches of

15

the West Riding. At Giggleswick James Carr, priest of the Rood chantry, endowed it with lands, and in 1507 leased from the prior and convent of Durham, to whom the parish church belonged, a half-acre of land on which he built a grammar school. Carr died in 1518, and at the time of the enquiry into chantries under Edward VI Richard Carr, who was probably his nephew, was incumbent of the Rood chantry, taught the grammar school, and was licensed to preach.[40] Sedbergh was founded by Roger Lupton, who was Provost of Eton from 1504 to 1535, and who linked the school closely with St John's College, Cambridge. That college had very strong northern connections – Bishop John Fisher, who really set it up, was a Yorkshireman from Beverley – and it will appear frequently in these pages.

There is a mention in a deed of 1524–5 of the chaplain and scholars saying mass in Sedbergh parish church, which must mean either that Lupton had made some progress in his scheme by that date or that there was a pre-existing school, but the formal foundation is somewhat later. In 1527 Lupton made a gift to St John's in return for which the college was to elect six scholars from the school, while the college was to choose the master, selecting him from the Lupton scholars if one of them was fit for the post. In the same year the abbot of Coverham granted the site of the school, and in 1528 the foundation ordinance sets out the endowment, and names the master who is to teach the grammar school and to be chaplain of the chantry in the parish church. The master was to teach 'without any exaccion or calenge of theyr stipend or wages besyde my allowaunce', though the children's friends might pay him to teach subjects other than grammar. In 1535 Lupton founded two fellowships and two more scholarships at St John's. He died in 1540.[41] The third school, the slightly earlier East Riding foundation of Pocklington, is similar in many ways to Sedbergh. It was founded in 1514, as part of the guild of the Name of Jesus, the Virgin and St Nicholas, by John Dowman, chancery lawyer and archdeacon. In 1525 five scholarships from the school at St John's College, Cambridge, were added. As we shall see, through some technical flaw in the

16

conveyancing, the property remained in the hands of the Dowman family and so it escaped confiscation when the chantries were abolished.[42]

The fate of other chantry schools will be discussed when the dissolution of the chantries under Edward VI is considered in the next chapter. In many cases the school was continued without any serious break, but in others the relationship between pre-Reformation and post-Reformation conditions is more indirect and more difficult to trace. At Skipton-in-Craven the school was traditionally founded in 1548 by William Ermysted, canon of St Paul's. Yet the schoolmaster, Stephen Ellis, had been the last chantry priest of Peter Toller's chantry founded in his will of 1492, and in 1560 Ellis secured the payment of £4.4.10 from the chantry stipend which had been withheld for some years.[43] At Wakefield, where the royal charter for a grammar school was not granted until 1591, there was probably a school connected with the Thurstone chantry, though it does not seem to have been continued by warrant of the chantry commissioners in 1548. It has been suggested that one of the curates of the parish took over the educational work of the Thurstone chantry priest.[44] An interesting example of this kind of transition can be seen at Leeds.[45] The traditional founder of Leeds Grammar School is William Sheafield who in 1552 left his copyhold lands for the support of a schoolmaster on condition that the parishioners built a schoolhouse and supplemented his endowment. Sheafield had been the last chantry priest of the chantry of St Katharine in Leeds parish church, founded by Thomas Clarell, vicar of Leeds 1430–69. Sheafield had been granted a pension of £4 in 1548 when the chantry was dissolved. The historian of the school has conjectured that at the dissolution the freehold lands were confiscated, but that the lord of the manor waived his rights over the copyholds. Sheafield then provided for the continuation of the school by leaving the copyholds in his will for that purpose. As we shall see, the subsequent fate of the chantry properties is often very difficult to unravel and the searches and negotiations continued over many years. The power of central government was often frustrated by the wiles of local

17

communities, who saw no reason to surrender valuable assets if they could find means to avoid doing so.

Notes Chapter 1

1. Leach, A.F. 1916: 329.
2. Orme, N. 1973 and 1989; Moran, J.A. Hoeppner 1985.
3. Orme, N. 1973: 60.
4. Orme, N. 1989: 231–2.
5. *EYS* vol. II: xxxi, 150.
6. Moran, J.A. Hoeppner 1985: 94–5.
7. Kreider, A. 1979; Riley, M.A. 1938: 122–65, 237–85; Wood-Legh 1965 does not deal with schools and almshouses.
8. Orme, N. 1973: 197.
9. Hey, D. 1986: 86.
10. *Ibid.*: 95, 119.
11. *Ibid.*: 173; for Roman Catholicism in the 16th and 17th centuries *see* pages 61–2.
12. Leach, A.F. 1896: 321–7; *see also* Leach, A.F. 1907 on Yorkshire schools, though he says himself that the information on pre-Reformation schools is not complete (pp. 415–16).
13. Wallis, P.J. and Tate, W.E. 1956: 64–104.
14. Orme, N. 1973: 293–325.
15. Jewell, H.M. 1982: 1–25.
16. Moran, J.A. Hoeppner 1985, App B: 237–79.
17. Moran, J.A. Hoeppner 1979.
18. Moran, J.A. Hoeppner 1981: 16.
19. Moran, J.A. Hoeppner 1985: 121.
20. *Ibid.*: 181.
21. *See* Ryan, L.V. 1963.

22. Kreider, A. 1979: 15–18.

23. Leach, A.F. 1907 and *EYS*.

24. Tate, W.E. 1963.

25. Raine, A. 1926: 63–4; *see also* pages 22–3, 33.

26. Orme, N. 1989: 206–7.

27. *EYS* vol. I: xxx, 31–2; Hamilton, D.H. (ed.) 1977: 29.

28. *EYS* vol. I: lx–lxi; Curtis, S.J. 1951: 74–6.

29. Leach, A.F. 1907: 446.

30. Dransfield, J.N. 1906: 191.

31. Leach, A.F. 1907: 481.

32. Wenham, L.P. 1958: 17–18.

33. Lawson, J. 1963: 31.

34. *Ibid.*: 32.

35. *EYS* vol II: 93.

36. Leach, A.F. 1907: 454; and *see* pages 54–5.

37. BIY Nom S/M 1685/10; 1688/1; 1706/13.

38. *See* page 6.

39. *EYS* vol II: xxx–xxxii, 109–30 (statutes), 149–60 (will); *see also* Guest, J. 1879: 106–19, 136–43.

40. *EYS* vol II: xxxix, xl, 239; Bell, E.A. 1912: 13–19, 22.

41. *EYS* vol II: xlii–liii, 287–316, 321–6.

42. Leach, A.F. 1907: 463–4; Leach, A.F. 1916: 287–8; Sands, P.C. and Haworth, C.M. (?1950): 8–22.

43. Gibbon, A.M. 1947: 12–14, 27–8.

44. Leach, A.F. 1907: 440; Curtis, S.J. 1954: 15; Peacock, M.H. 1892: 5.

45. Leach, A.F. 1907: 457–8; Curtis, S.J. 1953: 33; Price, A.C. 1919: 39, 51–66.

CHAPTER 2

Yorkshire and the Dissolution of the Chantries

The three-quarters of a century between the fall of Cardinal Wolsey in 1529 and the death of Queen Elizabeth in 1603 was a time of great upheaval in church and state in England. It began with the breach with Rome and the dissolution of the monasteries. Under Edward VI the pace of religious change quickened. There was a sharp but short-lived reaction under Mary, followed by the stabilization of the Protestant order under Elizabeth. The settlement of 1559 was to endure, but it was threatened, on the one hand by Catholic Recusancy and the growing power of the Counter-Reformation and on the other by the Puritan movement, whose supporters wanted to carry religious change much further than was permitted by the established system. In 16th century Yorkshire the danger came from the Recusants. The power of Puritanism was not to develop until the 17th century, when it became influential, especially in the woollen districts of the West Riding. But Catholics and Puritans, though they were influential and vocal, were only minorities. The great mass of Yorkshire people, whether clerical or lay, accepted with a more or less good grace what authority decreed for them. To desert the paths of obedience was painful and dangerous; it was more natural for the men of the time to conform and make the best of things. Only one man, Richard Snell from Bedale, was burnt in the county under the Marian persecution. He died at Richmond in September 1558.[1] Under Elizabeth, when the law identified the practice of Roman Catholicism with disloyalty to queen and state, the sufferings of the Recusants were far greater.

The schools, because of their close connection with the church, were greatly affected by these changes. The most crucial phase in their history was the dissolution of the chantries under Edward VI, though the current view among historians seems to be that these changes were less harmful to education that A.F. Leach, who really founded the modern study of the subject, had believed. Much more will be said about this later. Most of the chantry priest/schoolmasters went on teaching after their chantries had been dissolved, and some of those whose names were mentioned in the Edwardian certificates were still actively at work in Elizabeth's reign. We simply do not know in most cases what their personal opinions were. Most of them went on with their work whatever decrees came down from London.

Some men, of course, got into difficulties. A.G. Dickens has uncovered the case of William Senes, who was in charge of the song school at Jesus College, Rotherham, and who was arrested for heresy in August 1537. He was accused of attacking traditional rites and ceremonies, while he claimed that he had been loyal to the king against a disloyal group of local priests (all this, it is to be remembered, was very near the time of the Pilgrimage of Grace). It seems that Senes was brought to London and discharged by the Privy Council while Thomas Cromwell was the king's chief minister. After Cromwell's fall proceedings against him were resumed. He submitted himself to correction at York and did penance both in the Minster and in Rotherham parish church. After that he disappears from the record; he was no longer song schoolmaster when the college was dissolved in 1548.[2] In Dickens' view the story of William Senes suggests the existence in Rotherham of 'a serious but unheroic Protestant group'.[3] Under Elizabeth some schoolmasters got into trouble for their loyalty to the old religion. At Skipton Stephen Ellis, who had been priest of the chantry of St Nicholas, was deprived in 1561, perhaps because he was of Catholic sympathies,[4] and at Ripon John Nettleton was 'discharged' by the Court of High Commission, though he was to keep his office until a new master was appointed so that the boys should not be neglected.[5] Two masters of St Peter's,

York were of similar persuasion. John Fletcher, deprived for recusancy in 1574, was kept in prison for 20 years. Henry Pullen, appointed in 1576, was probably a Papist at heart. Four of the Gunpowder Plot conspirators, including Guy Fawkes, were educated under him.[6]

The dissolution of the monasteries after 1536 brought to an end the cloister and almonry schools which the monks had maintained for their own members and dependants. This certainly represented a loss to English education, though there is not much evidence about these monastic schools.[7] In the East Riding they were maintained by Kirkham and Bridlington priories.[8] A portion of the monastic wealth was used to establish six new dioceses, one of which, Chester, comes into our story because the archdeaconry of Richmond, covering much of the North Riding and parts of the West Riding, was transferred to it, and remained part of it until the diocese of Ripon was created in 1836.

Once the monasteries had gone by 1540 the last substantial block of church property left to be expropriated was the possessions of the colleges and chantries, and by the early 1540s greedy eyes were looking in their direction. The pickings, though much less than those offered by the monastic lands, were still in total considerable. It has already been argued that only a minority of the chantry priests were also teachers and that many of them were not themselves well enough educated to be able to teach very much.[9] The general statistics, however, do show what a major change took place when the chantries were swept away. Alan Kreider (1979) gives the following totals for Yorkshire for 1546–48.[10]

	Chantries	Stipendiaries	Free Chapels	Guilds	Colleges	Hospitals
	406	117	33	20	10	21
East Riding	82	11	7	4	5	7
North Riding and York	156	22	10	7	2	9
West Riding	168	84	16	9	3	5

Kreider estimated that in four sample counties (Essex, Warwickshire, Wiltshire and Yorkshire) 64 men or about 8% of the intercessory priests were engaged in teaching on the eve of the dissolutions. Only 18 men or 28% of that total seem to have been actually required to teach by their foundation ordinances. In many cases the earnings of the priests were small, and they always had to combine their teaching work with their other priestly duties.[11] In general their teaching work seems to have been popular with the parishioners, and the Edwardian commissioners generally did their best to ensure that it was continued.[12] Though the number of these schools in Yorkshire was not great, many of the chantry foundations like Hull, Sedbergh, Skipton, Pocklington and Leeds were important. They were to survive the changes of 1548 and to enjoy later histories of some distinction.

By the 1530s the chantries, like all religious institutions, were operating in a changing world. In 1536 a private act of Parliament enabled the Common Chamber of the city of York to suppress seven chantries and three obits, which the city had hitherto supported, because of the decay in its finances. This represented no doctrinal rejection of the intercessory principle, but is rather an illustration of the close control exercised by the city government over York life, of which the chantries formed an integral part.[13] At the same time as that York suppression took place, the doctrinal basis itself was coming under close scrutiny. Both the Ten Articles of 1536 and the King's Book of 1543 taught a very much modified doctrine of purgatory. In 1543 it was laid down that masses might not be said specifically for the soul of a particular person, which was to knock away the very linch pin upon which the whole system rested.[14] In parallel with these doctrinal changes there was an increase in the number of private suppressions of chantries. Some chantry priests exploited properties for their own personal gain or parishes used endowments for different purposes. In at least one place – Richmond in the North Riding – the townspeople took over and concealed chantry lands, determined, if they could do so, to avoid the losses which dissolution would bring.[15] Between 1539 and 1545 the government dissolved a number of colleges and hospitals, though there do not seem to have been any cases in Yorkshire. It does not appear that there was any principled policy behind these actions. They took place because some courtier or man of influence coveted the properties concerned.[16]

The general attack on the chantries was contained in two acts of Parliament, the first passed in 1545 at the end of the reign of Henry VIII, the second in 1547 in the first Parliament of Edward VI. The first act was a much more limited measure than the second, and concentrated to a large extent on the alienation of property by the officers of chantries and colleges which had taken place in the preceding years.[17] The preamble to the 1545 act described the misappropriation of the properties of colleges, chantries and hospitals by donors and founders, while priests and wardens had alienated lands and granted leases. The king, it was noted, had incurred heavy charges as the result of the wars with France and Scotland. It was then enacted that all chantries and colleges and their properties, chargeable to first fruits and tenths, which had been dissolved between February 4th in the 27th year of the king's reign and 25th December in the 37th year of that reign, were to be vested in the king and his successors. Covenants for the sale of lands were voided and money paid for the purchase of lands was to be repaid, while all gifts and surrenders to the king between the specified dates remained valid. Since much of the college and chantry property was misapplied by those who managed it and was not devoted to the charitable purposes for which it had been given, it was provided that the king might 'from tyme to tyme hereafter during his naturall lief' appoint commissioners to enter into these properties and take them into his hands. The commissioners were to make return into the Court of Chancery and the possessions thus acquired were to be under survey of the Court of Augmentations. The remaining provisions of the act were technical and need no further explanation.

The first object of this act was to staunch the wasting of assets which had taken place during the previous decade. The mention of the shortage of money in the royal exchequer suggests the pressing needs which led the king to act. There is a rather vague statement that the chantry endowments had not been used for the charitable purposes for which they had been given, but there is no sign of any doctrinal attack on intercessory prayers for the relief of souls in purgatory. The wording at least suggests that the king left himself considerable latitude on how the commissioners were to proceed. The enquiries were duly set on foot but very few chantries had been dissolved when Henry VIII died in January 1547, when the act lapsed. About a year passed between the passing of the act and Henry's death. Within that time more might have been achieved by more determined government policies.[18] Perhaps Henry VIII had aimed at little more than dealing with pressing issues like requests for lands from favoured courtiers.

The act dissolving the chantries passed by Edward VI's first Parliament was a much more thoroughgoing measure. Based on clear doctrinal assumptions hostile to the principle of intercessory masses, it set out a specific programme of reform, though, as we shall see, the financial resources of the government were insufficient for this to be carried through in any more than a fragmentary way. In its preamble the act pointed out the errors and superstitions which had resulted from

> devising and phantasising vain opinions and masses satisfactory, to be done for them which be departed, the which doctrine and vain opinion by nothing more is maintained and upholden, than by the abuse of trentals, chantries and other provisions made for the continuance of the said blindness and ignorance.[19]

The king would amend these abuses by using these resources to erect grammar schools, to augment the universities and to make better provision for the poor and needy.

The provisions of the act of 1545 were then recited (it must be remembered that it had lapsed with Henry VIII's death), and the king was given power to take possession of all chantry properties held within five years from the first day of the existing Parliament. These were to come into the king's hands 'immediately after the feast of Easter next coming'. Care was taken to see that nothing escaped. The king was to enjoy properties set aside for the maintenance of a priest during a limited time, though the rights of those who would enjoy the property after that time were safeguarded. He was to acquire the minor benefactions for the maintenance of anniversaries, obits and lights, and secular guilds and fraternities were to forfeit properties devoted to such purposes, though 'such corporations, guilds, fraternities, companies, and fellowships of mysteries or crafts' were exempted from the act. The government had originally intended to confiscate all the properties of these bodies, but that was prevented by opposition in the House of Commons.[20]

The positive provisions of the act centred on the duties of the commissioners who were to survey all the properties vested in the king. They were required to appoint a schoolmaster or preacher

> in every such place where guild, fraternity, (or) the priest or incumbent of any chantry *in esse*, the first day of this present Parliament, by the foundation ordinance or the first institution thereof, should or ought to have kept a grammar school or a preacher, and so has done since the feast of St. Michael the Archangel last past.[21]

The lands and tenements of the chantry concerned were to continue in succession to the schoolmaster or preacher for ever. The commissioners were required to endow vicars in parish churches which had been colleges or chantries. In populous parishes they were to assign lands for the maintenance of one or more priests to help the incumbent. Powers were given to allot pensions to the priests and stipendiaries of dissolved chantries, to continue benefits already given to the poor, and to allocate lands to fraternities and brotherhoods 'towards and for the maintenance of piers, jetties, walls or banks against the rages of the sea, havens and creeks'.[22] All such payments were to be made half-yearly by the king's receiver. The commissioners were to act 'beneficially' towards all persons entitled to benefit and their certificates

27

were to have the force of law. They were required to make a certificate of the lands thus acquired into the Court of Augmentations within a year of their appointment.

In a lengthy and complex piece of legislation there are many technical and detailed clauses which need not be noted. A number of exceptions were made. The act was not to apply to the colleges and halls of Oxford and Cambridge nor to any chantry within them, to St George's Chapel, Windsor, to Eton and Winchester, to chapels of ease with no property other than the churchyard and a house or close, to cathedrals (except for chantries and obits within them). Nothing in the act was to be prejudicial to 'the general corporation of any city, borough, or town within this realm'[23] which perhaps relates to the government's original plans to take over the properties belonging to guilds and fraternities. Provisions were made about properties within the Duchy of Lancaster, a clause which was important for Yorkshire where the duchy had extensive lands. The statute was not to extend to copyhold lands; as we have seen, this provided a loop-hole for the re-foundation of the grammar school at Leeds by William Sheafield, the former chantry priest.[24] Finally grants of chantry lands already made by the present king (Edward VI) and his father were confirmed notwithstanding the provisions of the two statutes on chantries.

It is valuable to look at the consequences of the chantry acts in a wide context in order to put the fate of the schools into the background of religious and social planning in the Reformation era. The events of these years in Yorkshire have been well documented by historians who have published documents relating to the commissioners' enquiries;[25] though much is missing, enough remains to tell us a lot about the schools in the county and to help us to form a judgment about the policies of Edward VI's governments towards education. Historians have been sharply divided in their assessments. For a long period the young king was regarded as a great founder of schools; his name appears in many school titles as it does in Yorkshire at Giggleswick.[26] A.F. Leach began his *English Schools at the Reformation 1546–8*, published in 1896, with a chapter entitled 'Edward VI:

Spoiler of Schools', and over the 90-odd years since that was written, successive historians have adopted positions at different points on a scale leading from one judgment to the other. Before these contrasting opinions are examined any further, it will be necessary to look in more detail at what actually happened to schools in Yorkshire between 1546 and 1553, when Edward VI died.

The certificates drawn up by the two sets of commissioners record a great deal about the teaching duties of the chantry priests, though they are not complete. The East Riding series has been lost,[27] and the 1548 series for the West Riding is fragmentary.[28] After the second enquiry had been made two officials, Sir Walter Mildmay and Robert Kellway, were directed to assign lands for the maintenance of schoolmasters and additional clergy for the parishes and to arrange for the payment of pensions to priests of the dissolved chantries. The King declared that it was his purpose

> to erecte diurse and sundrye Grammer Scoles in euery Countie in England and Wales, for the Educacone and brynyng uppe of youth in vertu and learnyng and godlynes, and also to make prouision for the releif of the pore, in such wyse as shall be thought mete and convenyent.

Since it was impossible at that time to make proper provisions for doing this, it was provided that schoolmasters and curates were to be paid the same yearly stipends as they already enjoyed, the money to come through the Court of Augmentations.[29] So the continuance arrangements were intended to be temporary, though no permanent arrangements were ever made and the fixed stipends then granted were to be paid for many years to come.

It is possible to put together from a number of sources a pattern of the Yorkshire chantry schools.[30] Two modern scholars, W.E. Tate and C.J. Kitching, have provided lists of schools,[31] and almost all of these are mentioned in Page's *Certificates*, in Leach's *Early Yorkshire Schools* and his articles in *V.C.H. Yorkshire*

29

vol. I, or in more than one of these sources. The schools thus named can conveniently be arranged in three lists:

A Schools appearing both in Tate's list of chantry and other schools continued in 1546 and 1548 and in Kitching's list of schools recommended for continuance at a fixed stipend			
Acaster Selby	WR	Northallerton	NR
Aldborough	WR	Owston	WR
Bedale	NR	Pickering	NR
Bolton-on-Dearne	WR	Pontefract	WR
Cawthorne	WR	Royston	WR
Giggleswick	WR	Sedbergh	WR
Hull	ER	Skipton	WR
Middleton	NR	Tickhill	WR
Normanton	WR	Wragby	WR

To this list of 18 schools should be added Rotherham, the continuance certificate for which is printed by A.F. Leach.[32]

B Schools not cited in the list of continuances, but included in W.E. Tate's list			
Crofton	WR	Romaldkirk	NR
Gargrave	WR	Rotherham	WR (but see above, List A)
Keighley	WR	Thirsk	NR
Kildwick	WR	Topcliffe	NR
Long Preston	WR	Wakefield	WR
Malton	NR	Well	NR
Richmond	NR	Worsborough	WR

C Schools located in other sources (as noted)[33]			
Beverley (a, b, c)	ER	Kirkby Malham (a, d)	WR
Bingley (c)	WR	Penistone (c)	WR
Bradford (c)	WR	Pocklington (c)	ER
Doncaster (c)	WR	Ripon (b, c)	WR
Hemsworth (c)	WR	York (St Peter's) (b, c)	–
Howden (c)	ER	York (Holgate's) (c)	–

The names of 44 schools appear on these three lists, though this must under-estimate the total number since the chantry certificates are incomplete. All or almost all the grammar schools survived the dissolution of the chantries, though, as we shall see, writing and song schools were less fortunate. Despite the ambitious plans suggested in the 1547 act, there were no new foundations in Yorkshire arising from royal initiatives. Only Archbishop Holgate's schools at Old Malton, York and Hemsworth (Lists B and C above), founded in 1546–7, reflect the influence of new ideas and the impact upon the county of Renaissance concepts of teaching and scholarship.[34] The stipends of the schoolmasters as laid down in the continuance warrants varied very much in accordance with the previous value of the chantry lands in each case. The highest were Hull (£13.2.2) and Sedbergh (£10.15.4). Giggleswick (£5.13.4) and Northallerton (£5.1.8) were in the middle of the range with Pontefract (£2.19.2) and Middleton (a miserable 18s.4d.) at the bottom.[35] It is clear that in Yorkshire, whatever may have been the case in other parts of England, the chantry schools formed a very important part of the total educational provision. Almost all the schools which have so far been mentioned in this study were involved in the dissolutions. Though there seems to have been a general desire on the part both of the commissioners and of local people to preserve the schools, the changes did present serious problems.

Before those problems are examined further, two examples will be given, one of a chantry certificate and the other of the arrangements for continuance. At Hull in 1548 the incumbent of Bishop Alcock's chantry was John Olyver, Bachelor of Arts, 46 years old, 'of honest conversacyon and lyvinge and well learned' ... 'th' above named John Olyver his bounden by his fundacyon therof, showed unto us, to kepe a free gramer schole and too teache and instructe all such youthe as resortethe thydder takinge for his payn in teachinge and for his salarye, as in the fundacion more plainlye apperethe, and so dothe according at this presentes'.[36] At Rotherham the Edward VI certificate records the clear value of the freehold land of Jesus College as £122.15.5½. The provost had an income, together with some allowances, of £13.6.8. Of the three teacher-fellows the grammar master had a total income of £10.15.4, the song master one of £7.8..8, the writing master one of £6.6.0. In the continuance certificate the income of the grammar master, Thomas Snell, was continued. The song master, Robert Cade, received a pension of £6 and the writing master, John Addy, a pension of £5. Arrangements were made to pay off the choristers, and the site and buildings, except the schoolhouse, were sold for £140, which included £32 for the lead roofs.[37] The Latin words appended to the settlement of Thomas Snell's salary, 'continuatur quousque', were used in many such cases. They may be translated: 'let it be continued until what time/until when'. That time was never determined, and the government, harassed by wars and inflationary pressures, was never able to complete the educational revolution envisaged in the act of 1547.

The pattern of change after 1548 was not uniform, and some schools fared much better than others. Some struggled on without any permanent endowment; others were quite quickly re-established with new foundations based on income from lands. In some places the local community was successful in concealing properties from the Crown and in using them to provide a permanent establishment for their school. Some schools were supported by the municipal authorities and others were rescued by the initiative of private individuals. Disputes about the former chantry lands went on well into the reign of Elizabeth, though by that time the gifts of many donors, both for new schools and for the support of old schools, had made these properties much less important comparatively than they had been in 1550.

The oldest of Yorkshire schools, the Minster School at York, was unaffected by the changes under Edward VI, though it was to be re-founded under Mary. In 1557 the dean and chapter acquired the hospital of Blessed Mary in the Horse Fair outside the city walls. Evidence was given that the hospital was in a dilapidated state, the master and two fellows were pensioned off, and a grammar school for 50 boys, to be called 'the school of the Cathedral Church of St Peter of York', was established in the building. The foundation deed, executed in that short period of Catholic reaction under Mary, urged that youth should be brought up so that

> in the church militant shepherds may everywhere be preferred who with the sword of the spirit, that is the word of God, may be able to drive away and put to flight the rapacious wolves that is, devilish men ill understanding the Catholic faith, from the sheepfolds or the sheep intrusted to them....[38]

The objective of official control is the same, though the ends to be attained are the opposite to those promoted by the Edwardian legislation.

In the other two major archiepiscopal foundations, Beverley and Ripon, the school seems to have survived, though the precise course of events is not always clear. At Beverley the burgesses petitioned the king in 1552 to grant lands for the support of the minster fabric and for a grammar school since the town was populous and there were many youths in it who might be brought up in learning. The lands for the support of the church were in fact granted, but nothing seems to have been done about the school. However in the 1560s and 1570s the town governors were making grants to support it, one of the many examples in the county of local concern for a local school.[39] Events at Hull ran on rather similar lines. There the master, John Olyver, was continued with the substantial salary of £13.2.2¾ when Bishop Alcock's chantry was dissolved, and the like sum was paid to his successors. Again there is evidence from the '60s and '70s of support from the town corporation.[40] Whether in both these cases the support began in the early Elizabethan period or whether it had been given from the time of the dissolutions it is not possible to say. In some parts of England the dissolution of guilds and chantries was followed by the grant to towns of a charter of incorporation, one of the duties of the new body being to manage the school. One example of this is the charter of 1553 to Stratford-upon-Avon in Warwickshire.[41] There are no Yorkshire examples of this precise development, though, as we shall see later, old chantry properties were sometimes recovered by local incorporated bodies which then gave some support to the school.[42]

Different foundations met very different fates, and it is difficult to understand why some were more successful than others in bridging the gap between the old order and the new. In most cases the presence or absence of powerful friends at court probably had a lot to do with the outcome. Two schools which had to survive on the masters' pensions and which were not re-endowed were Rotherham and Pontefract. Though both of them received some further financial support in Elizabeth's reign, it was not sufficient to make a major difference to their fortunes.[43] At Pontefract the master's continued stipend was only £2.19.2, a figure which, of course, reflected the pre-1548 chantry income. At Rotherham the grammar schoolmaster's salary of £10.15.4 was much better, though the song and writing schools which had formed part of Archbishop Rotherham's original structure had disappeared. It seems, however, that some kind of school for younger boys survived and was eventually merged into a charity school.[44] The grammar schoolmaster, Thomas Snell, had to go to the Court of Exchequer in 1561 to establish his right to his stipend, which had ceased to be paid in Mary's reign, and to claim his arrears, though he lost a part of what he was owed. It cost the inhabitants of the town 20 marks to obtain the decree.[45]

Two schools which obtained permanent endowments shortly after the dissolutions were Giggleswick and Sedbergh, though in the latter case success was gained only after a hard struggle. At Giggleswick the school, which had formed part of the chantry of the Rood, was re-founded at the petition of the vicar and other inhabitants of the town and parish in 1553. The Letters Patent created a grammar school with a master and usher. There were to be eight governors of whom the vicar was to be one. They were incorporated with perpetual succession and the power to hold lands. They were to have a common seal, to appoint the master and usher, and to have the power to make statutes with the advice of the bishop. They were granted former chantry lands at North Cave, Rise and Aldburgh in the East Riding to the annual value of £23.3.0, of which 63s. had to be paid as rent to the Court of Augmentations. The settlement was generous; the salary continued to the former chantry priest-schoolmaster Richard Carr had been £5.6.8. It is a reflection of the rather confused conditions created by all the transfers of property that some of the lands granted had formerly belonged to Bishop Stillington's college of St Andrew at Acaster Selby.[46]

At Sedbergh, as at Giggleswick, the schoolmaster's salary had been continued in 1548. In the Sedbergh case a resolute and in the end successful campaign was waged by St John's College, Cambridge, with which the school had been linked by its founder, to secure a permanent endowment. [47] First of all the college tried to save the existing lands. It told the Lord Protector, the Duke of Somerset, that the school was the only such foundation in a poor and barbarous country with no other school within 40 to 50 miles. If schools were abolished, the college argued, the university itself would perish. A fixed annual payment was much less desirable than an income from lands. The wills of the dead, if they were not superstitious, ought to be observed. Lands were better than a fixed stipend because the total income would be increased by fines paid on the renewal of leases. The stipend of £10 (approximately the sum granted to the master, Robert Hebbblethwayte) was not sufficient to tempt a man to leave the university. Who, enquired the college, was to pay this and what difficulties would the schoolmaster have in getting his money? The arguments which St John's put forward were a shrewd analysis of the difficulties which resulted from the abandonment of the original policy of re-foundation set out in the 1547 act.

The case, both for Sedbergh in particular and for the grammar schools in general, was eloquently put in sermons preached by Thomas Lever, Master of the College (1551–3), during 1550. In a sermon preached during Lent he went on to the attack

> There was in the North Countrey, amongst the rude people in knowledge (which be moste readye to spend their lives and goodes, in serving the King at the burnyng of a Beacon) there was a Grammer Schole founded, havyng in the Universitie of Cambridge of the same foundacion VIII scholarships, ever replenyshed with the scholers of that schole, which scole is now solde, decayed, and loste. Mo there be of lyke sorte handled. But I recyte thus only, because I knowe that the sale of it was once stayed of charitie, and yet afterwards broughte to passe by briberye, as I hearde say, and believe it, because that is only briberye, that customablye overcometh charitie.[48]

Success came in February 1551 with the establishment of a grammar school at Sedbergh by letters patent. The arrangements for its government were similar to those already outlined for Giggleswick. Robert Hebblethwayte was named as master 'in consideration that he was Scolemaster there before', and after his death the appointment was to lie in the hands of the master and fellows of St John's. The annual value of the properties transferred was £20.13.10, again as at Giggleswick a fairly generous settlement for Hebblethwayte's continued salary had been

£10.15.4.[49] He is another example of a chantry priest-schoolmaster who was to work for many years under the new order, remaining in office until 1585.[50]

In all the cases which have been mentioned the final result was the consequence of more or less clear decisions of official policy, though that policy, as we have seen, was not always consistent. There are many other cases which have to be placed in a kind of grey area where properties were concealed and all kinds of hole-in-the-corner bargains made with results which often took decades to clear up. The disposal of the chantry lands was in fact a very complex story, and the fate of the school properties is by no means the least complex part of it. Sometimes what happened came down to the decision of an individual. At Pocklington in the East Riding it was found, when the enquiry took place, that the property had never been properly conveyed and that legally it remained in the possession of the founder's nephew, Thomas Dowman. Consequently it was not confiscated under the act, and Dowman procured a private act of Parliament in 1551 to confirm the school's existence. The master was to be appointed by St John's College, and the master and usher were incorporated to hold the school lands.[51] At Almondbury near Huddersfield in the West Riding there had probably been a school in the chapel of St Helen which John Kaye in 1547 moved, with the consent of the parish, into 'the Scole howsse that now is' and obtained 'Mr Smyth a good scolar to com and teach Here'.[52] The rest of the transaction and the fate of the school until Letters Patent were granted to it in 1608 remain obscure. It would be a reasonable guess that other schools, as well as Almondbury, may have been preserved by the same kind of individual initiative at the crucial time of change. There were many people who, like John Kaye, were anxious that their parish should not lose its school.

There are many traces of similar activities by local notables, and their desire to preserve school and other chantry properties sometimes led them into devious paths. At Bradford the parishioners fought a straightforward battle in the Duchy of Lancaster Court, claiming that the school estates had been given for educational purposes and should not be confiscated. They were successful in maintaining their rights and letters patent were granted to them.[53] At nearby Bingley the chantry of St Mary seems to have escaped detection in 1547, perhaps because the parishioners concealed it. In a later deed of 1571 a group of donors granted properties for the maintenance of a schoolmaster, some of these going back to gifts of 1528–9. These actions were referred to much later in proceedings of the cCmmissioners for Charitable Uses in 1601 and 1622. It may be that the parishioners had concealed the rent-charges, hoping to benefit themselves from the enhanced capital value of the lands.[59]

What happened at Bingley is largely speculation. Events at Ripon and at Richmond can be more fully documented. In both cases, though the order of events is different, there was concealment, the subsequently formal establishment of a grammar school, and the successful defence of the endowments. At Ripon the school lands had been vested in the Rood or Holy Cross Guild. When the commissioners came to Ripon, these lands were concealed, since a group of local people gave information that they were school lands exclusively with no reference to the link with the guild which would have made the properties subject to confiscation. The parishioners might have succeeded in their deception without further difficulty had they not tried to dismiss the schoolmaster, Edmund Browne, himself a former chantry priest, who went to the Duchy of Lancaster authorities and told them that the properties were guild lands. Subsequently Browne was bought off with a money bribe, and in 1553 the parishioners obtained from the duchy a decree establishing a free school and providing that eight to ten of the inhabitants should be governors of it. Subsequently the governors purchased more chantry property from the Crown, and in 1555 obtained a royal charter which sets out the school's various endowments. But this was not to be the end of the story. Much later, in 1576, proceedings began in the Court of Exchequer to enquire whether the school lands had been the lands of the Rood Guild, and later a patent was issued granting these lands to two private purchasers. Legal proceedings continued for some years until in February 1583 the Attorney-General issued a 'nolle prosequi' in

38

the Court of Exchequer, and the governors remained in possession. A final decree followed in 1585. Such a long period of uncertainty about the ownership of former chantry lands was not unique.[55]

At Richmond the bailiffs and burgesses had, as early as 1544, taken over the property of most of the chantries and obits with the collusion of the priests who were granted pensions and whose intercessory duties were not interfered with. Only those foundations were left where a connection with the Crown would have facilitated discovery. The grammar school, taught by the priest of the chantry of the Blessed Virgin, John More, with a stipend of £6.13.4 paid by the bailiffs and burgesses, was declared to the commissioners who reported that it did not come under the act.[56] This major concealment of chantry properties was not likely to go unnoticed, and it was, in the latter part of Edward VI's reign, reported by an informer to the Court of Augmentations. He seems to have obtained a commission of enquiry, but nothing more happened until 1560 when the Crown brought an action against the bailiffs and burgesses of the town for intrusion into the chantry lands. The Crown found it very difficult to empanel a jury to try the case, and it was not finally decided until 1562 when a jury at York decided in favour of the townspeople. In the view of the modern historian of Richmond School that decision went clearly against the evidence and reflects the unpopularity of the Queen's government in the north.[57] The Richmond people had won, but perhaps they felt their position precarious, and they petitioned the Queen to establish a grammar school endowed with the lands in dispute. A charter of incorporation was duly granted in March 1567. This suggests in this case a somewhat more generous attitude on the part of government in London towards the disposal of former chantry lands, though that impression would not be borne out by the considerably later attempt, which has already been noted, to recover the Rood lands at Ripon.

Historians have differed widely in their assessment of the effects on education of the dissolution of the chantries. The pioneer in the modern study of the subject, A.F. Leach, believed that the government followed a policy of spoliation which did great damage to the schools. He pointed out in particular that, though grammar schools were preserved, the writing and song schools perished. Where school endowments had been confiscated and the masters continued on a fixed annual stipend, the effects of inflation worked very much against the interests of the schools. The salary in money was a steadily wasting asset whereas land would have appreciated in value as prices rose.[58] Leach's views were sharply criticized in a series of articles by Joan Simon, published in the 1950s.[59] Mrs Simon claimed that Leach had exaggerated the number of elementary schools which had been suppressed, and that he had under-estimated the educational provision made by the monasteries and over-estimated that of the collegiate churches. Once the chantry duties had been abolished, the schoolmaster was able to devote the whole of his time to teaching; he became a professional in a sense unknown before the Reformation. The sale of the endowments stimulated the market in land, and helped to increase the gifts of lay people who created schools which were under lay rather than clerical control. The Edwardian government had in fact instituted a national survey of schools. The schools re-founded after 1548 were, Mrs Simon wrote in a later book, 'conceived of as units in an educational system serving a protestant nation'.[60]

The idea that the chantry legislation created an embryo national system of education has proved attractive to other scholars. W.K. Jordan, like Mrs Simon, emphasised the secular purposes at which Reformation society aimed. Though he accepted that harm had been done when endowments had been replaced by fixed stipends, he argued that the commissioners had taken great care to safeguard the educational work of the chantries.[61] The changes had in fact increased rather than diminished the resources inherited from the Middle Ages.[62] Jordan attempted to calculate the net capital value of the chantry foundations. This, he believed, totalled £610,255.3s. in 38 counties, of which only £20,778.13s. was devoted to schools. As a result of the commissioners' work the former chantry wealth applied to schools was increased by 33% to £29,697.4s., though in Yorkshire and in some

40

other counties, it was actually reduced.[63] Jordan's financial calculations have been much criticized,[64] but his figures do lend some support to the view that the financial harm done by the changes can be exaggerated, though Yorkshire, it should be noted, went against the general trend.

Jordan regarded the educational inheritance passed from the Middle Ages as comparatively small in quantity; in his opinion the real spurt came under the Elizabethans. To Nicholas Orme the medieval contribution was much more important. He accepted the validity of many of the criticisms made against A.F. Leach, but he and Leach agreed in stressing the losses sustained by the failure to continue song and writing schools. A few localities may, in Orme's view, have suffered, but in general he thought that education was not harmed because the steady advance of private support and benevolence which will be examined later went forward without any check. Orme emphasized, as our Yorkshire examples have shown, that there was much concealment of properties and that the fate of individual schools depended very much on the help which they could command from men of influence.[65]

The fate of chantry properties in Yorkshire has been studied by C.J. Kitching.[66] Jordan argued that over the country as a whole the chantry lands were rapidly sold; not much of them was left when Edward VI died.[67] In Kitching's view much of the Yorkshire property took a long time to sell because, being held on long leases, it was not attractive to purchasers and because, on the Crown and Duchy of Lancaster manors, there was reluctance to sell land. However he agreed with Jordan that education and poor relief did not, over the longer term, suffer as a result of the changes.[68] Kitching took a generally favourable view of government policy and was sympathetic with the idea that it aimed to create some kind of national system of education. We know almost nothing, he argued, about the 'schools' kept by many of the chantry priests and no one at the time thought that the fixed stipends allotted to the schoolmasters would fall drastically in value as they in fact did as the result of inflation.[69]

Another historian of the North Country, A.G. Dickens, while he accepted some of the criticisms made against Leach's work,[70] took a rather different approach. He argued that the confiscations and the greed of the land speculators may well have done general harm to the Protestant cause and lowered the national morale. The monasteries, he thought, had often been regarded by their neighbours with very mixed feelings. The chantry dissolutions, on the other hand

> chiefly affected articulate and turbulent townsmen; they threatened ecclesiastical charitable and educational endowments, they demanded troublesome defensive action, they seriously modified parish life and intolerantly attacked the intercessory beliefs of a still considerable part of the nation.[71]

The Yorkshire rising of 1549, which took place in a small area north of the Wolds, may, in Dickens' view, have been partly caused by the abolition of the chantries of which there were many in the area.[72]

It is impossible to assess how deep such discontent was and how long it lasted. In Alan Kreider's judgment the dissolution of the chantries was 'a fascinating mixture of profit and loss, of progress and calamity',[73] though that, it must be noted, refers to the chantries as a whole and not specifically to their educational functions. In Yorkshire – and no wider judgment is attempted here of any large area – the grammar schools survived, though some of them fared much better than others. It is very difficult to trace the history of elementary schools because there is so little reference to them in the sources, but we know, for instance, that at Rotherham the writing and song schools came to an end, while at Ripon the song school did not survive the dissolution of the collegiate church.[74] Song schools of the traditional type had little place in the simplified worship of the reformed church, but it must be noted that, while stout efforts were made to preserve the grammar schools, there is little sign of similar efforts to defend education of the type which writing and song schools provided. It is true, of course, that in their lower classes the grammar schools did much elementary teaching, and thus served educational purposes more varied that the title 'grammar school' suggests. Many former chantry priests may have gone on teaching after they had been pensioned off, and this would not leave any trace in the records. However, once all these exceptions have been noted, the apparent neglect of elementary education through the period of change and reconstruction does represent a serious weakness. It must have been a serious loss to the town of Rotherham to forfeit two parts of the original triple structure so carefully planned by Archbishop Rotherham in his foundation deed.

The view that the dissolution of the chantries formed part of a plan to create a national system of education for a Protestant nation has already been mentioned. Something of that idea is certainly expressed in the Chantries Act of 1547, but it was never achieved, and indeed was probably beyond the power of Tudor government to achieve, given the resources available to them and the constraints, financial, international, inflationary, with which they had to contend. The very diverse fates of individual schools, as we have studied them, show the lack of any central directing power on the part of the state. This concept of a national system is often combined by recent historians with the argument that the changes represented a move towards lay control and a new status for the schools independent of the traditional association with the church. Certainly lay influence was greater after the Reformation than before it, and the governing bodies set up by royal charter were very largely lay in membership. Yet the majority of schoolmasters were still in holy orders, and often combined their teaching duties with pastoral responsibilities as vicar or curate of the parish, or they later left their schools to take livings. It was to be a long time before the schoolmaster appeared as an independent professional man.

Under Elizabeth and long afterwards he was required to be licensed by the bishop, a requirement which expressed the authority over him of both state and church, for in post-Reformation England it was very difficult to separate the two powers. If the control exercised over the schoolmaster enforced strict religious conformity, the same is true of the day-to-day life of the schoolroom. The life of the school was suffused with religion. Boys were taken to church; they learned the catechism and studied the Bible. It is difficult to see in the education of Elizabethan and Jacobean Englishmen the kind of laicization which some scholars have sought to find there. Indeed in some ways the inter-connections between religion and education were closer after the Reformation than they had been in the Middle Ages when the schools were neglected by authority because they posed no threat to it. After 1558 they stood in the front line of national politics.

Much space has been devoted to the dissolution of the chantries because this marked an important stage in the development of English education. Yet too much importance can be placed upon it if it is considered on its own. Before the events of 1545–50 took place charitable men and women had been founding schools, and they went on doing so at an accelerating rate so that the period from 1560 to 1640 marks the high point of private benevolence towards education as well as to many other good causes like the relief of the poor. The events of that period have still to be examined. The dissolution of the chantries and the fate of the chantry schools must be considered against that much wider movement and the striking growth in education which it produced in the three-quarters of a century before the Civil War.

Notes Chapter 2

1. Dickens, A.G. 1957 part II: 14–16.
2. Page, W. 1895: 380–82.
3. Dickens, A.G. 1959: 37–44.
4. Gibbon, A.M. 1947: 29.
5. *EYS* vol I: lxxii.
6. Raine, A. 1926: 78, 84.
7. Orme, N. 1973: 5, 258, 270–71; Moran, J.A. Hoeppner 1985: 114–15; Simon, J. 1966: 180.
8. Lawson, J. 1962a: 8.

9.   *See* page 12.

10.   Kreider, A. 1979: 14. A stipendiary was a priest bound to maintain services subject to the main services of the parish. He drew his stipend from a body of trustees. A chantry priest was his own governing body and was created as such under a licence in mortmain (Leach, A.F. 1896: 54–5).

11.   Kreider, A. 1979: 59–64.

12.   Rosenthal, J.T. 1974: 43–4, 47.

13.   Kreider A., 1979: 159–60; Dickens, A.G. 1947a: 164–73. An obit was a service on the anniversary of the death of the person commemorated.

14.   Kreider, A. 1979: 124–7, 152–3.

15.   *See* page 39 for events at Richmond.

16.   Kreider, A. 1979: 163–4.

17.   *Statutes of the Realm* vol III: 988–93.

18.   Orme, N. 1973: 273; Kreider, A. 1979: 177–8, 185.

19.   Gee, H. and Hardy, W.J. 1896: 328; Leach, A.F. 1911: 472–5; Sylvester, D.W. (ed.) 1970: 83–5.

20.   Kreider, A. 1979: 197–200.

21.   Gee, H. and Hardy, W.J. 1896: 338.

22.   *Ibid.*: 340.

23.   *Ibid.*:353.

24.   *See* page 17.

25.   Page, W. 1894, 1895; *EYS* 1898, 1903.

26.   Carlisle, N. 1818 vol II: 801.

27.   Kitching, C.J. 1972: 178–94.

28.   Tate, W.E. 1963: 11.

29.   The commission for continuance of schools is printed in Leach, A.F. 1896 Part II, pages vii–xvii. The quotation is from pages viii–ix.

30.   For the printed documents *see* Page, W. 1895 and *EYS*.

31.   Tate, W.E. 1963: 14–37; Kitching, C.J. 1970 Vol II, App IIIb.

32   *EYS* vol II: 184–5.

33. (a) Page, W. 1895; (b) *EYS* ; (c) Leach, A.F. 1907; (d) Leach, A.F. 1896 Part II: 306.

34. For Robert Holgate and his ideas *see* pages 117–20.

35. Kitching, C.J. 1970 Vol II, App IIIb.

36. Page, W. 1895: 520.

37. *EYS* Vol II: 182–6; Leach, A.F. 1896: 305.

38. *EYS* Vol I: xxxiii–xxxvi; *see also* Raine, A. 1926: 67–72; Aylmer, G.E. and Cant, R. (eds) 1977: 203. For a similar example *see* the Kirkby Ravensworth statutes of 1556, page 117.

39. *EYS* Vol I: li–liii, 113–16; Leach, A.F. 1907: 427–9.

40. Lawson, J. 1963: 44–9.

41. Fox, L. 1984: 8.

42. *See* pages 115–17 for the Sheffield Church Burgesses and the Rotherham Feoffees of the Common Lands.

43. *See* page 115.

44. Leach, A.F. 1907: 455–6.

45. The decree is transcribed in Guest, J. 1876: 8–12, and *see also* Guest, J. 1879: 334–6; *EYS* Vol II: 187–91.

46. *EYS* Vol II: 243–51; Leach, A.F. 1907: 461; Bell, E.A. 1912: 26–9.

47. For the following *see EYS* Vol II: 342–81.

48. *EYS* Vol II: 359–60.

49. Kitching, C.J. 1970: 81–2.

50. Lowther Clarke, H. and Weech, W.N. 1925: 33.

51. Leach, A.F. 1907: 464; Sands, P.C. and Haworth, C.M. (?1950): 17–22.

52. Hinchliffe, G. 1963: 23.

53. Claridge, W. 1882: 18; Leach, A.F. 1907: 471.

54. Dodd, E.E. 1930: 1–2, 11–13; Dodd, E.E. 1958: 31–2; Dodd, E.E. 1962: 92–9.

55. This is a very brief version of a complex story; *see EYS* vol I: lxiv–lxxiii, 176–93; Leach, A.F. 1907: 434–5; Rogers, P.W. 1954: 42–55.

56. For events at Richmond *see* Wenham, L.P. 1958: 20–23 and 1955: 96–111, 202.

57. Wenham, L.P. 1958: 23.

58. Leach, A.F. 1896: 96–7, 114.

59. Simon, J. 1954–5: 128–43; 1955–6: 32–48; 1957: 48–65; 1963–4: 41–50; Chaplin, W.N. 1962–3: 99–124; 1963–4: 173–83; Wallis, P.J. 1963–4: 184–94.

60. Simon, J. 1966: 240.

61. Jordan, W.K. 1961: 310–11; for W.K. Jordan *see* pages 94–5.

62. Jordan, W.K. 1959: 286.

63. Jordan, W.K. 1970: 191–3, 196–7, 198, 230.

64. *See*, for example, Feingold, M. 1979: 257–73.

65. Orme, N. 1973: 6, 278–9, 280–81, 283, 288–9.

66. Kitching, C.J. 1970; Kitching, C.J. in Heal, F. and O'Day, R. (eds) 1977: 119–36.

67. Jordan, W.K. 1970: 200.

68. Kitching, C.J. in Heal, F and O'Day, R. (eds) 1977: 130, 134, 135.

69. Kitching, C.J. 1970: 72–86, 92.

70. Dickens, A.G. 1959: 176.

71. *Ibid.*: 210.

72. Dickens, A.G. 1939: 151–69.

73. Kreider, A. 1979: 69–70.

74. *EYS* vol I: lxii–lxiii.

CHAPTER 3

Public Policy 1558–1714

The dissolution of the monasteries and the chantries represents the most spectacular exercise of royal power in the mid-16th century. At the same time the Crown was working steadily to regulate the public mind in order to produce a more ordered society, well-schooled in Christian truth as interpreted by official orthodoxy. The royal injunctions of 1536 and 1538 ordered the clergy to teach their parishioners the Lord's Prayer, the articles of faith and the Ten Commandments and to ensure that children were brought up to trades and occupations and not left in idleness. The Bible was to be kept in every parish church and the people encouraged to read it. Those clergy who had the means to do so were to support exhibitioners at grammar schools and universities, who might later be able to assist them in their cures. A sermon was to be preached in church every quarter and no one might preach without licence from the king, the archbishop of Canterbury or the bishop of the diocese.[1] Similar regulations were laid down (c. 1538) for the province of York by Archbishop Edward Lee

> Now everyone must be able to say the Pater Noster, Ave Maria, Credo and Decalogue in English before he may receive the Sacrament, and must teach the same to the children. A routine is laid down by which the curates and heads of congregations are to teach their parishioners in connection with the church services, and are to encourage those who could read to memorize also from the book.[2]

In 1545 the King's Primer, an elementary reading book to be used after the ABC, was published. In the royal injunction attached to it the king explained that inconvenience had been caused by the existence of many such books. It was therefore desirable 'to have one uniforme ordre of al such bookes throughout al our dominions, both to be taught unto children and also to be used for ordinary prayers of all our people not learned in the latyn tong'.[3] The same idea of a uniform order lies behind the two Edwardian Books of Common Prayer, and in 1553 a short catechism was issued, alongside the 42 Articles of Religion.[4] The policies embodied in these various documents were to be repeated many times in royal and episcopal injunctions during the rest of the century. Strict controls over preaching regulated what was said in the pulpit, the principal means of influencing a largely illiterate people. Regular instruction and catechizing ensured that ordinary folk were well schooled in the Christian faith. The whole programme created a kind of national education, though, for the vast majority, this was to be centred in the parish church and the family, not in the school.

For the small minority who attended grammar schools special provision was made. The core of their studies was Latin. In 1529–30 the Convocation of Canterbury ordered the adoption of a standard Latin grammar, though nothing was actually done until about 1540 when the king imposed the so-called 'Lily's' grammar, originally written for St Paul's School and adopted by Wolsey for his school at Ipswich.[5] The order was several times repeated, for example in the royal injunctions of Edward VI (1547) and in those of Elizabeth (1559),[6] and this grammar, later known as the Eton Latin grammar, reigned supreme in English schools until the mid-19th century. Though there may have been variations of detail, the general grammar school curriculum was thus highly standardized. On the religious side Alexander Nowell's Latin catechism for schools appeared in 1570 and was quickly translated into English. This paralleled at a more advanced level the simple catechism of the Prayer Book, and it was frequently mentioned in bishops' injunctions.[7] With a common Latin grammar and a set of catechisms designed for different levels of attainment, Church and State controlled a complete system of secular and religious instruction. In his *Largest Catechism* Nowell has the grammar schoolmaster telling the pupils that it was his duty

> not so much to instruct thee civilly in learning and good manners, as to furnish thy mind, and that in thy tender years, with good opinions and true religion. For this age of childhood ought, no less, yea, also much more, to be trained with good lessons to godliness, than with good arts to humanity.[8]

If this policy of moral and religious control were to be enforced effectively, the schoolroom needed to be supervised as closely as the pulpit. The policy of requiring schoolmasters to be licensed began under Mary. It was one feature of her programme which survived the changes made by her successor. The queen's articles of 1554 ordered the bishops and others in authority to suppress corrupt and hurtful opinions and to remove preachers and teachers who promulgated them. The same authorities were to

> examine all school-masters and teachers of children, and finding them suspect in any wise to remove them, and place Catholic men in their rooms, with a special commandment to instruct their children, so as they may be able to answer the priest at the Mass, and so help the priest to Mass as hath been accustomed.[9]

Similar policies were set out in Elizabeth's injunctions of 1559 in a form which was to be enforced, more or less effectively, at least until the end of the 17th century.[10] No one was to teach

> but such as shall be allowed by the ordinary and found meet as well for his learning and dexterity in teaching, as for sober and honest conversation, and also for right understanding of God's true religion.

All teachers were to bring up their children in 'love and true reverence of God's true religion' and to ensure that they learned such sentences of scripture as would lead them to godly living. The injunctions also repeated earlier orders for the exclusive use of the official Latin grammar and for regular catechizing by the parish clergy.

After the settlement of 1559 there were no real changes in public policy in religious matters until the Civil War. The Canons of 1571 repeated the same rules for the control of schools and schoolmasters as those laid down in the injunctions of 1559. They re-affirmed the idea that schoolmasters had a primary duty to promote the moral education of their charges, who were to be trained in habits of piety and hard work.[11] The system was reinforced by several acts of Parliament in the later years of the reign as fears of a Catholic revival grew. An act of 1580–81 imposed penalties on those who maintained schoolmasters who did not attend church. Any schoolmaster who taught contrary to the act was to be disqualified from teaching and to suffer a year's imprisonment.[12] An act of 1585 against priests and seminarists prohibited the sending of children abroad without permission of the queen or the privy council,[13] and another act in the first year of James I imposed a penalty of 40s. a day for keeping a school without a licence.[14]

This very brief survey of government policy from the injunctions of 1559 to the end of Elizabeth's reign is intended simply as a general background to a more detailed consideration of the policies of successive archbishops of York and their officials during the same period. Under Archbishop Thomas Young ((1561–8) the first of the Visitation Act Books (1561–4) contains details of the examinations of 57 schoolmasters before the vicar-general, John Rokeby, and Richard Barnes.[15] Some men were admitted to the highest category of qualification, some only to teach the rudiments, a few were rejected altogether. John Hunt, for example, schoolmaster at Beverley. was found to be sufficiently skilled in the Latin, Greek and Hebrew languages and was admitted to teach grammar and liberal accomplishments and sciences there. Richard Michill of Heptonstall, formerly of St Mary's Hall, Oxford, was found to be a good Latinist and was admitted to catechize and to teach grammar. Henry Langdayle, vicar and schoolmaster of Scarborough

52

had studied for four years at Benet (Corpus Christi) College, Cambridge under the Hebrew professor. He was found to know Hebrew as well as Latin and was admitted to catechize and to teach the rudiments of grammar throughout the diocese. A rather similar licence was given to Richard Hurst, schoolmaster at Almondbury, who was permitted to catechize and teach the rudiments of grammar. Hurst was also examined in the 39 Articles and subscribed to them.

Some of those examined were found, to a greater or lesser extent, to be unsatisfactory. Henry Jackson, curate of Norton (perhaps Norton near Malton), sought and received absolution from a sentence of excommunication. He was found to be ignorant of Latin and was not allowed to teach it. He was permitted only to catechize in the mother tongue. A similar judgement was passed on Christopher Henry, schoolmaster at Huddersfield... 'and the Engliysshe primer now allowed and the Englyshe accedens and no further'. Richard Collie, curate of Bagby (par. Kirby Knowle near Thirsk) and schoolmaster, knew Latin only moderately well and was not skilled in sacred reading. He was interdicted from teaching altogether.[16] A somewhat bizarre case was that of Edward Sandall, a York clergyman, who disobeyed the orders of the court. A year later he was brought up again, accused of disobedience and of being a corrupter of youth. Whereas, it was said, he should have read the Scriptures, 'he doth most comonlie use to reade the vaine bookes of the iiiior sonnes of Amon, Reynard the Foxe and such like'.[17] In 1570, a little later than the examples quoted, the Ecclesiastical Commission of York decided that John Lacye was 'unable and insuffyciente both for his learning and otherwise' to be master of the grammar school at Bradford. They therefore dismissed him from his office and ordered that he should not teach anywhere in the diocese nor receive a schoolmaster's stipend until he had received a licence.[18] An earlier decision of the commissioners (1564) throws some light on the parish clerk who often taught the children. The commissioners ordered the churchwardens of Hovingham to provide their parish with a clerk who might also 'teache Children Grammer and to write yf ned be'.[19] It is not clear whether this means English or Latin grammar.

There was an interregnum of almost two years between the death of Archbishop Young in June 1568 and the installation of Edmund Grindal (1570–76). Grindal came to the north in the period of tighter control after the failure of the rising of the northern earls. In the first few months of his rule the new archbishop was instructed to enquire into the Yorkshire schools to which the Crown was paying stipends. In the North Riding Grindal reported that the master at Bedale was efficient and the school well managed, though the schoolhouse was small and badly built. Soon afterwards the archdeacon of Richmond's commissary noted that a new master, who was also fit and able, had been appointed. The choice lay in the hands of the inhabitants of the town. At Northallerton the master, John Foster, who had been admitted by Archbishop Young, was fit and hard-working, and the school was kept in a suitable place. The archdeacon of Cleveland certified that it had a large number of scholars. Foster had been there for 20 years. He had been lawfully admitted and held the archbishop's licence.

In the East Riding the school at Hull was well built and well situated and efficiently managed by the master, Robert (or Richard) Baxter.[20] In the West Riding the master at Skipton, Stephen Ellis, had been displaced by the archbishop in 1561 and had removed to Lancashire, though there was some conflict of evidence whether or not he was still receiving his salary of £4.4.10 from the crown. The school was conducted properly and diligently by Roger Bolton who enjoyed a salary of £10.5.0 from lands given by the Earl of Cumberland and William Armistead (Ermysted). At Rotherham William Becke had left the town in 1568 and the townspeople had appointed Thomas Woodhouse who received the crown salary of £10.15.4. Both school and master were fit and suitable. At Acaster Selby William Jelletson (Gelatson), who had been in office when Bishop Stillington's college had been dissolved, was still schoolmaster, and received his annual salary of £8. He was efficient and the school was well-appointed. He must at that time have been about 60 years old; he was 38 when the college was dissolved. It was recommended by the archdeacon that the schoolmaster of Acaster ought to be appointed by the Queen or her officers.[21]

In 1571 Grindal carried out a primary visitation of his province, a duty which was carried out in much the same way by his two immediate successors, Edwin Sandys in 1578 and John Piers in 1590.[22] The archbishops' policies, deriving their authority partly from the royal injunctions and partly from their own powers as ordinary, enforced more detailed and effective controls than had existed before 1570.[23] Grindal asked for the names of all schoolmasters, both those who taught publicly and those who taught in private houses; whether they were diligent and of sincere religion; whether they were licensed; whether they taught King Henry VIII's Latin grammar, the Latin catechism and the appropriate sentences of Scripture.[24] The orders laid down by the injunctions mirror the form of the questions ...

> ... that no schoolmaster shall teach either openly or privately, in any gentleman's house, or in any other place, unless he be of good and sincere religion and conversation, and be first examined, allowed and licensed by the Ordinary in writing under his seal: he shall not teach anything contrary to the order of religion now set forth by public authority, he shall teach his scholars the Catechism in Latin lately set forth and such sentences of Scripture (besides profane chaster authors) as shall be most meet to move them to the love and reverence of God's true religion now truly set forth by the Queen's Majesty, and to induce them to all godliness and honest conversation.[25]

The Comperta et Detecta Book of Grindal's visitation of 1575 recorded nine unlicensed schoolmasters – five in the archdeaconry of York and four in that of Cleveland.[26] None were recorded in the archdeaconry of the East Riding. Two of these – at Drax and Crambe – were schoolmasters in private houses as was another master presented because he had not received Communion for 12 months. It is very likely that these were tutors in Catholic households. Two of the unlicensed men – at Adwick-le-Street and Huttons Ambo – were also curates. The master at Elland (par. Halifax) is not recorded as unlicensed; he 'standith contemptuouslie excommunicate and seeketh no restitucion'. The enquiries of Archbishops Sandys and Piers repeat much the same questions,[27] as do those of the Bishop of Chester, whose diocese covered parts of the west and north of the county.[28] In 1581 Bishop Chaderton asked whether parents brought their children to be instructed, whether the clergy were regular in catechizing, and whether schoolmasters were men of sincere religion, duly licensed and diligent in teaching.[29]

In theory the system should have been complete and all embracing. In practice things are unlikely to have worked out in so smooth a fashion since, in the northern province, the dioceses were large, the population in many areas sparse and scattered, and many of the people lukewarm in their acceptance of the newly established Protestant system. In 1599, for example, the Council of the North sent instructions to the city council of York directing them to enquire into the education of children of Recusants and non-communicants. The Queen had issued instructions that certain persons were to enter into recognizances that such education should be properly carried out.[30] Few actual schoolmaster's licences have survived, though the Exchequer records contain a contemporary registered copy of a licence issued in 1586 to William Gregson, described as 'literate', schoolmaster at Northallerton.[31] The modern historian of Hull Grammar School, John Lawson, has found no evidence that the schoolmasters of the early part of the queen's reign were formally examined and admitted, though the school was, as we have already seen, reported on in the enquiry of 1570 into schools where crown stipends were paid.[32]

The effectiveness of the licensing system for schoolmasters was related to the wider issue of the general efficiency of the system of church courts, of which the licensing procedures formed a part. That system had survived the Reformation almost intact, but its authority was seriously weakened by the growth of important groups, both Recusant and Puritan, who were hostile to the policies which it sought to enforce. The fact that there was opposition and controversy ensured that there was no shortage of business. Excommunication became more frequently used as a punishment than had been the case in earlier times; it has been calculated that 'hardened excommunicates and their families' formed nearly one-sixth of the population of York in the 17th century.[33] R.A. Marchant, in his work on the York church courts, concluded that the efficiency of church discipline varied very much from time to time and from place to place, with urban areas showing the highest levels of disobedience. The threat of excommunication certainly coerced some into compliance, but many ignored the penalty altogether.[34] The enforcement of the rules about licensing was likely to have met with the same difficulties as all the other regulations. In some dioceses which have been studied in detail this certainly seems to have been the case. D.A. Cressy thought that in the dioceses of London and Norwich it was 'by no means certain that ecclesiastical control over schoolmasters was consistent or comprehensive'.[35] Rosemary O'Day argued that in the diocese of Lichfield and Coventry licences were rarely applied for, and that in consequence the records reveal only a minimum in the total number of those who were actually teaching. The application of rules was, in her view, spasmodic and often the response to some special central initiative, while little attention was paid to the licensing of teachers in petty schools.[36] Such conclusions about other parts of England are not necessarily valid for the dioceses of York and Chester, which covered the county of Yorkshire, and the position there will be investigated later.[37] It is very unlikely that, either in York or anywhere else, the rules operated with the regularity and precision suggested by reading the injunctions issued by succeeding archbishops. Church and State were powerful in Elizabethan and early Stuart England, but they were not all powerful.

The system of licensing continued to work on the same lines throughout the 17th century. The Canons of 1604 required all schoolmasters to teach the Longer or the Shorter Catechism, to bring their scholars to listen to sermons in their parish church and to examine them on what they heard. The scholars were regularly to be taught appropriate sentences of Holy Scripture and 'the grammar set forth by King Henry the Eighth'.[38] Edward Cardwell, in his *Documentary Annals*, quotes a series

57

of episcopal orders in the 17th century requiring that schoolmasters be licensed, that they be well affected to the government in church and state, and that they bring their scholars to church. In 1695 Archbishop Tenison required the bishops of the province of Canterbury to take every possible care that there should be good schoolmasters in the public schools, 'not licensing any but such as upon examination shall be found of sufficient ability and...exhibit very satisfactory testimonials of their temper and good life'.[39] Archbishop Whitgift would have written much the same a century earlier. Though Cardwell's examples are all from the province of Canterbury, the position in the province of York was just the same.

The Puritan governments of the Commonwealth period used methods of control very similar to those employed by the Stuarts, though they worked through committees of ministers instead of through bishops. Under both systems those who refused to conform faced expulsion from their offices,[40] and, quite apart from issues of conformity in church and state, the same kind of disciplinary problems turned up under every regime. A good example is the case of Richard Jackson, who had been appointed master of Sedbergh School in 1648. There was a series of complaints and counter-complaints against him, and finally in March 1656 he was ejected from his office by the commissioners 'for ejectinge scandalous ignorant and insufficient Ministers and Schoole Masters for the Westriddinge and Cittie of York'.[41] The charges against him were that he was a frequenter of alehouses and had been drunk for several days at a time, while he had also left the school for three months, locking out his usher and scholars.

After the restoration of the monarchy in 1660 controls were further tightened by the so-called Clarendon Code. The Act of Uniformity (1662) required all incumbents and schoolmasters to make a declaration that they would not take up arms against the king and that they would conform to the liturgy of the Church of England. Any schoolmaster teaching without the bishop's licence was liable to be imprisoned and fined.[42] The Five Mile Act of 1665 forbade those clergy who had not conformed and made a similar declaration from coming within five miles of any city or corporate town or place where they had formerly been vicar or curate. Any person so restricted was not allowed to teach a school or to take boarders, again under penalties of fine and imprisonment.[43] Though there were several legal decisions at the end of the 17th century which limited episcopal authority, for example Cox's case (1700), which laid down that there was no ecclesiastical jurisdiction over schools other than grammar schools,[44] there was a Tory/Anglican revival under Queen Anne. This reached its climax in the Schism Act of 1714, which aimed to strengthen the system of licensing, though its provisions did not apply to tutors in noblemen's houses or to those teaching primary subjects and navigation. This act had a very short life and was repealed in 1719.[45]

Apart from the system of political and religious control which has just been outlined, there was another important area of state activity at this time which needs to be considered – the supervision of endowments given for charitable purposes. W.K. Jordan, in his work on 16th and 17th century philanthropy, has emphasized the importance of the charitable trust as the favoured means of safeguarding endowments for education and other benevolent purposes.[46] Two acts of parliament at the end of Elizabeth's reign (39 and 43 Elizabeth) had authorized the appointment under the authority of the Lord Chancellor and the Chancellor of the Duchy of Lancaster, of Commissioners of Charitable Uses to enquire into abuses of endowments and to make orders for their better management. The law was effectively enforced, and schools, like other charities, benefited greatly as a result. At a time when charitable giving had greatly increased, it was important to ensure that funds were properly applied for the purposes for which they had been established. In Yorkshire there were 35 such enquiries between the act of 1601 and the Restoration in 1660. These were all cases in which the word 'school' is explicitly used, and there may have been other cases of a more general kind which also possessed an educational element.[47]

This jurisdiction continued to operate during the Commonwealth which shows that its value was recognized by lawyers and politicians of very different opinions. An early example among Yorkshire·grammar schools is an inquisition of 1604 which listed the endowments at Penistone.[48] An inquisition of 1622 at Bingley named a committee of 13 inhabitants to control 'all the said charitable uses within the said towne & parishe'. They were to control all the rents and property of the trust and, when reinforced by 'two or more learned and sufficient preachers within the said Westrithing', they were to elect the schoolmaster. Later in the Commonwealth period there were two further inquisitions into property, one mainly concerned with the poor, the other with the school.[49] There were also two enquiries at Leeds. The first in 1621 led to the establishment of the Committee of Charitable Uses. The second in 1663 raised the numbers of the committee to 15; it had power to appoint and dismiss the master and to make laws for the government of the school.[50] At Skipton a Commission of Pious Uses was issued during the Protectorate; during the war years the building had been occupied by troops and the rents were unpaid.[51] At Bradford there was an enquiry by commissioners in 1655–6 into a dispute between the master and the usher. In 1658 this was followed by a petition from the inhabitants asking for a charter of incorporation, and this was granted by Charles II in 1662.[52] The work of the Commissioners of Charitable Uses during the 17th century marked an important exercise of state power which is often forgotten.[53]

Most 17th century Englishmen conformed more or less willingly to the policies laid down by the governments of the day, but there were important and continuing minorities – Roman Catholic at first and Puritan/Nonconformist later – who did not. The power of the state was exerted against those who dissented from official policy, and those who resisted were excluded from the national system of education. The Roman Catholics, except for their few years of official favour under James II (1685–8), suffered repression which was more or less continuous, though its severity varied from time to time. Before 1640 the Stuarts struggled hard to contain and to eliminate Puritanism, as Elizabeth had done earlier. After 1660 Anglican orthodoxy triumphed, and the Puritans were driven out of the official church and excluded from public life. They were seriously disadvantaged in education as in other ways; for example, they were cut off from the universities, but they succeeded in maintaining their own schools as they maintained their own churches. The most important of their educational institutions, the Dissenting Academies, rivalled the ancient universities of Oxford and Cambridge in the 18th century.[54]

Yorkshire was throughout the whole of this period an important centre of Roman Catholicism, and, by the beginning of the 17th century, the West Riding had become an important centre of Puritanism which was strong in the woollen district and in the area round Sheffield. In country districts the views of the local gentry were of crucial importance. J.T. Cliffe, in his study of the Yorkshire gentry from the Reformation to the Civil War, lists the education of 310 boys from these families between 1558 and 1642.[55] Of these 144 were educated in public grammar schools either inside or outside the county and another 52 in private schools or with resident tutors. The remaining 114 had received a Catholic education, a few (10) in schools in Yorkshire itself, considerably more (34) in Catholic schools overseas, but the great majority (70) from private tutors which makes it very clear why the government was so anxious to control tutors in private families. The Catholic total forms about 37% of the total number of pupils recorded in gentry families, though it is not suggested that this proportion can be extrapolated across the whole population of educated people. Though early Stuart governments took regular measures to prevent children being sent abroad to study, Cliffe has calculated that between 1568 and 1642 184 youths and 42 young women from 87 gentry families were sent to seminaries and institutions abroad to study, and that these, because of imperfections in the records, are minimum figures.[56]

It took some time, after the Elizabethan settlement of 1558-9, for the Roman Catholics to solidify as a defined group. Many families were divided, sometimes between the generations. Many assented in form to the official establishment while they retained some links with the ancient religion. By the end of

61

Elizabeth's reign the lines had become harder and more definite. A list of the Roman Catholics in the county in 1604 lists some 20 to 30 schoolmasters, some confirmed Recusants, others merely suspected of being so. Many of them were tutors in Catholic families. A long list of Recusants at Egton near Whitby notes: 'Jane Posgate doth keep in her house William Posgate her father, a Recusant who teacheth children...' These people were probably related to Nicholas Posgate, who had been martyred at York in August 1579.[57]

Early in the 17th century a Catholic school was suppressed in York Castle 'that had been catering for the surrounding countryside as well as the city of York, and took in *boarders*, and ran a grammar school curriculum that included music'.[58] York, as has already been suggested, was something of a Catholic centre. The Parliament of 1625 called before it a York schoolmaster who had 56 scholars, 36 of them Papists. The secret was that he was a licensed schoolmaster, the licence coming from an official 'who hath the keepynge of the schole duringe his life without privitie of the Arch Bishoppe'.[59] 14 Catholic schools are recorded in Yorkshire in the reign of Charles I and 6 in that of Charles II. In the promising years of James II the Jesuit, Henry Hamerton, opened a school for 60 scholars in York, which was attended by many Protestants, and he also supplied catechisms and books for the poor. After the Revolution of 1688 he was arrested, imprisoned and later bailed. He died at Ghent in 1718.[60] These Catholic schools were small and scattered and their existence precarious, and it was a matter of chance whether any evidence about them survived. In girls' education a continuing tradition was that created by Mary Ward, foundress of the Institute of the Blessed Virgin Mary, who died at Heworth, outside York, in 1645, and whose community later founded the Bar Convent in York which maintained a well-known school for girls.[61]

By 1600 Roman Catholics were completely outside the official system; until 1660 the Puritans were working inside that system to change it. J.T. Cliffe has again provided some statistics about Puritan sympathizers among the gentry and their education. He considered that in 1642 there were at least 138 Puritan families

62

within the Yorkshire gentry. Much the strongest concentration of them was in the West Riding with the smallest number in the North Riding where traditional Catholicism was strong. In the East Riding Puritanism was strong in Hull and Beverley and in a group of parishes along the Riding's northern edge.[62] Like other Protestant gentlemen, many who held Puritan opinions sent their sons to grammar schools like Beverley, Hull and Wakefield. Others used a private tutor or sent the boys to a clergyman who kept a private school. Naturally the clergymen selected would be those of appropriate opinions.

> Luke Robinson, the son and heir of Sir Arthur Robinson of Deighton, received part of his education under William Alder, rector of Aughton, who was eventually deprived of his living for nonconformity. Subsequently he entered the school of John Garthwaite who, after leaving Beverley Free School, had apparently established himself as a private schoolmaster in York.[63]

Some information is available about the Puritan clergy-schoolmasters of York diocese in early Stuart times. Garthwaite himself, who became headmaster of Beverley in 1614, was soon afterwards admonished for repeating the sermon preached in the morning to a company of schoolboys and others and for singing psalms.[64] Twenty years earlier, Richard Grange, schoolmaster at Ainderby Steeple near Northallerton, had been inhibited from teaching in the diocese because 'he had spoken diverse irreverent speeches against some part of the book of common prayer'. Later he served as curate at Thirsk and at Carlton Husthwaite, so he was not completely excluded from ministry. In the 1630s Thomas Rawson was headmaster of Sheffield Grammar School and assistant minister of the parish under the long-serving Puritan vicar Thomas Toller (1598–1635). In 1635 Rawson was brought before the chancellor for acting unlicensed as assistant minister and preacher and for not wearing a surplice. Some of those who had been in trouble later conformed. Nicholas Walton, schoolmaster and perpetual curate at Kirkby Malham, was admonished at the 1632 visitation and expelled by the Royalists during the Civil War. Yet he conformed at the Restoration. So did Francis Proude, perpetual curate at Hackness, a chapel built by Sir Thomas Hoby, from 1638 to 1680. Proude also taught a school where one of his pupils was Hoby's grandson, Francis. The triad of parish, school and tutorship is significant and was not uncommon.

Many Royalist and conforming clergymen were ejected during the Civil War and suffered considerable hardship, but after 1660, if they had survived their tribulations, they returned to their offices. The Puritans ejected in 1660–62 had no such good fortune; their exclusion was final. A.G. Matthews, in his modern edition (1934) of Edmund Calamy's account of the ejected and silenced ministers, lists 20 men from the diocese who were at the time of the expulsion or had earlier been schoolmasters.[65] Some of these conformed later. Among those listed by Calamy who did not conform were both the master, John Garnet, and the usher, Israel Hawksworth, of Leeds Grammar School, and Anthony Stevenson, rector of Roos, who had been master of Hull Grammar School from 1632 to 1645. Timothy Wood, vicar of Sandal Magna, had formerly been usher at Wakefield, and Rowland Hancock, vicar of Ecclesfield, usher at Sheffield. Some of those ejected like Peter Clark, rector of Kirby Underdale, subsequently ran their own private schools, and others, like James Calvert, vicar of Topcliffe, became chaplain and tutor in a private family. One or two practised physic, like Edward Richardson, curate and schoolmaster at Sawley near Ripon, who became an M.D. of Leiden and who died in Holland in 1677. At Penistone (WR) an ejected clergyman, Nathan Staniforth, became schoolmaster and parish clerk because the leading parishioners remained Puritan.[66] The last survivor of the ejected ministers was Nathan Denton, vicar of Bolton-upon-Dearne, who lived until 1720. In his early days he had taught a free school at Cawthorne. Puritan teachers like Anthony Stevenson of Hull naturally produced like-minded pupils. One of them, Alexander Metcalf, who had studied theology at Leiden, was ejected from Settrington near Malton in 1662. By his will he founded a scholarship at his Cambridge college, Clare, for boys from his old school, though the bequest did not become operative until 1725.[67] Finally, though he did not hold church preferment in Yorkshire, mention must be made of Richard Frankland, born at Giggleswick, who opened his academy at Rathmell, a few miles from his birthplace, in 1670, and who was one of the pioneers of the Dissenting Academy movement.[68] The history of Roman Catholic and Dissenting schools in the 18th century will be pursued in a later chapter.

Notes Chapter 3

1. Gee, H. and Hardy, W.J. 1896: 269-74 (Injunctions of 1536), 275-81 (Injunctions of 1538).

2. Baldwin, T.W. 1943: 38.

3. Sylvester, D.W. (ed.) 1970: 79, 82.

4. Wood, N. 1931: 169.

5. Orme, N. 1973: 255-8; Baldwin, T.W. 1944 vol I: 183; Leach, A.F. 1916: 309-10.

6. Frere, W.H. and Kennedy, W.M. (eds) 1910 vol II: 129; Frere, W.H. (ed.) 1910b vol III: 21.

7. Wood, N. 1931: 172, 174.

8. Baldwin, T.W. 1943: 216.

9. Frere, W.H. and Kennedy, W.M. (eds) 1910 vol II: 328; Orme, N. 1973:286.

10. Gee, H and Hardy, W.J. 1896: 417-42. The injunctions relating to schools are on pages 433-4; *see also* Frere, W.H. (ed.) 1910b vol III: 21; Sylvester, D.W. (ed.) 1970: 124-5; Wood, N. 1931: 56-7, 165.

11. Sylvester, D.W. (ed.) 1970: 125; Baldwin, T.W. 1943: 86; Wood, N. 1931: 62-3; Kennedy, W.P.M. 1924 vol I: cxlii.

12. Wood, N. 1931: 65; Montmorency, J.E.G. de 1902: 94.

13. Gee, H. and Hardy, W.J. 1896: 488; Sylvester, D.W. (ed.) 1970: 127-8.

14. Leach, A.F. (ed.) 1911: 528.

15. Marchant, R.A. 1969: 66.

16. Purvis, J.S. 1948: 103–104.

17. Quoted in Raine, A. 1926: 75–6.

18. Purvis, J.S. 1948: 108.

19. *Ibid.*: 190

20. Lawson, J. 1963: 47 says 'Robert'.

21. *EYS* vol II: 74–83, 98–100, 193–4. The schoolmaster's name is also given as 'Gegoltson' (see page 15).

22. Kennedy, W.P.M. 1924 vol I: lxxiii–iv.

23. Marchant, R.A. 1969: 129.

24. Frere, W.H. (ed.) 1910b vol III: 270.

25. *Ibid.*: 291; Wood, N. 1931: 63.

26. Sheils, W.J. (ed.) 1977: vi, 6, 25, 33, 42, 63.

27. Kennedy, W.P.M. 1924 vol II: 93–4, 98; vol III: 261, 262, 264.

28. For the diocesan boundaries *see* page 23.

29. Kennedy, W.P.M. 1924 vol II: 113, 118–19.

30. Wood, N. 1931: 70–71, 300–301.

31. Tate, W.E. 1956: 431; and *see* pages 71–2.

32. Lawson, J. 1963: 47–8; and *see* page 54.

33. Houlbrooke, R. in O'Day, R and Heal, F (eds) 1976: 245; and *ibid.*: 23–4 (Introduction).

34. Marchant, R.A. 1969: 212–13, 220–21, 235.

35. Cressy, D.A. 1973: 129–30.

36. O'Day, R. 1973: 115–32; O'Day, R. 1982: 169–70.

37. *See* Chapter 4 'The Mechanism of Licensing'.

38. Baldwin, T.W. 1943: 87–8.

39. Cardwell, E. 1844/1966. For Tenison's letter *see* vol II: 387.

40. *See* Stephens, J.E. 1971: 181–6 and 1967: 253–62; Hull, J. 1984: 45–65.

41. The Jackson case is dealt with very fully in *EYS* vol II: 386–415; *see also* Lowther Clarke, H. and Weech, W.N. 1925: 43.

42. Sylvester, D.W. (ed.) 1970: 163–5.

43. *Ibid.*: 165–7.

44. Montmorency, J.E.G. de 1902: 171–2.

45. Costin, W.C. and Watson, J.S. 1952 Vol I: 121–3.

46. Jordan, W.K. 1959: 18–19, 116, 118.

47. Public Record Office *Lists and Indexes* no. 10 (1899) lists all the cases and prints the two statutes; *see also* Montmorency, J.E.G. de 1902: 71–2.

48. Dransfield, J.N. 1906: 192–3; Addy, J. 1958b: 511.

49. Dodd, E.E. 1930: 20–21, 35; Vincent, W.A.L. 1950: 95–6.

50. Price, A.C. 1919: 71–3.

51. Gibbon, A.M. 1947: 42–3.

52. Claridge, W. 1882: 30–32.

53. *See also* Stephens, J.E. 1984: 4–19.

54. For the Dissenting Academies *see* pages 262–3.

55. Cliffe, J.T. 1969: 69.

56. *Ibid.*: 195–9.

57. Peacock, E. 1872: 97–8.

58. Beales, A.C.F. 1963: 78.

59. *Ibid.*: 201.

60. *Ibid.*: 249.

61. Oliver, M. 1960: 212–13; and *see* the sections on girls' education, pages 152–3, 267–9.

62. Cliffe, J.T. 1969: 262.

63. *Ibid.*: 266.

64. Marchant, R.A. 1960: 37, 250, 269–70, 290.

65. Matthews, A.G. 1934: 99, 118, 163, 211, 217, 246, 253–4, 410, 462–3, 542.

66. Ex inf. Professor David Hey; for Staniforth *see also* page 134.

67. For Metcalfe *see* Lawson, J. 1963: 140–42. For exhibitions and scholarships *see* pages 114, 130, 154–5, 228.

68. *See* pages 262–3.

CHAPTER 4

The Mechanism of Licensing

Before the working of the licensing system is reviewed, the ecclesiastical organization of the county must be explained. The greater part of Yorkshire lay in the diocese of York, which also included Nottinghamshire, though no Nottinghamshire material has been included in this study. In 1541 the archdeaconry of Richmond had been transferred from York to the new diocese of Chester. That archdeaconry, a very extensive area, stretched from the Lancashire/Cumberland coast to parishes within a few miles of the city of York. In Yorkshire itself it covered Swaledale and Wensleydale in the North Riding, and in the West Riding the area around Boroughbridge and Knaresborough, excluding the liberty of Ripon, and the far north-west from Clapham and Bentham to Sedbergh. The records of the diocese of York are in the Borthwick Institute at York and those of the archdeaconry of Richmond are in the West Yorkshire archives at Leeds. Both these sources have been used, but because the two sets of records are rather different in nature, they need to be discussed separately. The York records will be examined first, the Richmond/Chester records later. For the diocese of York much use has also been made of material published by Dr J.S. Purvis.[1]

Before the licence was issued the schoolmaster had to submit a testimonial and a nomination from those entitled to make the appointment. If these were deemed to be satisfactory and the licence was issued, he then had to make a formal subscription to certain articles. The process of licensing can be looked at from two different aspects: first of all the actual subscription itself, and secondly the nomination and testimonial which preceded subscription and the grant of a licence. It has been calculated from the subscription books in the diocesan records that there were 138 subscriptions made by schoolmasters in the period 1598–1640 and 674 for the period 1660–1703.[2] Another scholar, J.E. Stephens, has calculated that before 1642 subscription involved at most 27% of schoolmasters and that between 1660 and 1700 subscriptions generally exceeded 40%.[3] In the more detailed study contained in his Ph.D. thesis[4] Stephens concluded that between 1605 and 1627 few schoolmasters in the diocese subscribed, but that the visitations of Archbishop Richard Neile (1632–40) revealed a number of schoolmasters who had not complied with the regulations and led to an increase in the number of subscriptions.

In 1662 there were 137 subscriptions after the long intermission caused by the Civil War, and there was an extensive review in Archbishop Frewen's visitation of 1663. But in later archiepiscopal visitations comparatively few schoolmasters exhibited their licences, nor do they appear frequently in the records of visitations by the archdeacons. The archdeacons themselves do not appear to have taken much interest in the schools, and there is no sign of the authorities attempting to extend their control over schoolmasters.

A typical example of a subscription from the Restoration period is the following (from the Nominations). I have quoted it because the man licensed, Christopher Sollitt, will appear later in this chapter

> I Chrofer Sollitt now to be lycensed to teach a grammar school at Scarborough in the diocese of York doe willingly and ex animo subscribe to the 39 Articles of the Church of England & ye 3 first Clauses of the second article menconed in the 36th Canon & to the declaracon & acknowledgement menconed in the Act of Uniformity aforesaid & every clause contained in them & every of them. Witness my hand this 21st day of April 1676
>
> Christo: Sollitt

Let every Curate and grammar schoolmaster (licensed?) as above subscribe: & besides their subscriptions they must take the oathes of allegiance & supremacy and read the declaration for renouncing the Covenant.[5]

Reference has already been made to the Schism Act of 1714.[6] On 1 August 1714 the Vicar of Leeds John Killingbeck testified that seven schoolmasters of the town had taken the sacrament of the Lord's Supper and made application for licences, 'apprehending themselves to be under the obligation of takeing licences by vertue of the late Act of Parliament, for the preventing the Growth of Schism ... I do heerby testify that they all live in constant communion with the Established Church: and do believe them all to be sufficiently qualifyd both as to Learning and sobriety for their Respective charges'.[7]

There are no books of licences in the diocesan records, though it was common to note on the nomination letter that a licence had been granted ('Emanavit licencia' or some abbreviation of those words). The licence granted to Jeremy Gibson, headmaster of Wakefield Grammar School, by Archbishop Tobias Matthew (5 June 1607) has survived. After reciting that Gibson had been elected schoolmaster by the governors of the school after the resignation of his predecessor, and that they had submitted his election to the archbishop under seal, Matthew admitted Gibson to the office of master of the school, to teach grammar and 'good' authors and to enjoy the rights attached to the post. Trusting in Gibson's sound doctrine and good morals, the Archbishop accepted and agreed to the election and granted a licence and faculty under the seal of his vicar-general.[8] There is among the Nominations another licence dated July 1690 to Joseph Ellythorpe for the mastership of Bridlington Grammar School. This is in poor condition and in places difficult to read. It was granted by Henry Watkinson, vicar-general of Archbishop Lamplugh. It is drawn up in a similar but not identical form to the Wakefield licence of 1607, and it makes use of some of the same Latin phrases. It is endorsed with a note that the licence was exhibited at the visitations of 1693 and 1702, in accordance with the practice laid down for such occasions.[9]

The information about licensing is of interest to the modern scholar from two rather different points of view. First of all, it provides valuable information about the official system of controlling schools and teachers. Secondly it helps to answer the question how many schools and schoolmasters there were and where, in a very large county, parts of which were remote from large centres of population, these schools were located. It is difficult totally to separate the two aspects, though initially attention will be concentrated on the first of them – the official control side. The statistical information as a whole will be analyzed later. It is enough for the moment to say that the latest authority has calculated that by 1700 there were over 300 grammar schools in the county, though some of these will have varied in academic status from time to time.[10] By about the same date rather more than 100 elementary schools and teachers had been recorded in the diocese of York and about another 60 for the archdeaconry of Richmond, giving a total of perhaps 150/160 for the whole county, though there will have been many 'petty' or elementary schools and even more individual teachers who have left no record behind them.

Although the licensing system was clearly never complete, it does provide a lot of information not only about official policy, but also about parish life. In this discussion attention is concentrated not on the subscriptions themselves, but rather on the lesser known aspects of the nominations and testimonials which initiated the whole process, because these tell us a lot about the local background and about the intentions of patrons and parishioners. If the York Nominations and Testimonials are taken together, only four have survived before the collapse of the episcopal system during the Civil War.[11] After the Restoration the totals recorded are as follows: 1660–66, 21; 1670–79, 20; 1680–89, 60; 1690–99, 87; 1700–09, 92; 1710 –14, 45. Between 1663 and 1707 16 more were recorded in parishes within the peculiar jurisdiction of the Dean and Chapter. These figures give an average for each decade of the '60s and '70s of about 20 and for the decades between 1680 and 1714 of about 80.

These totals for the years after 1660 are substantial, but, if they are compared with the figures of grammar and elementary schools already cited, it would appear, as has already been shown by the figures quoted for the subscriptions, that a number of masters must have slipped through the net. Nor is it possible to judge how complete a picture these figures give of the total number of licences granted. John Lawson, in his history of Hull Grammar School, says that there is no record of the episcopal approval of the two masters appointed soon after the charter of 1611, though it seems unlikely that they escaped the need to obtain it. After 1622, Lawson says, the masters for a century or more went to York after their appointment with letters of nomination under the seal of the corporation, and that the same was true for the ushers in the 40 years after 1662.[12] Yet the Nominations at York only record three Hull ushers: John Catlyn (1661), Robert Wilson (1683), and Thomas Elcock (1691), and no masters at all.[13] Catlyn's testimonial is of particular interest because of its reference to the events of the Civil War.

> These are to Certifie whome it may Concerne: That John Catlyn of Kingstone upon Hull, dureinge the late troubles, and rebellion, and to the present time, hath behaved himself as a faithfull and loyall subject to the King's most excellent Majestie; and alsoe that he is a person fitly qualified, and endowed for the undertakeinge the charge of a Grammer School, and thereupon as in order to the encouragement of learninge, and the procurement of a licence, for the said John Catlyn to use and exercise his facultie wherewith God hath enabled him that way, wee whose names are here underwritt have thought it requisite to subcribe this testimonial.[14]

One direct comparison which can be made between two 17th century sources is that between the Nominations and Christopher Wase's collections. Wase's information was collected in the mid-1670s, and he lists 65 endowed grammar schools in Yorkshire, 55 of these in the diocese of York, 10 in the diocese of Chester.[15] The Nominations material only becomes really useful, as we have seen, after the Restoration. Of the 55 York diocese grammar schools in Wase, 14 appear in the Nominations (taking 1676 as the terminal date),[16] and there are 11 more grammar schools in the Nominations for the same dates which are not in Wase.[17] The general impression once again is that the licensing system must in many cases have worked in the late 17th century as it was supposed to do, but that there were many exceptions to it. The available evidence does not really permit any conclusion firmer than that, particularly because none of the lists which can be made are likely to be complete.

The more prominent grammar schools can be traced in the York Nominations for the period up to 1714 as follows. There are seven such schools which appear four times or more (Wakefield, Giggleswick, Leeds, Sheffield, Bridlington, Heptonstall, Batley). Eight appear two or three times (Bingley, Otley, Hipperholme, Bradford, Acaster Selby, Skipton, Guisborough, Almondbury). Five only appear once (Halifax, Rotherham, Beverley, Doncaster and Archbishop Holgate's at York, though in the last case there is other evidence about masters' licences).[18] Hull is not well represented, but, as we have seen, there is other evidence to show that the masters after 1662 were licensed. Beverley, which was an important school, is represented only by one reference to an usher. Another important East Riding school, Pocklington, does not appear at all. Neither do Ripon nor St Peter's York, though in those cases there may have been some special relationship with the Archbishop in the first case and with the Dean and Chapter in the other.

It has been argued that, in another diocese (Lichfield and Coventry), little attention was paid to the licensing of masters in elementary or 'petty' schools.[19] This does not seem to have been the case either in the diocese of York or of Chester. The York records contain many examples of nominations to teach in elementary schools. Both the words 'petty' and 'private' are sometimes used. It is

74

not possible to distinguish between a village elementary school and a more exclusive school to which parents who could afford to pay larger fees sent their children. But in many cases an ordinary village or town elementary school is clearly what is meant in the documents because the word 'petty' is used or reference made to a school to teach English. Examples come from Handsworth (1663), St Mary Bishophill Junior, York (1664), Person (Parson) Cross, Ecclesfield (1675), Killington (Kellington) (1675), East Harlesey (1675), Sheffield (1689), signed by both the vicar and the grammar schoolmaster, Thorne (1691), Burton (par. Royston) (1694), Rothwell (1695), Sutton-upon-Derwent (1698), Northowram (par. Halifax) (1705), Hull (1706), Harpham (1707), Hampsthwaite (1709). There are other village schools where the level of teaching is not mentioned, but which, since they do not appear in any of the lists of grammar schools, are likely to have been elementary; three examples are Great Ouseburn (1662),[20] Altofts (par. Normanton) (1705), and Riccall (1707).

Sometimes the wording of a letter or replies to the articles of an enquiry explain a lot about the way in which the system worked. J.S. Purvis quotes a respondent who explained that he had a licence to teach a petty school but that he was not licensed to teach a grammar school and had never sought to teach Latin except in one limited case where he thought he was allowed to do this by the terms of his existing licence.[21] In another undated document some of the parishioners of Long Preston near Settle explained that they lived several miles from their parish church, that they had built a chapel of ease and maintained a minister for it, and they now sought the archbishop's permission to have their children educated within the same chapel because they could not afford to maintain them elsewhere. The petition was signed by the vicar of the parish and the minister of the chapel and the names of 25 parishioners were attached to it.[22]

There are other cases too where the nomination letters explain the local circumstances which had led the petitioners to ask for a licence. In 1664 the two bailiffs with the vicar and churchwardens of Scarborough petitioned for a licence for

William Lacy who had asked to settle in the town in order to teach English, arithmetic and the rules of navigation, and who had taken the oath of allegiance before the bailiffs. He had himself travelled abroad, and was well qualified to teach navigation to the mariners whose numbers in the port were constantly increasing. 'We do hereby certifie,' they wrote, 'that we do approve and allow of the said William Lacy to teach school as above said in this Towne, humbly desiring he may be admitted and lycensed thereunto by authority, to practise the same accordingly.'[23]

A letter of 1690 about the school at Attercliffe (par. Sheffield) once again brings out the differences between licences for a petty school and for a grammar school and the competition offered in the closing years of the century by the Dissenters. The curate Daniel Leech explained that he had hoped to see the official, 'Mr Squire',[24] at the visitation at Doncaster, but since he had not done so, he had been under the necessity of writing.

> There is one Jonathan Shuttleworth, who now teaches School in Attercliffe, who desires to have a license for that purpose, and he is one that is very fit for that employment. He would willingly have had a license for teaching of Grammar, but enquiring of the Clerkes which were at the visitation he was discouraged from it by reason of the greatness of the fees. The place is very mean having nothing belonging to it besides a Schoolhouse, besides which some of the Dissenters have brought in another to teach school there in a place which is fitted for a meeting house; which is no little prejudice to that which was wont to be the public school. I desire you therefore to send the said Mr. Shuttleworth a license to teach a petty school in the school of Attercliffe for he is not willing to be at the charge of the other. But I desire you to send it forthwith by this bearer, who will pay the ffee for it, which I am informed is half a crown. I pray you seal it up in a paper, and direct it to me without acquainting the bearer what it is. I pray you fail not to send it speedily ...[25]

In the following year (1691) 23 inhabitants of Thorne asked for a licence for John Wilburne to teach an English school for the benefit of the poorer people who wanted their children to be taught 'but are not in a Condicion for sending them to the Grammer Scoole'.[26] In both the Attercliffe and the Thorne cases there is a note on the letter saying that the licences had been granted.

The next matter to be discussed is what kind of people initiated the process which ended with the grant of a licence. Sometimes the school had an individual patron who acted in the same way as the patron of a living. Examples include William Hustler of Heworth, 'the true and undoubted Patron of the perpetuall free Grammer Schoole of Bridlington' (1661),[27] Sir John Blande, 'ye undoubted feoffee and Patron of ye ffree Grammar School of Kippax' (1690),[28] and R. Monckton of Felkirk (1708), though in that case the date of the licence endorsed on the letter of appointment was four years later than the appointment itself.[29] At Bank Newton (par. Gargrave) in 1694 the nomination was made by Henry Colthurst, himself the founder of the school, supported in this case by the vicar of Giggleswick who testified that the master 'is a constant frequenter of Divine Service according to the Present Establishment of the Church of England at his parish of Giggleswick'.[30]

The most common procedure was nomination by the trustees or governors of the school foundation. Where such a corporate body existed, they were the natural and proper people to act. A typical example is the election and nomination in 1697 of Charles Daubeny as their master by 'the Electors and Governors of the free Grammar School of Sheffield'... 'And that Wee do look upon him as a person fitted by his Conformity to the Church by law established and sufficiently in the knowledge of the Latin and Greek tongues to instruct the youth as aforesd in the sd School.'[31] Sometimes action was taken by the incumbent acting on his own or by a group of the local clergy. In 1689 the rector of Thornton in Pickering Lythe asked for a licence for Thomas Wilson to teach the free school there. This was accompanied by a general testimonial from the rector and from another man, together with a college testimonial under seal from the master and fellows of

University College, Oxford.[32] In 1675 the nomination of Henry Hunter by the patron, the Duke of Buckingham, to the mastership of the school at Helmsley was accompanied by a supporting letter from six of the York parochial clergy. Presumably Hunter had come to Helmsley from York.[33]

Some of the letters sent to York were signed not only by those in official positions like incumbents and school trustees, but by a wide selection of local people in a way which suggests that – sometimes at least – there was widespread concern in the community about the fate of the local school. An interesting example from Scarborough will be quoted later in another context.[34] J.S. Purvis quotes two such cases. In 1679 28 inhabitants of Whitby certified that Christopher Stephenson, whom they had formerly supported for a licence to teach in the town, was not a nonconformist and a consorter with Quakers but a constant churchman and no associate of 'phanaticks otherwise then all others doe in ordinary Communicacion'. In 1698 a request that John Bowcocke, who had already taught the Clerk's School in Skipton for almost two years, might be granted a licence was signed by the Constables, the Churchwardens both old and new, the Overseers of the Poor, the Collectors for the land tax and the window tax, various gentry and other townsmen, the local physician and probably the apothecary.[35] Such support must have been a strong tribute to Bowcocke's efficiency and success as a teacher.

Occasionally there are nominations for individuals without reference to a particular school. In 1663, for example, the vicar of South Kirkby certified that Alverey Bingley was of good behaviour, a sound churchman, and able to teach grammar and Latin authors, and asked that he be granted a licence to teach both Latin and English. The letter is endorsed: 'let him a lycense for a Gramer School and let him come & make the declaracon'.[36] In 1703 the vicar of Kildwick (WR) certified (in Latin) that he had examined Peter Allcock of Pembroke Hall, Cambridge and found him competent to teach boys both Greek and Latin.[37] Sometimes, it appears, such a general request was a way of helping a man who could not earn his living in other ways. There are two such examples among the papers of the exempt jurisdiction of the Dean and Chapter. In 1665 the curate and churchwardens of St Sampson's, York, sent a letter testimonial for William Waudby, 'he being but in a low condition is desireous for to teach a school desireth a license for that purpose'.[38] A year later seven inhabitants of Market Weighton certified that Robert Darrell

> is a good honest and feeble creature And is in no manner of way able to undergoe any hard or toilsome paines for his living Therefore we the Inhabitants of the aforesaid towne of Market Weighton whose names are hereunder written; knowing him to be a man of a very good depportment and civill behaviour: And able to undertake the office of a Schoole Maister would intreat the Court to grant him a license ...[39]

There are a few nominations of curates to be schoolmasters in the same parish, a fairly common practice of the day. At Kirkheaton in 1688 the rector and four parishioners asked for a schoolmaster's licence for their curate.[40] In 1695 35 of the freeholders and inhabitants of Armley (par. Leeds) asked for a similar licence for their curate and further requested for his 'better encouragem^t & maintenance..yt no other person whatsoever may be licensed or allowed to teach School in ye town of Armley..'[41] A similar recommendation combined with a restriction on other competitors can be found at Horsforth (par. Guiseley) in 1699.[42] At Thorne in 1709 there seems to have been a change-round in the parish offices. Three of the trustees of the schoolhouse 'Purchased by us and Sev^{r}all other Inhabitants of the said Town att our own proper Costs & Charge' asked that their minister Robert Jellison, who 'hath but a small Competency by his Curacy', should replace the existing schoolmaster, Benjamin Tennant. However Tennant was not to be totally dispossessed because a request was also made for a schoolmaster's licence for him, as well as a licence for him to be parish clerk.[43] This suggests that the town of Thorne at that time could support two schoolmasters. This combination of the offices of parish clerk and schoolmaster is commonly found in the records. J.S. Purvis cites cases at Filey (1578),[44] at Skipton (1699) and at Rudston (1675).[45]

Examples among the nominations include Wales (1668), Kirby Misperton (1675), Skirlaugh (1690), and Barwick (1696).[46] In the last parish the curate nominated John Hemsworth for the joint offices, 'having been sufficiently recommended to me for his good life and conversation, as also for competent learning to teach a Petty School, and discharge a Parish Clerks place ... which places during the time of his probation he hath discharged to the satisfaction of me and others of the Parish of Barwick.' These appointments, as in the Barwick case, were certified by the incumbent or his curate.

In some cases recommendations were made after a man had already been teaching for some time, which suggests that sometimes the licence was regarded as a certificate that the master was acceptable to the parishioners on a long term basis. The circumstances at Wragby in 1662 were unusual in that they reflected the disorders of the Commonwealth years. The minister and four others certified that their schoolmaster, who had already taught there for upwards of 11 years, was a man of good abilities and loyal to the King.[47] More than 30 years after Church and King had been restored there was a similar delay a Brighouse in making application for a licence. In 1694 the vicar of Halifax, the curates of Elland and Rastrick and nine others certified that Anthony Akeroyd of Brighouse had already taught a petty school there for six years 'in wch he hath soo prudently demeaned himself that the Inhabitants of Brigghouse aforesd are desireouse that he may be there continued to teach his Schoole as aforesd ...' They also petitioned that a Quaker who had surreptitiously obtained a licence to teach in the same place might be 'made Incapable of teaching there any longer'.[48] Four years later, in another part of the West Riding clothing district, the vicar and curate of Kirkburton with 13 parishioners pleaded the rather similar case of Jonathan Swallow. He had been formerly licensed to teach a petty school at Honley in the parish of Almondbury. He had then been persuaded to teach a petty school at New Mill in Kirkburton parish, and, after teaching there for some time, 'being unmindful to pᵣsume to teach there any longer without lycence: Humbly desireth he may (att this opportunity) obtaine

& have lycence to & for the same'. Swallow's application was supported by the usual testimonials to his ability, morals and conformity to the laws of the Church of England.[49]

A few unusual cases stand out among the mass of the Nominations which are on the whole stereotyped both in form and in content. There are a few references to 'private' schools (Upper Poppleton 1663; Kettlewell 1675); in both cases the incumbent signified his approbation for the school.[50] It is not at all clear in these two cases what the term 'private' implies; perhaps it means a more selective and more expensive school as opposed to the village petty school, though all schoolmasters depended to a greater or a lesser extent on the fees which they could charge. And – a very considerable rarity – there is one application for a licence for a woman (Armley, par. Leeds, 1688). It is unusual enough to be quoted; it is a letter from William Tottie at Leeds to 'Mr John Preston in ye Minster Yard York'.

> After hearty respects to you ect I intreat you to send to me a licence for a woman to teach Schollers who is a very honest woman and of good repute and behaviour her name is Susanna ye wife of Samuill Murgatroyd of Armley in ye pish of Leeds. She begann to teach since Candlemas, only teaches petty Schollers, pray send it by ye first returne of Carrier and ye prijs what it costs and you shall be pd. honestly when comes to my hand...[51]

One town whose problems with its schoolmasters are revealed in the records is Scarborough. The subscription of Christopher Sollitt to teach a grammar school there (1676) has already been recorded.[52] Only a year later there were complaints that he was negligent and careless and treated his pupils in a barbarous fashion. As a result he had only about eight or ten boys, most of whom were his near relations. There was, the complainants urged, a much greater demand for education than could be met by one master and his usher, and there had usually been three Latin or grammar schools in the town.[53] In the same year (1677) the bailiffs and churchwardens asked for a licence for Bryan Bales to teach a grammar school since

81

there was a great need for an efficient schoolmaster. The request was accompanied by a letter signed by 62 inhabitants, making very similar points to those made by the bailiffs, and affirming that they were all well satisfied with Mr Bales. Rather strangely perhaps, in the light of the comments already recorded about Mr Sollitt, they explained that there was plenty of room for him to teach a Latin school as well.[54]

The Scarborough people seem to have had little more success with John Phillips and with 'Mr Urquhart', for whom applications were made in 1690, than with Mr Sollitt.[55] In 1691 Coote Ormsbye[56] wrote to explain that Mr Searle, who seems to have been another schoolmaster, had left the town, and that 'poore Mr Phillips cannot gett any number of Schollars to come to him having not above a dozen & that all English schollars which Mr Searle had more than fifty'. Consequently Ormsbye asked that a licence to teach in Scarborough might be granted to the (unnamed) bearer of the letter

> who is one of those poor Episcopall men who have been ejected in Scotland for not submitting to presbytery & has taught a public free Schoole in ye Kingdom for 12 yeares & is a Master of Arts in one of those universities & is in Deacons orders in ye Church of England & recommended to me by some of the clergy of Durham...he is a very sober discreet person & has taken ye oaths to King William & Q Mary at his ordination by ye Bishop of Durham & is ready to take them over againe at his receiving his licence.

Ormsbye also asked that the bearer might be given a licence as curate of the parish. It would be best, Ormsbye thought, that he and Mr Phillips should join together in teaching the same school, and he did not doubt that they would both find 'a competent Mayntenance'. As for Urquhart, who was living with a woman who was not his wife, 'we will have nothing to do with him'.[57]

Sometimes, as we have seen, the application for a licence included the request that the recipient might be protected against other competitors. In 1691 Thomas Elcock, who had been licensed as usher of Hull Grammar School, had complained to the mayor about an unlicensed teacher, Thomas Baynham, and when the mayor failed to take action, Elcock approached the archbishop's official and asked him to intervene. Two years later in 1693 the mayor, George Bacchus, and ten other signatories wrote to thank the archbishop for sending an inhibition against Baynham, but they pointed out that he had ignored the order and continued to teach in the same place. Since the mayor and his fellows were well satisfied with Robert Pell the grammar schoolmaster, they asked that further steps be taken to remove Baynham. Despite a further inhibition Baynham was still teaching 30 years later in nearby Sculcoates. He had, according to John Lawson, been licensed to teach a grammar school there, but this is not recorded in the Nominations.[58]

The events marking the change-over from one master to another are noted on several occasions. At Thornhill in 1698, since the previous master William Beevor had 'gotten somewhat better preferm^t in Norfolke', Lord Halifax had presented Gamaliel Batty to succeed him. Batty would deliver up Beevor's licence to the Archbishop's chancellor, and the request was made for a new licence for Batty to teach the school.[59] At Fishlake in 1706 the minister, John Hall, had received a letter from the new master, and replied to him as follows

> Taking it for granted yt you are qualified according to ye will of ye Donour I wd advise you to come away this day or to-morrow and take your Nomination from ye Trustees and go and take License upon yt and come wh all imaginable speed to take care of ye schoole. As to other matters shall talk wth you w^n you come and give you further assurance of my friendship. If you love your Selfe do not delay.[60]

But Mr Hall does not explain the reason for the urgency in the matter. At Acaster Malbis in 1688 two trustees gave notice that James Heblethwaite was not to have any salary nor to teach the children from 'Maday' of that year because he was not a

83

single man 'but Married & a reader of divine service' contrary to the will of the donor. Instead Robert Thomlinson, who was a single man, was to teach and receive his share of the endowment.[61]

This analysis of the York Nominations has led into many different aspects of education in 17th century Yorkshire. The material about the archdeaconry of Richmond is much less abundant, and the picture it presents is therefore less clearly defined, though many of the same points emerge as in the York examples. The Richmond material consists of cause papers, churchwardens presentments, and the deanery Compert books which record presentments made at visitations.[62] In addition there is now a printed version of the enquiry into the Yorkshire parishes of the diocese in Bishop Francis Gastrell's 'Notitia Cestrensis'.[63] Though the 'Notitia' cover a period slightly later than the terminal date of 1714 which has been used here, they lie so close in time to the other material used in this chapter that it seems appropriate to cite them. This Richmond material is richer on the statistical than on the official control side, though it does provide valuable material about licensing as well. What is interesting about it from both aspects is that it relates largely to village schools in remote and sparsely populated areas of the county. Wase listed ten grammar schools in the archdeaconry of Richmond, only five of which appear in the Presentments and Compert books.[64] Of the two most important schools, Sedbergh and Richmond, Sedbergh does not appear in them at all, because there are for this period no records in the West Yorkshire Archive Service collection for the deanery of Lonsdale in which it lies. Though there is a reference to William Wainwright, clerk, who was teaching without licence at Richmond in 1689, he does not appear to have had any connection with Richmond School.[65] The 'Notitia' mention both Richmond and Sedbergh, and in addition Tanfield from Wase's list. But in this part of the county it is the village schools which dominate the picture as we see it through the records, whether their masters were licensed or not.

As at York there is some information for the years before the Civil War, but the material becomes much more abundant after 1660. At Eriholme (Eryholm, par.

Gilling) in 1614 the churchwardens said that the parish had no schoolmaster other than their minister who taught privately. He had had a licence, had decided to stop teaching, but had been strongly pressed to start again, '& since he hath required no licence'.[66] At Kirklington in 1626 the schoolmaster Anthony Ibbotson, had shown his licence to the commissary. Since he was Bachelor of Arts, he may have taught some Latin.[67] The writing of the presentment from Stanwick St John (1623) is faint and difficult to read. It seems to say that their curate (Sir) John King, a very poor man and a Scot, had been hired only for a time and his wages were but small. It was hoped therefore that the ordinary would not put him to the charge of taking out a licence... 'his doings and honest behaviour is known to all parts of the country'. The churchwardens appear to be asking for an exemption for him because he was a poor man and under particular difficulties.[68] The churchwardens of Riccall in the same year presented their vicar for not catechizing the children and Matthew Chester for teaching without a licence.[69]

The Compert books begin after the Restoration, and the evidence about the licensing of schoolmasters in the latter part of the century is rather conflicting. The churchwardens' presentments record licensed masters at Nun Monkton, Marton and Grafton, and Stanley (?South Stainley) in 1680,[70] at Gilling (Hartforth) in 1674,[71] at Kirkhammerton, Great Ouseburn and Whixley in 1681.[72] At Downholme the churchwardens say that they have no free school; 'ye Schoole yt is is taught by oᵣ Min:'. At Boroughbridge in the same year there was a school taught in the church.[73] In neither case is there any reference to the master being licensed. The Compert books for the deaneries of Richmond and Catterick (1664, 1675, 1679) record a number of unlicensed masters: in 1664 at Burneston, Kirklington, Patrick Brompton and Well, where the man presented, William Pratt, was a Quaker as well.[74] In 1675 neither the schoolmaster not the parish clerk were licensed at Ainderby (Steeple), and there were other cases of unlicensed teachers at Grinton, Kirby Wiske and Ridmar (Redmire and Bolton).[75] In 1679 there were again unlicensed masters at Well and at Burneston. In the latter case the offender, Robert Ashton, curate of

Leeming, was himself a cleric.[76] And finally – a reference to a Chester parish in the York records – the churchwardens of Masham in 1690 asked for a licence for their schoolmaster, John Moore, who had formerly been licensed... 'therefore we humbly desire his Admission, so yt he may remaine amongst us'.[77] Perhaps this Masham example illustrates the tendency already suggested to use the licence as confirmation that the master is permanently accepted in his office.

Various papers dealing with schools in the archdeaconry during the first two decades of the 18th century have survived, but these make comparatively few references to schoolmasters' licences. In the cause papers, for example, the minister and churchwardens of Knaresborough certify in 1717 that there were in the parish a grammar school and no less than six private schools, but they do not explain whether or not the masters were licensed.[78] In the same year the vicar and churchwardens of Aldborough certified that there was no free school nor any such endowment in their parish and its chapelries of Boroughbridge and Dunsforth, and they continue – in somewhat self-righteous tones –

> Where any private Schools are held in any of the above sd Premises tis by the Nomination and Certificate of the Incumbent Vicar to the Ordinarie: for a License to such a Master of Teaching in any Parte of the sd Parish, or of the Chappelries belonging to either of them.[79]

From the information provided by the Compert books of 1719 and 1720 it is doubtful how far that statement reflected current practice.[80] Both books contain a good deal of information about schools, but in one or two cases only, for example a grammar school at Bedale, is the master specifically said to be licensed. There are many more schools – Marske, Bolton, Patrick Brompton, Nun Monkton in 1719; Ainderby, Bowes, Danby Wiske, Forcett, Coverham, Hipswell, Wensley in 1720 – where the schoolmaster was not licensed. And in other cases in 1720 – Romaldkirk, Smeaton, Pickhill, Scruton, Tanfield – it was not known whether the master was licensed or not. Reference has already been made to Cox's case (1700) which laid down that there was no ecclesiastical jurisdiction over schools other than grammar schools,[81] and it may be significant that one of the few cases where a licence is specifically mentioned is that of the grammar school at Bedale.

In the case of the Richmond parishes Bishop Gastrell's 'Notitia Cestrensis' ignores the question of licensing even more completely than the records which have already been quoted. The 'Notitia' contain a lot of information about schools, and, from the statistical point of view, they are a very valuable source. Yet it is remarkable, particularly in the light of the history of the 50 years before 1720, that the 'Notitia' say nothing at all about licensing, which must mean that the subject was not important to those who initiated the enquiry. There does seem to have been a divergence in practice here between the dioceses of York and Chester. Perhaps the system became discredited because it did not always provide a guarantee of efficiency. One of the very few licensed masters in the 1719 Compert book was 'Mr Lluellin' of Thornton Watlass. He, we are told,

> neglects his School and is a drunken pson, and of very ill life and conversation, neither goes himself, nor causes his scholars to go to Church either on Sundays or holy days.

In the margin there is an entry in a different hand of the one Latin word 'fugit'. So Lluellin ran away in the end; his licence had not protected the parish of Thornton Watlass from a thoroughly unsatisfactory schoolmaster.

Notes Chapter 4

1. Purvis, J.S. 1948, 1953, 1959.
2. Lahey, P.A. 1982: 1–6.
3. Stephens, J.E. 1983: 90–94.
4. Stephens, J.E. 1975.
5. BIY: Nom SM 1676/1 (Scarborough); cf Subscription Book 1606–27 – Philip Spark, Wakefield, 1607; John Ashemore, Old Malton, 1622.

YML: Subscription Book 1660–1726 – John Catlyn, Hull 1686, John Grundy, Almondbury, 1686.

6. *See* page 59.

7. Purvis, J.S. 1959: 57 (Plate 24).

8. Peacock, M.H. 1892: 119–20.

9. BIY: Nom SM 1690/11 (Bridlington).

10. *See* pages 96–7.

11. The four are Wakefield (1607), Giggleswick (1642), Sandal Parva (Kirk Sandal) near Doncaster (1642), Slaidburn (in the Forest of Bowland) (1644).

12. Lawson, J. 1963: 79.

13. BIY: Nom SM 1660/1, 1683/3, 1691/3.

14. Purvis, J.S. 1959: 53 (Plate 22) reproduces this testimonial.

15. Wallis, P.J. 1952: 102–104.

16. Hull, Coxwold, Guisborough, Bradford, Calverley, Giggleswick, Halifax, Heptonstall, Leeds, Normanton, Otley, Sherburn, Skipton, Wakefield.

17. Sandal Parva, Slaidburn, Bridlington, Wragby, Kilham, Helmsley, Kirby Moorside, Kirk Leavington, Cawood, Darton, Scarborough.

18. *See* Jewels, E.N. 1963: 22–7.

19. R. O'Day's comments, *see* page 57.

20. This comes from the York records, though Great Ouseburn was in the archdeaconry of Richmond.

21. Purvis, J.S. 1959: 65 (Plate 28). The date is 1686, but the place is not specified.

22. *Ibid.*: 89 (Plate 40).

23. BIY: Nom SM 1664/2. The text of this is damaged and difficult to read.

24. Elsewhere described as 'Proct^r in ye Court of York' (Nom SM 1691/3).

25. Nom SM 1690/10. For Daniel Leech *see* Hunter J. 1869: 409. Leech was curate of Attercliffe from 1673 to 1708.

26. Nom SM 1691/2.

27. Nom SM 1661/4.

28. Nom SM 1690/14.

29. Nom SM 1708/8.

30. Purvis, J.S. 1959: 55 (Plate 23).

31. Nom SM 1697/1.

32. Nom SM 1689/8.

33. Nom SM 1675/5.

34. *See* pages 81–2.

35. Purvis, J.S. 1959: 51, 63 (Plates 21, 27).

36. Nom SM 1663/5.

37. Purvis, J.S. 1959: 45 (Plate 18).

38. Nom SM (Dean and Chapter of York) 1665/1.

39. Nom SM (Dean and Chapter) 1666/1.

40. Nom SM 1688/4.

41. Nom SM 1695/7.

42. Nom SM 1699/7.

43. Nom SM 1709/4.

44. Purvis, J.S. 1948: 194.

45. Purvis, J.S. 1959: 67 (Plate 29), 85 (Plate 38).

46. Nom SM (Dean and Chapter) 1668/1; Nom SM 1675/1, 1690/7, 1696/3.

47. Nom SM 1662/4.

48. Nom SM 1694/8.

49. Nom SM 1698/8.

50. Nom SM (Dean and Chapter) 1663/1 (Upper Poppleton was in the parish of St Mary Bishophill Junior, York); Nom SM 1675/3.

51. Nom SM 1688/7.

52. *See* pages 70–71.

53. Purvis, J.S. 1959: 91 (Plate 41).

54. Nom SM 1677/1.

55.   Nom SM 1690/2; 1690/6.

56.   It is not clear who Ormesby was. He was not vicar of Scarborough (see list of vicars in Rowntree, A. (ed.) *The History of Scarborough* (1931): 94–7). Perhaps he was an influential parishioner or the agent of Lord Bridgwater, patron of the living.

57.   Nom SM 1691/6.

58.   Nom SM 1691/3; 1693/1; Lawson, J. 1963: 102–103.

59.   Nom SM 1696/5.

60.   Nom SM 1706/12.

61.   Nom SM 1688/1.

62.   *See* Purvis, J.S. 1953: 48.

63.   *AR* (Butler, L.A.S. (ed.) 1986/1990). Francis Gastrell was bishop of Chester 1714–25.

64.   The ten are Bedale, Briscall (?Briscoe), Brudnell (?Brignall), Kirkby-on-the-Hill (K. Ravensworth), Richmond, Romaldkirk, Tanfield, Flaxby (par. Goldsborough), Knaresborough, Sedbergh. The five which appear in the Presentment/Compert Books are Bedale, Kirkby-on-the-Hill, Romaldkirk, Flaxby, Knaresborough. For the Wase lists *see* Wallis, P.J. 1952:102–104.

65.   WYAS: RD C/14 (Compert Book Richmond and Catterick deaneries, 1689). Wainwright is not mentioned in Wenham, L.P. 1958.

66.   WYAS: RD/CB/8/16 (Richmond Churchwardens' Presentments).

67.   WYAS: RD/CB/8/76.

68.   WYAS: RD/CB/8/130. 'Sir' means 'Dominus' or Bachelor of Arts.

69.   WYAS: RD/CB/8/89. It is difficult to understand why Riccall should be found in these papers since it is in the East Riding and the diocese of York.

70.   WYAS: RD/CB/8/43, 44, 49.

71.   WYAS: RD/CB/8/55.

72.   WYAS: RD/CB/8/50, 56; 72.

73.   WYAS: RD/CB/8/53, 54.

74.   WYAS: RD/C/ 2.

75. WYAS: RD/C/ 10.

76. WYAS: RD/C/ 11.

77. BIY: Nom SM 1690/9.

78. WYAS: RD/AC/1/5/44; *see also* pages101–102.

79. WYAS: RD/AC/1/5/30.

80. The returns from 1713 to 1732 are contained in a single volume (RD C/23), though there are no entries for some years.

81. *See* page 59.

CHAPTER 5

The Distribution of Schools in the 17th Century

After studying the licensing system as an apparatus of public control, the next step is to estimate the number of schools of different types in the county, to explain how they were founded and administered, and to say something about the history of individual foundations, both large and small.

Recent historians have shown that there was a widespread national movement to found schools and to increase educational opportunity in the 80 years before the outbreak of the Civil War in 1642. Lawrence Stone, for example, has spoken of 'The Educational Revolution in England 1560–1640'.[1] This argument has been most fully developed in a series of books by the American scholar W.K. Jordan.[2] Jordan saw the foundation of schools as part of a great movement of national philanthropy, the primary purpose of which was the relief of poverty. Education played a part in this process because the acquisition of knowledge broke the circle of ignorance and dependence and made social and economic progress possible. It also promoted the triumph of Protestant principles and helped to extinguish the lingering remains of Popery. Jordan argued that the chief agents of these changes were the wealthy London merchants whose benevolence extended over the whole country, with particular concentration on places where they had been born and grown up. Yorkshire was one of the sample counties which Jordan selected for detailed examination. The foundation of many schools helped it to progress from primitive conditions in the late Middle Ages to a much more sophisticated economy by the outbreak of the Civil War. Population was growing again under Elizabeth and the early Stuarts. The fortunes of both Hull and York revived, and the woollen industries of the West Riding expanded steadily. In the reign of James I about 6,000 people lived in the extensive parish of Leeds, most of them in the town itself. The progress made by the Sheffield cutlery industry was marked by the incorporation of the Cutlers' Company in 1624.[3]

W.K. Jordan calculated that between 1480 and 1660 £243,650.14.0 was given for charitable benefactions in Yorkshire, of which £75,812.8.0 or 31.12% was devoted to education.[4] £48,572.16.0 of this had been spent on grammar or elementary school foundations.[5] In the 40 years before 1640 32 schools had been founded or endowed in the county, while donations of various kinds had been made to 23 more.[6] As a result of these developments, with the exceptions of two mountainous and thinly peopled areas, 'no boy in 1660 could have lived more than 12 miles from an endowed school with all the opportunities that were opened to youth by its beneficent presence.'[7] The accuracy of Jordan's statistics has been much attacked, particularly since he based all his figures on an assumption of constant levels of prices in an age when inflation was high and long-continued.[8] He has also been criticized for exaggerating the part played by the London merchants and for over-emphasizing the religious – and especially the Puritan – impulse behind the efforts of charitable donors.[9] Yet, when all the qualifications have been made and the effects of inflation have been taken into account, Jordan's work does substantiate the general picture of development and change in the period between the accession of Elizabeth I and the outbreak of the Civil War.

Jordan also emphasized the growth in the number of endowed schools. There had always been from medieval times, and there continued to be in the future, many schools and many teachers who flourished for a longer or a shorter period according to the success or otherwise of individual effort. Endowments might be abused or misused, but they did provide a constant background of stability for succeeding generations, and for that reason alone the years between 1560 and 1640 laid a foundation which has been important for English education ever since. Jordan has charted one of the major social movements of modern English history, and Yorkshire participated in it as much as any other part of the country.

Several calculations have been made of the number of grammar schools in the county, though the suggested totals differ widely between different sources. For elementary schools no hard statistics exist, though an attempt will be made to offer some estimates which take the story a certain way, but cannot claim to tell the whole of it. Grammar schools were fewer in number, more prestigious and much easier to identify. Christopher Wase in the Restoration period listed 65 endowed grammar schools in Yorkshire which break down as follows: City of York, 1 (St Peter's); East Riding, 6; North Riding, 12; West Riding, 46.[10] Nicholas Carlisle in 1818, after the attrition in the number of grammar schools which took place through the 18th century, listed 52 such schools:[11] City of York, 2 (St Peter's and Archbishop Holgate's); East Riding, 3; North Riding, 16; West Riding, 31. Since Wase listed 30 schools which are not in Carlisle and Carlisle listed 17 schools which are not in Wase, the two lists taken together provide a grand total of 82 endowed grammar schools.

Exact comparisons between later lists are difficult to make because different lists use different terminal dates. J.E.G. Montmorency (1902), using the figures from the *Digest of Schools and Charities for Education* presented to Parliament in 1842, calculated a total for the county of 102 grammar schools and 242 endowed non-classical schools. The same source also provides a total of 258 educational charities not attached to endowed schools.[12] These totals cover the foundations of the late 17th and the 18th centuries, and so cover a wider time-span than Wase. A.F. Leach, in his substantial contribution on schools to the *Victoria History of Yorkshire*, vol I (1907), wrote separate histories of 99 schools founded before 1714; these are mostly grammar schools, though a few of them seem to have been of a lower status. Leach also listed, without giving any detailed notice of them, 18 other schools founded before the Reformation, so his total of grammar schools founded before 1714 amounts to some 110/115. His list of 'Elementary Schools founded before 1770' will be discussed later.[13]

W.A.L. Vincent (1950) gives a list in an appendix which, he says, 'contains the names of grammar schools which existed in England and Wales between 1600 and 1660', that is a period of time very similar to that for which Wase collected his figures. Vincent's list gives 155 schools in Yorkshire.[14] P.J. Wallis and W.E. Tate (1956) provide the fullest and the most carefully documented account thus far available.[15] They included only schools which existed before 1700, which takes in a period 40 years later than Vincent's deadline. Their criterion for inclusion was, in most cases, that a school had sent at least one pupil to, or had had as a master a member of, one of the universities. Inclusion did not mean, Wallis and Tate explained, that a school functioned permanently as a grammar school, nor did evidence from different dates imply a common institutional identity nor a continuous existence over the intervening period. Their list is not confined to endowed schools and is therefore more inclusive in its nature than the older lists which are generally so restricted. It is clearly very difficult, when considering this 17th century evidence, to draw a precise line between schools of different types, and different historians have interpreted the data in different ways. For example, there are about 20 schools which appear as grammar schools in the Wallis/Tate lists which Leach includes in his list of 'elementary schools founded before 1770'.[16] It is always important to remember Rosemary O'Day's warning that it is impossible to impose a rigid pattern on schools which covered a multiplicity of types and were responsive to many local pressures.[17]

Yet, when all these limitations have been borne in mind, Wallis and Tate do present a total number of grammar schools in the county far higher than that given by earlier writers. They claim that their tables extend the number of such schools by more than 100%, and they argue that even this higher figure underestimates the true total.[18] At the same time they warn against the dangers involved in simply adding up their examples. If that be done with the consciousness in mind of the dangers involved in the procedure, the total number of grammar schools comes to 335 (City of York, 17; East Riding, 59; North Riding, 85; West Riding, 174). Of these 66 had been mentioned before 1548 (City of York, 4; East Riding, 8; North Riding, 14, West Riding, 40). However inexact all these totals may be, the great increase in numbers after the middle of the 16th century does testify to the great expansion of schooling in the subsequent period. There may be reservations about accepting such a massive increase in the number of grammar schools as that suggested by Wallis and Tate, particularly on the grounds that some of the schools listed may have functioned as grammar schools for only brief periods. However, they do make a strong case for claiming that the earlier estimates were too low.

The problem of continuity is even more of an issue in the case of elementary or petty schools. Here the great bulk of the evidence has been gathered from the diocesan records and will be presented in the same way as before: York first, Chester (archdeaconry of Richmond) second. Some further material has been collected from other sources, especially from A.F. Leach's articles in *VCH Yorkshire*. Some of the petty schools were permanently endowed institutions, but in the majority of cases, as in the York Schoolmasters' Nominations, the information we have relates to individual masters who might or might not be succeeded by someone else when they died or moved away. A reference to the same place at different times might encompass different schools or indeed not refer to an established school at all. A Nomination tells us something about an individual teacher at a particular point of time. It may or may not have reference to a permanent institution.

On the other hand the 60 elementary schools listed by Leach as founded before 1714 were all permanently established structures. These, like the grammar schools figures already cited, are figures for the whole county; they include schools in the dioceses of both York and Chester. A few examples from Leach will provide a picture which is characteristic of the whole series. Once again the difficulty in defining the exact function and academic level of a school is to be noted. At Halton

97

Gill (par. Arncliffe, WR) in 1619 Henry Fawcett of Norwich gave £10 yearly to the minister for teaching poor men's children and reading the service. In 1630 William Fawcett added another £13.6.8, 'having built a schoolhouse where the 'rudiments of grammar' should be taught'.[19] At Kirkby Malzeard in 1640 Gilbert Horseman left a rent-charge of £5 to maintain five poor scholars, and in 1716 Gregory Elsley gave the schoolhouse which he had built and certain lands for teaching ten poor children.[20] In 1705 Ralph Lowther gave £100 for the support of the curate of Sawley (par. Ripon) for 'carefully teaching and instructing gratis to read English and to write 6 poor boys or girls'.[21] In 1710 Miss Dorothy Wilson of York made bequests to several places in and near the city, giving by will

> £20 yearly for teaching 20 poor boys in the testatrix's house at Foss Bridge End in York, also £20 for clothing them in blue cloth faced with green. Further she gave 10 cattle-gates in Skipwith Holmes, if a schoolhouse were provided there, and 20s. half-yearly to a school dame in St Dyonis' parish for teaching 6 poor children to read, and a further bequest to Nun Monkton School.[22]

The York Schoolmasters' Nominations for the years 1607 to 1714 include rather more than 100 examples which explicitly in some cases and implicitly in others refer to elementary schools (including so-called 'private' schools under that heading). These schools do not appear in the Wallis/Tate lists, and are therefore separate from the grammar schools already discussed. Of this total of about 100 only seven (Northowram (par.Halifax); Hepworth (par.Kirkburton); Felkirk; Hampsthwaite (two different schools); Aston; Catcliffe (par. Rotherham)) appear in Leach's list of elementary schools, so it is reasonable to argue that the Nominations reveal the existence of about 100 schools/teachers in the diocese of York in addition to the 60 named by Leach for the whole county. The totals for the archdeaconry of Richmond will be discussed later.

It would be a tedious task to list these 100 teachers and the places where they taught, but by grouping them into areas it is possible to obtain an interesting picture of the distribution of elementary schools in various parts of the diocese. As might be expected, since the district was already thickly populated, the largest group (about 40 cases) was to be found in Leeds and the clothing district, that is about two-fifths of the whole. The nominations came from the towns – Leeds itself, Wakefield, the great parish of Halifax with its dependencies of Brighouse, Elland, Luddenden and Sowerby, Dewsbury, Huddersfield with its neighbouring villages of Longworth and Golcar. There are smaller places too – Heptonstall, Kippax, Knottingley, Harewood, Brotherton, Thorner, Mirfield and Calverley. Hull and the East Riding are well represented with some 16 cases, almost all of them in the villages such as Barmston, Warter, Skirlaugh, Hayton, Hunmanby, Swine, Rise and Flamborough. There are about ten cases from what we now call South Yorkshire – several from the Sheffield area, one from Wentworth and two from Thorne. There is a similar number from York and its environs, two from city parishes and the remainder from the surrounding villages such as Colton (par. Bolton Percy) and Upper Poppleton. The smallest group of seven is from the North Riding beyond the environs of York, and half of these are petty schools in Whitby. This was a very thinly peopled area, and much of the diocese lay in the diocese of Chester. Perhaps too, since this was the traditionally Catholic part of the county, there was an inbred reluctance to conform to the system and a tendency for teachers to stay outside it if they could.

This analysis of the York Nominations provides at least some indication how many petty schools there were, though no doubt many others escaped the licensing net. It also shows that schools and teachers were widely spread, and that schooling was provided in many villages as well as in the towns, though in the smaller places particularly the reference to a schoolmaster in a certain year does not mean necessarily that there was an established school in that village. The evidence for the archdeaconry of Richmond leads to rather similar conclusions. There were a few well-known schools in this part of the county, but most of those mentioned were village schools in quite remote places. The Richmond sources are the parish

99

presentments and the Compert books in the West Yorkshire archives which have been used for the discussion of licensing. There is further material from Leach's list of elementary schools and the 'Notitia Cestrensis' of 1714–25.[23]

The papers in the West Yorkshire archives mention schools and teachers in 68/69 different places. Many villages are mentioned more than once, and, particularly when there is a gap of a number of years between such references, there may not have been any continuity between the institutions so named. However, each place has been counted only once which may if anything underestimate the total number of schools/teachers which can be traced. Leach's list of elementary schools names ten in the archdeaconry. Three of these are already included in the West Yorkshire archives numbers, so that Leach adds seven new names to the previous total of 68/69, which gives a grand total from all these sources of about 75. Of this number 27/28 appear in the Wallis and Tate list of grammar schools,[24] so that if that number be deducted, we are left with a figure of about 50 elementary schools, or rather fewer than that.

If the schools so far mentioned are then compared with the information given in the 'Notitia', this total can be slightly increased. The presentments mention about seven schools which the 'Notitia' do not include, but the 'Notitia' add nine more, many of them like Austwick and Newby in Clapham parish, West House Green and Burton-in-Lonsdale in Thornton-in-Lonsdale parish, and Howgill in Sedbergh parish in the far north-western deanery of Lonsdale for which there do not appear to be any papers for this period in the West Yorkshire archives. This total of nine does not include a few more of the 'Notitia' schools which are in the Wallis and Tate lists. The conclusion seems to be that there were about 60 (50 *plus* 9 from the 'Notitia') elementary schools in the archdeaconry at the end of the 17th/beginning of the 18th centuries. The grammar schools have already been accounted for in the figures for the whole county.

This rather tedious calculation, though it has been worked out from two different bases, does not claim to offer any more than a general guide to the number

100

of elementary schools which can be traced in the archdeaconry of Richmond by the early years of the 18th century. It is difficult to avoid repetition from different lists, to be certain whether these do or do not refer to the same school, and there is the constant danger of double-counting the grammar schools. However, once these reservations have been made, the totals cited probably take the discussion about as far as the evidence will carry us. It is clear from the entries in the 'Notitia' that many villages had no teacher or school at all. It is perhaps surprising that so many schools existed in remote places. Before we leave the archdeaconry it will be interesting to flesh out the picture with a little more detail.

The longest entries in the 'Notitia' generally refer to the grammar schools and other endowed schools. At Burneston there was both a free school (presumably a grammar school) and a petty school.[25] The 'Notitia' writes

> Here is a free school founded and endowed by Matthew Robinson Vicar in 1680. Salary to Master £16 p.a. paid out of lands with another school adjoining for a petty master who has 9s. per month allowed him and £5.8s. 0d. given by the said Mr. Robinson and every year a purple gown. Nomination of a Master is vested in the vicar for the time being...The Master ought to be a graduate in one of the Universities or within a year of taking his degree, to be examined and approved by certificate under hand of Ministers of Bedale, Kirklington and Burneston before he be accepted. The founder likewise intended that he should be a clergyman that he might assist the vicar. The Vicar of Burneston to have 2 votes in the choice of a master, the other Trustees have each one. There is a good Schoolhouse, Chamber and Garden for the Master and he is paid for each scholar outside of the parish 20 shillings p.a.[26]

In 1717 the minister and churchwardens of Knaresborough certified that the borough contained a free school 'founded in the Reign of Kg James the first by Dr. Chandler Rect[r] of Agmondesham in Buckinghamshire, And endow'd by him with £20 pr annm for one Master'. The master was appointed by the 16 governors. In addition there were six teachers in 'private schools', three in the borough and three in 'the out hamletts', one of the teachers in the second group being a woman and a Quaker.[27] There is no evidence about the level of work done in the private schools; it is probably wise once again to remember that the lines were often very imprecise. The very rare reference to a woman should be noted, as also the fact that she was a Quaker.

Both Burneston and Knaresborough schools appear in the Wallis and Tate list of grammar schools, as do other endowed schools mentioned in the records like Hartforth (par. Gilling), Kirkby Ravensworth, Wath, Lartington (par. Romaldkirk), Ripley and Flaxby (par. Goldsborough). Probably many of these lay on the borderline between grammar and elementary, filling different roles for different pupils and at different times. Some of these schools (or at last schools in the same places since it is not possible to be certain that different references always refer to the same school) are called 'English' or 'petty' in the records; for example Garsdale,[28] and Goldsborough and Ainderby Steeple,[29] though all these places have an entry in Wallis and Tate. In several cases a town or a village had a grammar school and other schools as well. Knaresborough and Burneston have already been mentioned. The 'Notitia' entry for Sedbergh records the grammar school, one of the most prominent in the county, plus two petty schools

> Given by Mr Holme Rector of Lowther £100 for an English School for boys and girls not yet fully settled. *An. 1724* By Mr. William Burton of this town £40 more for the same use. *Certificate An. 1725.* Here is also a private school for teaching the younger children endowed only with £2 p.a.[30]

The Compert book for 1719 recorded for Bedale a grammar school with an endowment of £20 per annum, a charity school at Aiskew (Ascough), and another in Bedale itself, 'not taught by the Curate but by other psons'.[31]

The endowments given or bequeathed for village schools were often small in value. At Cleasby near Darlington, John Robinson, Bishop of London 1714–23, had built the church and founded a school which he endowed with £10 per annum. He also built a house for the master. That was a generous provision.[32] At Thornton Watlass the master had £5/6, at Barningham £4.4.7½.[33] Some had much less. At Howgill (par. Sedbergh) the master's salary was 40s. plus a little close of the value of 4s.[34] At Patrick Brompton there was

> a little school erected in 1707 by Samuel Atkinson to which he left a close of 20s. p.a. at Newton. Given since by Samuel Clark of London £3 p.a. Master nominated by parish. The £3 p.a. was given for teaching 6 poor parish boys. The Curate generally teaches.[35]

In some cases (Clapham, West House Green (par. Thornton-in-Lonsdale), Ingleton) the schoolhouse had been built by the inhabitants,[36] and the school was supported both by the parish and by individual benefactions. At Barton Cuthberts (par. Gilling), for example, there was

> a schoolhouse and garth belonging to it worth about £1 10s. p.a. purchased at the charge of the town for a master to teach their children, who has also the interest on £50 p.a. left by Thomas Smithson for teaching ten poor children.[37]

In many villages the schoolmaster had no such support, either public or private, to depend on. The Compert books mention a number of such cases. At East Witton there were three private schools, two English, one grammar ... 'Noe Endowmᵗ to any of them'. At Eriholme there was an English school 'for the use of the Neighbours, but uncertain and inconsiderable'.[38] The same picture is revealed in the Cause Papers. These two examples come from 1717. At Kirkby super Moram there was a school taught by Mr William Sharpe, curate of Skelton in the parish of Ripon, but it was not free and there was no 'Salary, Rent, Pension or Exhibition' belonging to it. At Whixley the curate and churchwardens reported that we have a private school taught by our Curate, but the profits will not find both Meal & Apparel, without further assistance from children's parents (as we believe), but no sufficient salary or settled Maintenance for a teacher.[39]

Similarly the 'Notitia' record that at Ainderby Steeple there was a petty school with a master who taught reading and writing, 'but without salary or pension'.[40] Such schoolmasters must have found it very difficult to survive financially. Frequently a man doubled as curate and schoolmaster. Others probably augmented the meagre sums they could earn from school fees by doing other work, though clearly, since there were number of men in this position, it must have been possible for them to make some sort of living.

This material from the York and Richmond records provides the greater part of what has been discovered about Yorkshire elementary or petty schools in the late 17th/early 18th centuries. A little more can be added from other sources so far traced, and no doubt more could be found from parish records and other local material. John Lawson has traced schools in the East Riding at Acklam, Marton, Otteringham and Skipsea from the Visitation Act books of 1600.[41] The modern editor of the 'Notitia', in an appendix on the Archbishop's liberty of Ripon, noted three township schools in addition to Ripon grammar school. These three schools were at Pateley Bridge, Sawley and Winksley. Each had a small endowment, and the school at Sawley was taught by the curate.[42] Similar schools can be traced in several towns. At Skipton the Clerk's School, which was usually taught by the parish clerk, had been founded in 1555. J.S. Purvis prints a testimonial of 1698 for the master, John Bowcocke.[43] At Beverley there are several references in the borough records for the 1670s and 1680s to the school attached to St Mary's Church.[44] At Wakefield the Storie petty school was established in 1674 by the grammar school governors as a result of the bequest of John Storie of Hasleborrow in Derbyshire. The governors appointed a schoolmaster to teach 12 boys who were 'to be admitted as Free Petty Scholars till they are fit for the Free Grammar

School'. In 1703 the governors decided to spend some of their funds on educating some of the poorest children in the town. At first these were split up among several teachers, but later a schoolhouse was built and William Lambert, master of the scholars under Storie's bequest, was appointed master of the petty school at the substantial salary of £20, with a dame as assistant at £10 a year.[45]

These developments in Wakefield take us into the story of the Charity Schools which will be dealt with later.[46] By the end of the 17th century the pattern of education was changing considerably from that which had existed at the beginning of the Civil War. In Yorkshire new schools had continued to be founded. Leach gives an account of 41 new foundations between 1640 and 1714 – 28 of them in the West Riding, 11 in the North, 1 in the East and 1 in the Ainsty.[47] All of these were located in villages and small towns because schools had been established earlier in the larger centres. In the country as a whole grammar schools were declining in comparative importance, and more attention was being given to elementary education, to more modern and practical studies, and to the setting up of private schools with a more liberal curriculum than that offered by the traditional grammar school. The growth of the private school was to some extent the result of the Civil War and its aftermath. During the Protectorate Charles Hoole, formerly headmaster of Rotherham Grammar School and the best known writer of his day on the grammar school curriculum, had kept a successful school in London, as did many others of the displaced Anglican clergy.[48] After the Restoration many Dissenting ministers, displaced in their turn, did the same, and this became more common as the burdens of the Clarendon Code became lighter after 1689.

The split between Anglican and Puritan was an important influence in breaking up the shared social and educational background from which the early Stuart grammar schools had drawn much of their strength. It is possible that one reason for the decline in grammar school numbers was the increasing difficulty experienced by poor men in securing livings.[49] If this were so, there was less incentive for such men to go to university and therefore fewer attractions in pursuing the full grammar school course up to university entrance. Certainly university matriculations fell, at Cambridge more sharply than at Oxford, and it was at Cambridge that most Yorkshire boys had gone to study. J.A. Venn estimated that from 1600 to 1699 Cambridge welcomed 30,000 freshmen and Oxford 31,000; from 1700 to 1799 the comparable figures were 16,000 and 25,000. Matriculations which in 1620 had been about 450 a year at Cambridge had fallen to about 190 in 1700 and to about 150 in 1750.[50] Such a fall must have meant that many grammar schools had entirely ceased to train boys for the university or at best produced a candidate at only infrequent intervals. In any grammar school, even the largest and most successful, the number of university candidates in any one year can never have been very large. Yet the training of those boys set the tone for the whole work of the school, and if they were to disappear or become very few in number, much of the rationale for the maintenance in that school of the full classical curriculum vanished. The pupils who remained were likely to demand a basic English curriculum and to leave school at an early age.

One modern writer has spoken of a pattern among schools of 'the survival of the fittest'.[51] On the whole the larger better-known schools went on in the 18th century very much as they had done in the 17th, though individual schools always had their times of good and bad fortune. As we shall see, many of the Yorkshire grammar schools went on sending boys to the universities throughout the 18th century, and the more successful of them attracted boarders from prominent local families. The concentration of such boys into a few 'public schools' was a 19th century rather than an 18th century phenomenon. From the later 17th century the smaller and less successful schools dropped out of the race and settled for a purely local role in teaching the elementary subjects. It is not possible to document this development in detail in the case of any particular school, but what happened in many places over a long period of time is suggested very well by what Nicholas Carlisle wrote in his survey of 1818 about Batley Grammar School. The system of education there, he wrote, was such as is generally followed in Grammar Schools...But *Classical* learning here is now, and for some time past, has been little regarded – the Inhabitants being persons engaged in business, and almost entirely of the lower class of labouring people. Reading, writing, and arithmetic are, therefore, all that they wish for in the education of their children, with very few exceptions.[52]

After the Restoration there were those who claimed that too many scholars were being produced and who argued, like Thomas Hobbes in *Behemoth* (1679) that the universities were to blame for the Great Rebellion since the teaching of the classics had taught men to identify liberty with republicanism.[53] Christopher Wase's unfinished enquiry into grammar schools, which has already been referred to,[54] was part of a movement to defend the grammar schools against these charges. In his book *Considerations concerning Free Schools as settled in England*,[55] Wase maintained that endowments were advantageous because they enabled men to be trained for the highest offices and for the service of the state, while it was desirable that the sons of the gentry should attend the grammar schools. Men were sent out from the schools and universities 'ingag'd in the strictest bonds of allegiance', and 'the late Civil Commotions' did not prove that the country was overstocked with scholars. It was important, he argued, that the country should not neglect the benefits which it had received from the schools.

But have we not Free-Schools in almost every Market-Town? Did we depreciat benefactions received: we should be unthankful to God and unjust to the memory of many worthy Patriots, Ornaments of their Profession, who have so far extended these provisions towards the preparing of youth for business religious and secular; of which benefit, others more directly, but the whole Country in some measure partakes. Lastly we should ill deserve of that Faith, whose Charity we dishonor'd.[56]

Wase published his book but he never completed and published his statistical enquiry. It has been suggested that he abandoned it because he had met with opposition, and he feared that to press ahead might do more harm than good to the cause he wished to defend.[57] The grammar schools experienced no direct attack in the later 17th century, but their role in the 18th was to be less central than it had been in the years before the Civil War. There was a strong demand for new studies like modern languages and mathematics which, because of their traditional curricula and teaching methods, they were unable to meet. The gap was filled by the growth of private schools, more sensitive to the demands of the clientele which patronized them, more adept at meeting changing needs. One of Wase's correspondents reported that there were fewer pupils in the free schools of Warwickshire than in earlier years because many masters had begun to teach private schools.[58] Increasingly such schools were set up for girls as well as for boys. Some of the boys' private schools retained a largely classical curriculum, but others emphasized more practical and vocational studies. A similarly utilitarian impulse lay behind the expansion of elementary education at the end of the 17th century through the creation of the charity schools which aimed to provide for the poor, both boys and girls, not only the skills of literacy, but religious training and sometimes vocational expertise as well. By 1700 the traditional grammar school had been supplemented and in part replaced by schools of several different types. It remains to examine in later chapters how all these developments affected educational patterns in Yorkshire.[59]

Notes Chapter 5

1. *See* Stone, L. 1964: 41–80.
2. Jordan, W.K. 1959, 1960, 1961, 1962. For Jordan *see* pages 40–41.
3. Hey, D. 1986: 131–5, 139, 150–52, 154–5.
4. Jordan, W.K. 1961: 440 (Appendix Table III).
5. *Ibid.*: 348.
6. *Ibid.*: 338–9.

7. *Ibid.*: 348.

8. *See* Jordan, W.K. 1959: 34 for his argument on this topic.

9. Feingold, M. 1979: 257–73.

10. Wallis, P.J. 1952: 102–4.

11. Carlisle, N. 1818 vol II: 778–920.

12. Montmorency, J.E.G. de 1902 App II: 243–7.

13. *See VCH Yorkshire* vol I (1907): 415–500 for Leach's articles on schools.

14. Vincent, W.A.L. 1950 App A: 133–4.

15. Wallis, P.J. and Tate, W.E. 1956: 64–104.

16. It is impossible to give a precise figure because it is not always certain whether the two sources are describing the same school, but this figure of 20 is approximately correct.

17. O'Day, R. 1982: 40.

18. Wallis, P.J. and Tate, W.E. 1956: 65–6.

19. *VCH Yorkshire* vol I (1907): 491.

20. *Ibid.*: 492.

21. *Ibid.*: 494.

22. *Ibid.*: 495. The schoolhouse at Foss Bridge End still exists; the present building dates from 1812.

23. For the 'Notitia Cestrensis' *see* page 84.

24. *See* pages 96–7.

25. *See also VCH Yorkshire* vol I (1907): 487.

26. *AR*: 70 (Catterick deanery).

27. WYAS: Cause Papers (RD/AC/1/5/44 – Knaresborough, 1717). 'Agmondesham' is Amersham, and *see also VCH Yorkshire* vol I (1907): 482.

28. *AR*: 103.

29. WYAS: RD C/23 (Compert Books 1719, 1720).

30. AR: 101.

31. WYAS: RD/C 23; and *see AR*: 68.

32. *AR*: 111.

33. *AR*: 89, 109.

34. *AR*: 103.

35. *AR*: 83.

36. *AR*: 98, 99, 104.

37. *AR*: 135-6.

38. WYAS: RD/C 23.

39. WYAS: RD/AC/1/5/24 (Whixley); *ibid.*/27 (Kirkby super Moram). For the latter *see also AR*: 51.

40. *AR*: 108.

41. Lawson, J. 1959: 3.

42. *AR*: App 1: 155–6.

43. Gibbon, A.M. 1947 App C: 144–7; Purvis, J.S. 1959: 51 (Plate 21); *see also* page 78.

44. Dennett, J. (ed.) 1932: 153, 156, 173.

45. Walker, J.W. 1966 vol II: 373–4.

46. *See* Chapter 10.

47. *VCH Yorkshire* vol I (1907): 483–8.

48. For Charles Hoole *see* pages 145–8.

49. O'Day, R. 1982: 198; and *see* page 181.

50. *See VCH Yorkshire* vol III (1959): 214.

51. O'Day, R. 1982: 204.

52. Carlisle, N. 1818 vol II: 780.

53. Watson, F. 1916: 128; Lawson, J. and Silver, H. 1973: 179–80.

54. *See* pages 73–4.

55. Wase, C. 1678.

56. *Ibid.*: 110.

57. Vincent, W.A.L. 1969: 39. Chapter II of Vincent's book deals with Wase's enquiry.

58. *Ibid.*: 205.

59. For an expansion of these points *see* Chapter 8.

CHAPTER 6

Individual Founders and Foundations

The effects on the schools of the dissolution of the chantries has already been discussed in an earlier chapter.[1] Some schools like Sedbergh, Giggleswick and Pocklington had been re-founded with substantial endowments. Others like Pontefract, Rotherham and Hull had been left with nothing beyond an annual pension for the master, the real value of which was to decline steadily as time went on. Yorkshire shared fully in the national movement between 1560 and 1640 to found and endow schools, but the pattern in the county was rather different from that in other parts of England. There were few large donors, but a great deal of community effort in collecting money and providing buildings. Some well known schools such as Wakefield were launched with a large number of small gifts, and it was quite common for the founder to provide an endowment for a master and for the town or village to build the schoolhouse. The outstanding individual benefactor was Robert Holgate, archbishop of York 1545–54, who was, from one point of view, the last of the great medieval churchmen in the tradition of Thomas Rotherham and from another, the pioneer of the new ideas of the Renaissance in the curriculum which he laid down for his schools at York, Old Malton, and Hemsworth.

W.K. Jordan has made much of the importance of the great London merchants. He estimated that 10 out of 103 endowed schools in the county were founded by London merchants and tradesmen.[2] Among these were Coxwold

(1604), founded by Sir John Harte, a grocer who had been lord mayor in 1589–90, Burnsall (1605), founded by Sir William Craven and his wife, Dame Elizabeth, and Topcliffe (1635), founded by William Robinson, a merchant.[3] None of these was of major importance. In general the impetus behind the Yorkshire schools of the 16th/17th centuries seems to have been strongly local in its motivation.

A general survey of elementary schools has already been attempted in the previous chapter, though it is not possible to provide any detailed picture of particular schools of this kind. Much more is known about the grammar schools. Though most of them still remain little more than names, there are some 25 to 30 among them which have a recognizable history and personality. Some of these histories will later be examined, including, so far as is possible, both larger and better known and smaller and more obscure schools.

The thread of continuing local support comes out strongly in the case of schools which had been left in a weakened condition as a result of the abolition of the chantries and religious houses. At Beverley, after the collegiate church had been suppressed, the school was continued by warrant of the commissioners.[4] In 1552 the burgesses petitioned for a grant of lands to provide for the support of the minster and for the establishment of a grammar school since there were so many young people in the town who needed to be brought up in learning. The lands for the upkeep of the minster were granted, though there is no record of what happened about the school. In the 1560s and 1570s the town accounts record payments to the schoolmaster; in 1572, for example, the Town Governors agreed to appoint a master to teach the 'petties' so that the grammar schoolmaster might not be required to do such work. In 1602–3, after a gap in the accounts, the town was helping to maintain an exhibitioner at Cambridge, and in 1606–7 a new schoolhouse was built. The same pattern of municipal support continued in later years. In 1612–13 the schoolmaster was paid £10, more money was spent on exhibitioners at Cambridge, and Erasmus's *Adages* were bought for the schoolhouse.[5] The question of school books and school libraries will be further discussed later.[6]

Two of the re-founded schools already referred to were Pontefract and Rotherham.[7] At Pontefract the master's continued stipend, reflecting the old chantry income, was only £2.19.2, which was clearly insufficient to maintain an efficient teacher. In 1583 a decree of the Chancellor and Council of the Duchy of Lancaster consolidated the Pontefract income with that of four other small schools to produce an income for a master and usher at Pontefract of £25.7.2.[8] The decree claimed that the combined incomes would suffice to maintain 'a meete learned and sufficient School-master and Usher' in Pontefract which was both an important borough and the seat of a major royal castle. The townspeople had made suit for this change and had promised to build, furnish and repair a suitable schoolhouse. The Chancellor of the Duchy was to appoint the schoolmaster who was to be paid £20 a year and the remaining £5.7.2 was to be paid to an usher chosen by the mayor and townspeople with the agreement of the schoolmaster.

At Rotherham the grammar schoolmaster had to go to the Court of Exchequer in 1561 to establish his right to his stipend, and the decree cost the townspeople 20 marks to obtain.[9] In 1584 William West, the seneschal of the Earl of Shrewsbury, the great local magnate, arranged for the re-purchase of some of the old chantry lands, partly by paying for them himself, partly by general subscription, and in 1589 the 12 Feoffees of the Common Lands of Rotherham were set up to manage the properties. They spent their income partly on the relief of the poor, partly on the maintenance and repair of bridges, and, from the end of the 16th century, partly on repairing the fabric of the schoolhouse.[10] The accounts of the two greaves show payments for 'mossinge and ridgeinge the Scholehouse' (1598), for a quart of wine and sugar at the putting in of a new schoolmaster (1620), for two 'dixionaries', a calfskin to cover them, and a payment to the book-binder (1621). In 1632 the threat of a legal action against the legal validity of the purchase of the lands in 1584 cost the feoffees no less than £7.6.6 in fees and travelling expenses to London.[11]

There is some evidence to suggest a lingering feeling of resentment in the town over the fate of Archbishop Rotherham's bequest. In a document of about 1591 a local clergyman, Michael Sherbrook, rector of Wickersley, himself an old boy of the school, described the original foundation and the poor state into which the building had fallen, being then used as a malthouse.

> Now let every one consider what great loss this was to such a Town, and the Country round it, not only for the Cause of learning, but also for the help of the Poor; that now in the Town is not a few: for there are many more than there was then.[12]

And long after Sherbrook's time Charles Hoole, the Rotherham schoolmaster of the 17th century, recounted the story of the fight in 1561 for the schoolmaster's stipend, and added

> I remember how often and earnestly Mr. Francis West, who had been clerk to his uncle, would declame against the injury done to that school, which indeed (as he said) ought still to have been kept in the college, and how when I was schoolmaster there he gave me a copy of the foundation, and showed me some rentals of lands, and told me where many deeds and evidences belonging thereunto were then concealed, and other remarkable passages, which he was loth to have buried in silence.[13]

The old order, which Mr. Francis West still lamented in the days of King Charles I, had enjoyed a brief re-birth in the reign of Queen Mary (1553-8).[14] In 1555 Rotherham's neighbours in Sheffield had been re-granted by letters patent certain chantry lands which were to be administered by the 12 Capital Burgesses of the town and parish.[15] Like the Feoffees of the Rotherham Common Lands, the Burgesses spent money on education. There are several references in their accounts for Elizabeth's reign to a school and schoolmaster. Sheffield grammar school was endowed in 1603-4 under the will of Thomas Smith, and in 1619 the Church Burgesses transferred the schoolhouse and croft to the school Governors.[16] As in so

116

many instances in Yorkshire schooling was provided through the co-operation of several agencies, one of which, in this Sheffield case, drew its income from pre-Reformation religious sources.

The traditionalist language used in the re-foundation deeds of St Peter's School, York, has already been cited.[17] The tones of an older Catholic England can be heard even more loudly in the foundation the previous year of the school and hospital at Kirkby Ravensworth (Kirkby Hill) near Richmond. These were set up by John Dakyn, archdeacon of the East Riding, as executor of William Knight, bishop of Bath and Wells (d. 1547) and others.[18] In May 1556, after the Mass of the Holy Ghost had been celebrated and Dakyn had preached on the text 'Except the Lord build the house...', the first guardians, master and almspeople were chosen. The schoolmaster was required to recite with his scholars prayers and collects in Latin every day, to say mass at least twice a week in the parish church, to pray for the good estate in life and for the repose of their souls after death of King Philip and Queen Mary, of John Dakyn and other members of his family, of Bishop Knight and of Robert Holgate, late archbishop. He was to instruct his scholars in such Latin authors as inculcated piety and good morals, and when he was admitted to his office, he was to swear

> that I will not read to my scholars any reprobate or corrupt bookes or workes set forth at anie time contrarie to the determination of the universal or catholic church, whereby they might be infected in their youth with anie kind of corrupt doctrine, or els be induced to insolent manner of living.[19]

Dakyn died on 9 November 1558 and Robert Holgate, whose name appears on his bead-roll, three years earlier on 15 November 1555. Holgate was probably born at Hemsworth near Pontefract in the West Riding about 1481.[20] He became a canon of the order of St. Gilbert of Sempringham, prior of Watton in Yorkshire and master of the order. In 1537 he was appointed bishop of Llandaff and he was President of the Council of the North 1538–50. He succeeded Edward Lee as archbishop of York in 1545. He had been generously pensioned off after the suppression of his order, and in October 1546 he was given letters patent for the foundation of 'three free and perpetual schools', one at Old Malton in the North Riding, one at Hemsworth, and the third at York.[21] The deed of foundation of the York school begins by setting out the arrangements for the establishment of the three schools with a total endowment for the three masters of £56, 'over and above all charges and reprises' – that is, £12 for the York master, £24 for Hemsworth, £20 for Old Malton.[22]

The York school was to be sited in the Close, and the master was to teach 'Gramer and other knowledges and Godly Lernyngs' to his scholars without any fee or charge. The schoolmaster was then named. He and his successors were to be a body corporate with a common seal, and were to be appointed by the archbishop with provisions for other nominators to act in case he failed to name a master within the prescribed period. The schoolmaster was to understand Hebrew, Greek and Latin and was to teach them to his scholars, with especial emphasis on the 'Latin Tonge and Gramer'. The introduction of Greek and Hebrew should particularly be noted since this expresses the new scholastic ideals of the Renaissance as they had been set out by pioneers like John Colet, the founder of St Paul's School in London. It has been said that this is the first reference to the teaching of Hebrew in schools, something which became fairly common later in the century. The teaching of Greek is much more important because it brought Holgate's schools into line with the practice of the leading grammar schools of the time. Certainly for conservative Yorkshire, this all sets a very new tone. It is interesting to compare Dakyn's Kirkby Ravensworth statutes of a decade later which only mention the teaching of Latin.

Arrangements were then laid down for the more detailed conduct of the school at York. The usher was to be paid by the master. The school hours were to be from 6.30 a.m. till 11 a.m. and from 1 p.m. to 6 p.m. in summer, with a later start and an earlier finish in winter. The master and the usher were to be present in the school at all times. The prayers to be said during each day were laid down, and each Sunday or holy day the master and his scholars were to attend the cathedral or parish church. Regulations were made about the dismissal of the master, about the school property and the grant of leases, about the disposal of any surplus funds which were to be used to repair the highways or to assist the poor. The master might be a layman, married or unmarried, or a priest, though if he were married, his wife might not be kept within the cathedral close. Finally the scholars were to practise writing, and the master and usher were to teach only those boys who could read, though it was laid down that some of the scholars might be appointed to teach reading.

These provisions at Holgate's York school have been set out in some detail because they are fairly typical of many of the deeds and statutes for schools made during the ensuing 50 to 75 years. Two frequently repeated clauses are the provisions about prayers and church attendance, and the requirement that the master and usher should not have to teach reading. The provision that the master might be a layman can be found elsewhere, though most 16th century masters were in Holy Orders.

The later years of Holgate's own career were troubled. He was deprived of his see in 1554 because he had married, and was imprisoned. In January 1555 he was released after he had offered £1,000 to the Queen for his liberty. In his petition for release Holgate mentioned the creation of the three free schools and his share in setting up two more. One of these was probably East Retford (in Nottinghamshire and in his diocese) and the other was Sedbergh, which he may have helped to save.[23] In his will he established a hospital for 20 poor men and women at Hemsworth where he had already founded a school.[24] Holgate was a major benefactor of education and charities in Yorkshire who is now little remembered. In one sense he stands in the tradition of the medieval founders like Thomas Rotherham. In another he looks to the changes of a new age. His three schools were founded in 1547, just before the suppression of the chantries, yet they stand very largely clear of the rituals and ceremonies of the old order. He saw the academic curriculum in terms of the new movements of his time. In both respects he

119

forms a sharp contrast with his archdeacon and contemporary John Dakyn of Kirkby Ravensworth whose foundation we have also examined. Holgate was not an heroic figure but he was a creative one because he was the pioneer in introducing ideas of Renaissance education into Yorkshire.

Dakyn and Holgate were not the last members of the old hierarchy to found schools. In 1558 Owen Oglethorpe, bishop of Carlisle, who died in 1559, founded a school and almshouse at Tadcaster.[25] He has his place in national history because he crowned Queen Elizabeth. In 1561 Robert Pursglove, the last prior of Guisborough and bishop of Hull, founded a similar school and almshouse at Guisborough in the North Riding. In the statutes which he drew up Pursglove directed that the master should be a priest, though an unmarried layman might be appointed if a priest could not be obtained. The master was to teach the scholars free, though he might take 4d. on admission. Thereafter no other payment was to be compulsory, though he might accept voluntary offerings. The school was to be divided into four forms, the lowest for 'young beginners, commonly called 'Petits''. The master was not to teach them himself, but to assign some of his older scholars to instruct them. In the top two forms no language was to be spoken in the schoolhouse save Latin 'saving only in the teaching of the lower Forms'.[26]

The contents and wording of foundation deeds, royal charters and statutes do not vary very much between the different examples which might be quoted.[27] The statutes were the most important documents of all because they controlled the day-to-day running of the school. Sometimes no statutes had been drawn up at all, and such an omission usually created problems. The Wakefield statutes date from 1607.[28] They begin as was usual with provision about the election and duties of the governors. The schoolmaster was to be a master of arts. He was to take his scholars to church and to teach them Latin and Greek, though boys were not to be forced to study more advanced subjects until they had grasped the basic elements of learning. He was to ensure that his pupils were clean in person and that their manners were good. He was to be paid 40 marks a quarter plus entrance money and money from fines if the school could afford that. The rules for the usher were parallel to those for the master. He was to teach the rudiments of Latin and the Latin grammar, writing and the making of translations. He was not to be responsible for more than half the scholars. He was to be paid 50 shillings per quarter with the same rules for augmenting the basic salary as in the case of the master. No scholar was to be admitted unless he could read and could be 'promoted to the accidence'. The master was not to take more than 20 'foreigners' as pupils and the usher not more than 10, and they were to retain the fees which the foreigners paid. The rules about prayers and the hours of school were similar to those already cited for Archbishop Holgate's school at York. The master was allowed 24 days of absence during the year and the usher 16. Later amendments (1615–16) strengthened the master's control over the usher, provided that scholars were to attend the parish church on Sundays and that they were not to maintain 'any notorious points of Popery' nor to use any Popish books or writings.[29]

The Giggleswick statutes which are slightly earlier (1592) are very similar to these.[30] Their main interest is that they examine the qualifications of the master at some length. He was to be 'a man fearinge God, of true religion and godlye conversacion, not gyven to diceinge, cardinge, or other unlawfull games'. He was both to teach his scholars and to catechise them 'to thende their obedience in lyfe may answere to their proceedings in godly litterature'. He should, in so far as the scholars could understand them, use only the Greek, Latin and Hebrew languages in the school. Finally, a very important provision in a society in which patronage and local interest were very important,

> ...he shall indifferently in schoole endevour himself to teache the poor as well as the riche, and the parishioner as well as the stranger, and as his said schollers shall profytt in learninge, so he shall preferre them accordingly, without respecte of persons.

It is interesting to note that these Giggleswick statutes seem to have been taken over word for word for the smaller and later foundation of Otley (about 1610–11).[31]

The three West Riding schools of Wakefield, Halifax and Sheffield all provide good examples of foundations which became firmly established as a result of community effort involving large numbers of people. At Wakefield there was probably a pre-Reformation school connected with the Thurstone chantry in the parish church.[32] Though there is no evidence that the school was continued by the chantry commissioners, teaching probably continued in the town. In 1591 a royal charter was obtained with the Saviles, a prominent local family, playing an active role. A schoolmaster was at once appointed, but it took from 1591 to 1605 to provide an endowment and a building. The Saviles gave generously, including the school site, but many of the bequests were quite small. There were in total 46 bequests between 1564 (long before the grant of the charter) and 1611, and the gifts continued during the early years of the school's history. By about 1611 £350 had been collected in money, plus rents of about £50 a year and a share in scholarships at University College, Oxford and Clare College, Cambridge. The school's historian claimed that almost everyone of importance in the town and neighbourhood had given something to the school, and that in the end a 'laye' or local rate had been levied to bring in more money and to complete the endowment.[33]

At Halifax the process was similar, but it took much longer, and a leading role was played by two successive vicars of the parish, John Favour and Henry Ramsden. The royal charter was granted in 1586, but no schoolmaster was appointed until 1600. A subscription had been launched, but initially response was slow. In 1598 Lord Shrewsbury and others gave six acres of land and a house recently built for a schoolhouse. As at Wakefield there were a large number of small subscriptions and legacies. Favour collected about £350 in all, and gave to the

122

school Latin and Greek dictionaries and a large volume Bible. Ramsden collected about another £195 in 1635 for the purchase of lands.[34]

At Sheffield, as we have seen, support for the school had been received during Elizabeth's reign from the Church Burgesses. A royal charter was granted in 1604 after Thomas Smith's benefaction of 1603.[35] In 1606 an assessment to meet the costs of the new foundation amounting to £108.18.3 was raised from 473 individuals, who paid between 2d. and 40s. each. A survey of the town's population in 1615 gave a total of 2,207 people, so all or almost all the male adults must have paid.[36] One common form of local community action all through the 17th century was to collect money for building. At Ilkley, for example, an arbitration award in 1607 decided that a bequest should be used to maintain a schoolmaster. In 1635–6 13 inhabitants made an agreement to build a schoolhouse.[37] The fact that such arrangements were quite common suggests a strong local interest in schooling and a readiness to spend money on supporting it.

Although many schools were founded after 1550, most of these were in smaller and more obscure places. Schools had been established in most of the larger centres before that time. Since there were so many grammar schools in the county, only a few selected histories can be treated here, first of all some half dozen of the larger schools and then a similar number of the smaller foundations. The careers of old boys, in so far as anything is known about them, will be examined in the following chapter on 'Teaching and Learning'. The three important East Riding schools of Hull, Pocklington and Beverley form a good group with which to begin.

Both at Hull and at Beverley the town authorities took a good deal of interest in the school during the reign of Elizabeth. At Hull after about 1569 they made up the master's stipend to £20 a year, and in 1579 school fees were introduced in order to pay for an usher.[38] In 1580 the Corporation built a gallery in Holy Trinity Church to seat the master and his scholars, and in 1582–3 a new schoolhouse was begun which was largely paid for by Alderman William Gee, who left a benefaction (1602–4) to augment the master's stipend. In fact this gave the school only limited help because the Corporation paid over only an annual fixed sum and took the rest of the rents from the Gee property for themselves. In 1611 the mayor and aldermen were given by charter the right to appoint the schoolmaster, and in 1630 they acquired the schoolhouse, the ownership of which had been disputed as being concealed chantry property. In 1599 and 1602 the master, Robert Fowbery, was allowed an increase in salary. In 1612–13 he petitioned St John's College, Cambridge, for the mastership of Pocklington and when he did not get it, he moved to the mastership of the grammar school at Newcastle-upon-Tyne where he died in 1623.[39]

The first third of the 17th century was a prosperous period for Hull grammar school, which numbered about 100 boys in the 1630s, many of whom went on to Cambridge. A considerable number of them came from the leading merchant families, though the school never seems to have attracted the sons of the East Riding gentry as Beverley and Pocklington did. In 1657 John Shoare became master. He conformed at the Restoration, and was succeeded in 1664 by his usher, John Catlyn, whose strong Royalism during the Civil War has already been recorded.[40] In Catlyn's time the Corporation restored and re-equipped the schoolhouse, and the master started a school library. However he had a long continued dispute with the bench of alderman about the appointment and control of the usher, and he was eventually dismissed from the mastership in 1676.

Catlyn's successor, Robert Pell, elected in January 1677, went on until he died in 1716. Pell's very long reign was not a successful period in the history of the school. A smaller proportion of boys went on to Cambridge, and there is evidence of competition from private schoolmasters.[41] A return of 1680 to the bench of aldermen showed a total of only 29 boys, 21 of them in the bottom two classes which the usher taught. Most of them still came from the merchant families of the town, though there were boys from lower social groups as well. One prominent old boy of this period was Thomas Watson, fellow of St John's and later bishop of St

David's, who died in 1717. He had planned to provide a further endowment for the school, but when he died nothing had been done.

This rather depressed period at Hull under Pell coincided with a prosperous period at Beverley. Neighbouring schools often went up and down in relation to one another because they drew to some extent on a common catchment area. Most of the available information about Beverley comes from the borough records.[42] In 1578 Robert Brockelbank, teacher of the grammar school at Hasyll (Hessle), was appointed master at an annual salary of 20 marks with an usher who was to be paid 40s. a year plus a fee of 4d. (later raised to 6d.) for every scholar in the school. Brockelbank died within a few months and the mayor and governors paid his executors 53s. In February 1609 the Great Order Book of the town contains a memorandum of an action in the Exchequer at York between the town and William Ellis, who had taught scholars to the detriment of the public schools. It was agreed that Ellis should leave to teach four 'gramer schollers', who were named, until they left him. Thereafter he was not to teach grammar in the town any more, but only 'accidence' and other inferior books to prepare children for the grammar school. Perhaps, as a sop to Mr Ellis, the mayor promised that he would try to obtain £10 for him out of the town's benevolence for his diligent preaching at St Mary's and elsewhere.

In 1664 Francis Sherwood, schoolmaster, had his salary of £26.13.4 reduced to £13.6.8. Perhaps this was done because three years earlier he had been appointed assistant at the Minster at a salary of £16. Sherwood was required to provide an usher for the school at his own charge. Clearly there was a close linkage between appointments at the school and at Beverley Minster. In 1667 Elias Pawson, 'Lecturer of this town', was given a Christmas gift of £6.13.4 and was asked to go to the free school as often as he wished and examine the progress of the scholars in learning. When Pawson died in 1678, he was succeeded as lecturer and minister of St John's by Stephen Clark, sometime schoolmaster of Cottingham. In 1670 the Beverley schoolmaster, John Forge, had been authorized to nominate an usher because the school had increased to about 50 scholars and he could not manage them all himself. The usher's salary was to be £6.13.4. He was to be examined by Mr Pawson and then approved by the Corporation. Later in the century the usher's salary was increased to £10.

When Forge died, he was succeeded by Joseph Lambert, assistant at St John's, at an annual salary of £20 plus £10 given in Dr Metcalf's will. The son of every free burgess who paid to the poor was to pay at least 2/- quarterly. It was also laid down that Lambert was to hold no other church appointment while he was schoolmaster. In 1703 an order was made that the post of usher at the grammar school and assistant curate at the Minster must remain two distinct places. Perhaps this desire to avoid such pluralism reflected the fact that numbers were high at the school and that there was plenty of work to do there without undertaking additional clerical duties. The same sense of prosperity may lie behind the order of 1691 that the schoolhouse was to be made more warm and convenient for the master and scholars, and another order of 1702 for taking down part of the Minster wall so that the south end of the grammar school might be enlarged.

The third East Riding school, Pocklington, suffered very varied fortunes.[43] Under Anthony Ellison (?1558–81) there were about 140 boys in the school at one point. When Martin Briggs (1600–13) accepted the living of Barmston and resigned, the townspeople complained that the numbers had been brought down from 80 to 'two children, the eldest not exceeding twelve years'. Under Robert Sedgwick (1630–50) 18 boys entered St. John's, most of them being gentlemen's sons, though the average school life of a boy at this period was very short. His successor Edward Lluellen (1650–57) was outstandingly successful. He probably had about 100 boys in the school at any one time. Since he kept an admissions register, more is known about the parentage of the boys than is usually the case. The ages at entry ranged from 6 to 18, the largest number being between 8 and 15. The average age was 12½. Many of the boys came from good Yorkshire county families – Hesketh, Fairfax, Savile, Beaumont, Darcy, Vavasour – but the social

126

range was wide. Parents also included clergy, merchants, yeomen, and a few blacksmiths, butchers and tailors.[44]

Under Lluellin's successor Rowland Greenwood (1657–60) numbers fell away rapidly. The townspeople complained that there were only eight or nine little boys in place of six or seven score, of whom three-quarters 'hath been tablers, gentlemen sonnes, which was a great benefitt to our Towne'. Under the long reign of Thomas Ellison (1664–93) things must have got better again since in his time 44 boys went up to St John's and nine to Peterhouse. One serious problem for the management of Pocklington school was that no statutes had ever been made, though the founding Act of 1551 had laid down that this was to be done. In 1613 St. John's asked the archbishop to approach the Crown so that action might be taken, but nothing was achieved. Consequently authority was divided between the master and usher, St John's who appointed the master, and the vicar and churchwardens of the parish. The weaknesses of the system were shown when John Clarke, master 1660–64, with his usher, granted a long lease of some of the school's property to Sir John Reresby at a very low rent in return for a bribe and perhaps the promise of preferment. Thomas Ellison began legal proceedings in 1680, and it took 23 years of litigation before the lease was annulled and some of the arrears recovered. The proceedings, wrote the school's historians, 'show the weakness of a system which allowed the master and usher, acting as a corporation, to mismanage the school's property in this way'.[45]

Leeds, Wakefield, Giggleswick and Sedbergh were four of the major schools in the West Riding. Wakefield, as we have seen, had been endowed through the gifts of many members of the local community. Leeds had received benefactions from William Sheafield and from William Ermysted (1555), who had also endowed the school at Skipton, but as at Wakefield local people were generous as well.[46] In 1624 John Harrison, the Leeds merchant and benefactor, built a schoolhouse. The establishment of the Committee of Charitable Uses (1621/1663) has already been described.[47] The committee had responsibilities for the repair of the highways and the relief of the poor as well as for the maintenance of the school. The decree of 1663 gave them power to appoint and dismiss the master and to make 'laws and orders' for the good government of the school. After 1691 the master received a salary of £50 and the usher £20/£25. The hours of schooling for 1710 are recorded: 7 a.m. to 11.30 a.m. and 1 p.m. to 5 p.m. from Lady Day to Martinmas, 8 a.m. and 11.30 a.m. and 1 p.m. to 4 p.m. from Martinmas to Lady Day. These are longer than a modern school day but shorter than the hours laid down in Archbishop Holgate's foundation deed at York.[48]

At Wakefield the Savile family had played a large part in the foundation. George Savile, the first Spokesman of the governors, gave

> the great deske in the myddle of the schole, and a plate dyall which standith in the courte, and the Queen's arms in a frame which be in the upper end thereof... He also did give the great large Dictionary, made by Bishop Cowper, called in Latine *Thesaurus Linguae Romanae*, etc... item one bedstead of waynscott carved and wrought, made at the charges of the governors standing in the master's chamber.[49]

The school suffered considerably during the Civil War; probably 10–15% of its property was lost.[50] The master, Robert Doughty (1623–63), collected the rents and managed the estates during this period, and the school owed a lot to his devotion to duty. In an affidavit dated 14 Feb. 1653 Doughty and the only surviving governor of that time, William Waler, described how the room over the church porch in which the school deeds were kept had been broken into 'by the soldiers and some malevolent hands'. The records had been scattered about and some of the seals plucked off. Doughty and Waler therefore asked, at the request of the present governors, that the accounts should be carefully examined and the rights of the school confirmed in a court of record.[51]

Doughty had taught Charles Hoole, the schoolmaster of Rotherham,[52] and in the half century which followed the school trained some very distinguished men –

John Radcliffe benefactor of the University of Oxford, Richard Bentley the great classical scholar, Joseph Bingham the church historian, and John Potter, archbishop of Canterbury (1737–47). One of the most successful of the masters was Thomas Clark (1703–20), to whose care, it was said, 'the sons of the principal gentry in the county of York were entrusted'.[53] In 1717 the governors decided that, as there were about 160 boys in the school, the usher's salary was to be paid to the schoolmaster who was then to pay to the usher and to another assistant £30 each.

A memorandum on school routine drawn up in 1695 gives an interesting picture of the school at that time. There was to be a monitor at each end of the school, the office to continue for a week. On Sundays the monitors were to see that the boys behaved themselves in church and that there were 'no idle persons' hanging about the school. On week-days they were to call the boys into the school at the usual times, to see that they sat in their proper places and that they made no noise. They were to write down all offenders 'such as swear, curse, use filthy and obscene words, give bad names, fight, game for money, break the Scole windows, teare the school books, speak English, come late or are absent'. They were to put away the school books, to see that the doors were locked, and to ensure that boys did not go out more than two at a time to relieve themselves.

The master's duties were also carefully specified. He was to ensure that the monitor did his duty and to see that the boys behaved themselves out of school and treated their elders and betters with respect. He was to support the authority of the usher, to have prayers morning and evening and to be present when they were said, and to see that a chapter in English was read in the morning and another at one o'clock in the afternoon. He was to correct the school exercises carefully and himself to make exercises from time to time for boys to imitate. He was to see that those who were able to make speeches and declamations repeated them from memory and that, in repeating their lessons, the boys did not prompt one another. He was to insist on good writing and 'true Orthography', and to ensure that those who could read Greek made use of a lexicon and not of a Latin translation of the

129

passage. Finally he was to permit no one other than himself or the under master 'to send for ale, or Club in the Schole Chamber During schole time, it being a thing of ill Example to the Schollars, and discredit to the Schole'.[54]

The boys of Giggleswick School benefited from several exhibitions founded in the early 17th century. The school had a close connection with Christ's College, Cambridge. One Burton exhibitioner of the college who came from the school was Richard Frankland (1630–98), one of the pioneer tutors of the Dissenting Academies.[55] Under William Walker (1648–56) 25 boys went to Christ's and 3 entered St John's in a single year (1652). Under John Armitstead (1685–1712) 27 boys went up to Christ's alone. He persuaded the governors to allow him to collect the rents from the school estates, which was generally an undesirable practice because it confused the personal interests of the master of the time with the longer term interests of the foundation. When Armitstead's successor, John Carr (1712–43), was appointed, an agreement was made between him and the governors. He was to observe all the school statutes. The governors were to appoint the writing master at their meeting in March. When the masters received any rent from the property at North Cave and Rise, they were to inform at least one of the governors, to give an acquittance and enter the money received into 'the schoole booke'. Other rents they were to keep for themselves, giving an acquittance for them. Restrictions were also placed on the expenses which might be incurred at the governors' meeting in March.

Sedbergh, despite its remote location, was one of the most successful of Yorkshire schools all through this period.[56] From the time of the long headmasterships of Robert Hebblethwaite (1544–85) and John Mayre (1585–1623) it sent up a steady stream of boys to St John's College, Cambridge, many of whom became fellows of the college. Under Gilbert Nelson (1623–46) there were 50/60 boys. He was accused of neglecting the school because he also had a living; sequestered as a delinquent in 1646, he died two years later. A rare personal portrait of him as headmaster and teacher has survived in Peter Barwick's life of his brother, John, Royalist propagandist and later dean of St Paul's. Nelson was, in Peter Barwick's view

> a very good man, but that he did not constantly attend the school, for his salary not being sufficient to maintain his wife and family, he engaged also in a cure of souls to the great disadvantage of his scholars. What time he could afford them he taught them Latin very well, Greek indifferently. He was a very pleasant facetious man, and by his merry comment rendered so very agreeable what uses to give most uneasiness to learning, that his scholars became fond of their books, though never so hard. They were wonderfully delighted when he undertook to explain any of the dramatic poets, particularly Terence or Plautus, for whatever in them seemed difficult to the weaker capacity of the boys, he expounded with so much wit and merriment that all who had the least ingenuity were extreamly in love with that sort of learning. In order also more thoroughly and clearly to explain the meaning of those poets, whether comedians or tragedians, he used to teach such of his scholars as he found fit for it to tread the stage now and then for their diversion, and act the several parts of those plays; without which kind of knowledge he knew he might fit them for the lives of monks or hermits, but not to bear any offices in the state, or perform the duties of a civil life.[57]

The deprivation of Richard Jackson (1648–56) for drunkenness and neglect of duty has already been considered.[58] One reason why it had been difficult to deal with Jackson's case was that Sedbergh was another of the schools for which no statutes had been made. The school's highest point of success was reached under Posthumus Wharton (1674–1706) under whom the numbers reached 122, many of them sons of the local gentry. He himself belonged to a well-known local family. He had been usher to Edward Fell (1662–74) and was only 24 years of age when he was appointed by the governors because the patrons, St John's, had failed to appoint within the stipulated time. A suit in Chancery brought by one of the tenants

(1681) led the governors to make a strong defence of their headmaster.[59] They denied that he had extracted payments in respect of boys, though it was customary to offer a gratuity when a boy entered. Wharton had not demanded payment for certificates when boys went to St John's as scholars, nor had he admitted boys for a short time so that they might qualify for such awards. He had not endeavoured to get the schoolhouse rebuilt out of the school revenues, and he had built a house for the master to live in with his own money. He had received fines paid on the renewal of leases with the governors' permission. He worked, the governors claimed, extremely hard, being in school with the boys at 6 a.m. or at 7 a.m. in the depth of winter. The school endowment was £97 per year. There had always been an usher who was paid about £30 a year and, except when the usher was ill, Wharton had never used the older boys to do his teaching. He had brought honour to the school and, through his boarders, money to the town. If he were to leave or to die, 'most of the boyes would, upon the uncertainty of the fitness or aptness of his successor (comeing generally and immediately from the said Colledge and consequently untryed in that respect) go to other Schoolmasters of good established repute in their calling'.

The histories of the smaller and less prominent schools largely replicate the picture which has been given of the larger foundations, and only a few examples will be given. It is surprising that St Peter's York, the most ancient of Yorkshire schools and situated in the county capital, was always so obscure. Under Elizabeth it had been under strongly Catholic influences. The schoolhouse in the Horse Fair was abandoned during the siege of York during the Civil War and the school settled in the Bedern inside the city walls. The school seems to have received a very inadequate return on its endowments, and this may have had something to do with the low level it reached during the 18th century.[60] Some of the schools which had survived the fall of the chantries were re-established at different times. One of these was Almondbury near Huddersfield. By about 1600 the school had ceased to exist, and in 1608 the vicar and gentry of the parish petitioned the king for the establishment of a grammar school, for which money had been collected, and for the grant of the schoolhouse and ground. To obtain the letters patent cost £44.8.10, which was probably met by a levy.[61] About 1700 a set of statutes was drawn up. These conform very much to the general pattern, though it is perhaps worth noting that no boy was to be admitted as a scholar 'who shall not be able to read plainly and distinctly the psalter or Psalms of David in English and be fit to begin the Accidence.'[62]

Another school which had links with a chantry was Worsborough near Barnsley where copyhold land was surrendered in 1560 to support Sir William Wolley as schoolmaster. In 1632 John Rayney left property to the Drapers' Company to pay £30 a year to the lecturer at Worsborough and £13.6.8 to the grammar schoolmaster. The master was to teach both grammarians and 'petties', and to pay his usher and a scrivener for part of the year.[63]

Batley was one of several schools founded by clergymen.[64] William Lee, vicar of Stapleford in Cambridgeshire, who had been born in the parish of Batley, conveyed land at Gomersal to 12 trustees in 1612. The endowment deed required the master to teach children to read English and to write as well as to teach Latin and Greek and to prepare those who were capable for the university. The school was to be free to parishioners; children from outside the parish were to pay such fees as their parents and the schoolmaster agreed. The annual value of the endowment was £16.10.0 and the master was to receive £15, so the endowment made no provision for an usher. In 1685 Robert Laycock was appointed master and duly received his licence. Laycock failed to teach the boys properly and punished them savagely, so the trustees dismissed him. He then appealed to the Archbishop, but as there is no official pronouncement on the case in the records at York, the trustees' actions were presumably upheld.[65] Some other cases of brutal schoolmasters will be cited later.[66]

The upheavals caused by the Civil War in a number of schools, notably Wakefield, have already been noted. One school which was considerably affected was Skipton, which was a Royalist garrison town. In 1654 Edward Browne was nominated as master by Lincoln College, Oxford. The college later complained that he had been much abused and attacked by the usher, that the school was neglected, and the rents not paid. Thomas Barker, master from 1621 until he was displaced in 1646 and then again from 1661 to 1674, practised as a physician in the town during the Commonwealth period. Perhaps this period of rapid change and disorder encouraged John Collier (1656–9) to let school property at long leases with a low rent and a high fine, which of course benefited him at the expense of his successors since he received the fines and they had to suffer the low rents. These leases were finally quashed in a law suit of 1699.[67]

In the Restoration period Nathan Staniforth (1668–1702) built Penistone up to a school of 60 boys.[68] Under his successor John Ramsden (1702–26) the parish built a new school. The agreement between him and the feoffees of the school on his appointment has survived.[69] Ramsden promised to teach the children of parishioners the 'Rudiments of ye Latin and Greek Tongues, with ye Rhetorick according to ye Foundation of ye said School'. He also promised to teach them to read English so that the school might be 'of Generall Use to ye poorer sort', as had been the practice for many years. He undertook to allow a salary to the usher, who was to teach 'ye said English tongue', and to ensure that the usher did his work properly. There then followed a number of provisions of the usual kind about holidays, about supervising the boys' behaviour, and about ensuring that they learned the church catechism. Ramsden promised to resign if he became unfit to conduct the school, and finally he promised that, while he remained master, he would not enter into holy orders without the consent of the feoffees. That final clause may have been a relic of Puritan feeling in an old Puritan area, or it may have reflected the feoffees' fear that if the master took orders, he would look for a curacy and then neglect the school. It should also be noted that, both in this Penistone example of 1702 and in the much earlier Batley deed of 1612, the school was to teach English as well as Latin and Greek. Perhaps these smaller grammar schools tried to cover a wider curriculum than the formal definition of their function suggested.[70]

Notes Chapter 6

1. *See* Chapter 2: pages 28–31.

2. Jordan, W.K. 1961: 349.

3. Jordan, W.K. 1960: 234, 237, 241.

4. For Beverley at this time, *see* Leach, A.F. 1907: 427–9 and *EYS* vol I: li–liii, 113–16.

5. *EYS* vol I: 129.

6. *See* pages 146–9.

7. *See* pages 34–5.

8. *EYS* vol II: 47–9.

9. Guest, J. 1876: 8–12.

10. Mackenzie, M.H.1971–9: 350–59.

11. Guest, J. 1879: 388, 392, 394.

12. Dickens, A.G. (ed.) 1959: 127 (Sherbrook, M. 'The Fall of Religious Houses'); *EYS* vol II:191–2; Guest, J. 1879: 96; Dickens, A.G. 1981: 299.

13. From Hoole's *Scholastick Discipline* (*EYS* vol II: 230–31.).

14. For a re-appraisal of the religious policy of Mary's reign *see* Duffy, E. 1992: chapter 16.

15. Hunter, J. 1869: 239–43.

16. Wigfull, J.R. 1925–8: 336–43; Moore Smith, G.C. 1929–37: 145–60.

17. *See* page 33.

18. For John Dakyn *see* Dickens, A.G. 1957, Part I: 7–8. Dakyn sentenced Richard Snell, the only Marian martyr to be burnt in Yorkshire.

19. For Dakyn and his foundation *see* Whitaker, T.D. 1823 vol I: 118–21.

20. The Dictionary of National Biography gives the main facts of his life, and *see* page 31.

21.   *See* Carlisle N. 1818 vol II: 817–20 (Hemsworth); *ibid.*: 858–9 (Old Malton); *ibid.*: 919 (York) for the letters patent and the school foundations.

22.   For the York foundation deed *see* Jewels, E.N. 1963: 10–16.

23.   For the re-foundation of Sedbergh *see* pages 35–6.

24.   For Holgate's career in general *see* works by Dickens, A.G. 1937: 428–42; 1941: 450–59; 1959: 174–7; 1981: 335–6. *See also* Lawson, J. 1962a: 12; Jordan, W.K. 1961: 311–12. There is an article on Holgate in Wilkinson, J. (n.d.): 269–308.

25.   Curtis, S.J. 1952: 69–81.

26.   Carlisle, N. 1818 vol II: 805–6.

27.   For the Skipton foundation deed of 1548 *see* Gibbon, A.M. 1947: 24–5, 137–43. For the Elizabethan royal charter of Richmond *see* Wenham, L.P. 1958: 140–42.

28.   Peacock, M.H. 1892: 54–75; Simon, J. 1966: 329–30.

29.   Peacock, M.H. 1892: 77–8.

30.   *EYS* vol II: 254–9.

31.   Cobley, F. 1923: 39–47.

32.   *See* page 17.

33.   Peacock, M.H. 1892: 7–48; Jordan, W.K. 1961: 321.

34.   Cox, T. 1879: 7–25; Jordan, W.K. 1961: 326.

35.   *See* page 116.

36.   For these figures *see* Hunter, J. 1869: 148; Wigfull, J.R. 1929–37: 287–92; Jordan, W.K. 1961: 326.

37.   Salmon, N. (n.d.): 14.

38.   This section on Hull is based on Lawson, J. 1963: chs. II and III.

39.   Fowbery belonged to a Northumbrian family (*see* Mains, B. and Tuck, A. 1986: 19).

40.   *See* page 73.

41.   *See* page 83.

42.   The following is largely based on Dennett, J. (ed.) 1932.

43. The following is based on Sands, P.C. and Howarth, C.M. (?1950): 23–61.

44. *See* lists of occupations in *ibid.*: 51.

45. *Ibid.*: 60.

46. For Leeds *see* Price, A.C. 1919; for William Sheafield *see* page 17.

47. *See* page 60.

48. *See* page 118.

49. Lupton, J.H. 1864: 59–60.

50. For the general history of the school *see* Peacock, M.H. 1892.

51. Lupton, J.H. 1864: 79–80.

52. For Hoole, *see* pages 145–8.

53. Peacock, M.H. 1892: 133; and *see also* page 189.

54. Peacock, M.H. 1892: 237–9.

55. For Giggleswick *see* Bell, E.A. 1912. The Burton rent-charge had been purchased from the Clapham (1603) and Tennant (1604) exhibition endowments.

56. Lowther Clarke, H. and Weech, W.N. 1925:27–59; *EYS* vol II: lxxx–lxxxv.

57. *EYS* vol II: 384–5; Lowther Clarke, H and Weech, W.N. 1925: 36–7.

58. *See* page 58.

59. For the following *see EYS* vol II: 425–37; Lowther Clarke, H and Weech, W.N. 1925: 56–7.

60. Raine, A. 1926: 89–102.

61. For the earlier history of the school *see* page 37, and Hinchliffe, G. 1963: 31–7.

62. Dyson, T. 1926: 20–1.

63. Wallis, P.J. 1958: 147–63; Wilkinson, J. 1872: 320–21. For Obadiah Walker's gift of books to the school *see* pages 148–9.

64. Others were Burneston (1680), Catterick (1662) and Wath (1684), all in the North Riding (*AR*: 70, 72, 90).

65. Lester, D.N.R. (n.d.): 10–17, 31–9.

66. *See* pages 140–141.

67.   Gibbon, A.M. 1947: 38–45.

68.   Addy, J. 1958b: 513–14; *see also* page 64.

69.   Dransfield, J.H. 1906: 196–7. The agreement is dated Feb. 9 1702 (1702–3).

70.   Vincent, W.A.L. 1969: 74.

CHAPTER 7

Teaching and Learning

The last three chapters have examined the development of Yorkshire schools from 1558 to 1714 – the systems of public control, the numbers of schools of different types, the histories of some of the individual foundations. It remains to look at the system from the inside, so as to speak – to examine the processes of teaching and learning and to say something about the careers of people about whose education we have some knowledge. It has to be said at once that such people are very few in number and a small proportion of those who attended school.

The primary purpose of education, as has already been made clear, was moral and disciplinary. Young people were trained to be faithful Christians and loyal citizens, obedient to authority in both church and state. The round of Bible-reading and religious observance formed a major part of the scholastic programme at every level. All learning was closely linked with religious instruction, and for the men of that time it would have been impossible to separate the two.[1] Education began in the family, which had the primary responsibility of ensuring that sound religious and moral foundations were laid.[2] Great emphasis was placed on the teaching and learning of the catechism by all children and young people, whether they were to receive formal schooling or not. Such schooling of all kinds was for a minority, but the catechism – in theory at least – was for all, and that is why catechizing ranked very high among the duties of the parish clergyman.[3]

In one sense therefore all the parish clergy, incumbents and curates alike, had an important teaching function. Many of the clergy were teachers in the more professional sense since they provided most of the masters in grammar schools and even some in petty schools just as their predecessors had done in the Middle Ages. It is difficult to assess the position of the schoolmaster as a professional man in Tudor and Stuart times. Kenneth Charlton has argued that the teaching profession became increasingly secular both in membership and in outlook. Teachers were no longer priests first and teachers in their spare time. 'The staffing of schools ... was now generally a matter of choosing men who wished to devote their lives to the teaching of children...'[4]

This argument is related to the claim that the Reformation changes had aimed at creating a secularized educational system organized on national lines. No attempt can be made here to argue the case as it applies to the whole country because the purpose of this book is much more limited than that. So far as the Yorkshire evidence is concerned, it would be difficult to substantiate the claim. The great majority of Yorkshire grammar schoolmasters were in holy orders. Many curates taught school themselves, as did many parish clerks, the incumbent's right-hand men in conducting the services of the church. Schoolmasters moved on from schools to livings, and in many cases attempted to fulfil both sets of duties at the same time, which was said to lead, as in the case of Gilbert Nelson of Sedbergh,[5] to the serious neglect of their pupils. The whole atmosphere of all the schools was heavily religious and at least semi-clerical. The teachers who, by devoting themselves over many years to their schools, were helping to build up a professional framework of teaching and learning, were doing so within the constraints of a firmly Anglican structure. Any lay ethos of education lay a long way in the future; in Yorkshire it hardly existed until the days of the 18th century private schools.

Schoolmasters like clergymen in general varied a great deal in quality. If many were devoted and hard-working, others were either negligent or brutal or sometimes both at once. At Archbishop Grindal's visitation of 1575 it was reported that the schoolmaster of 'Gysburne' (Guisborough) 'hath forced many scholars to go from him by his cruell beatinge of them'.[6] J.S. Purvis has cited several examples from the turn of the 17th/18th centuries. Where complaints were made, they often involved severe punishments. At Kirkburton in 1716 the schoolmaster was accused of striking boys severely on the head, knocking one boy's tooth out and giving another a great swelling on the chin. At nearby Kirkheaton in 1695 the schoolmaster, who was also the curate, was accused of favouring some children above others and of not correcting them in an equitable manner, of shutting the school up and going away, and of appropriating money which he should have spent on repairs to the building. At Kirkby Ravensworth in 1701 the deponent complained that after eight years in the school

> hee made so little progress in learning, that hee did not understand the Construccion of the Book call'd Cato, nor the English Rules of Grammar, which hee imputed to the Negligence ignorance or ill method, of the said Mr Horne, for that other Schollars were equally short with this deponent as hee verily believes, in their Books in the said School.

At Kirkby Malhamdale (1712), because the schoolmaster had spent so little time in school teaching his pupils, he had 'hindered some well disposed persons from Augmenting the Salary of the said Schoole'.[7]

The question of literacy in the 16th and 17th centuries has been most fully discussed by David Cressy.[8] He argues that the progress of education in general was irregular rather than steady, with periods of advance alternating with periods of regression. Literacy, as a major component of the whole field, followed a similar course. There was, Cressy thinks, a period of general advance from about 1560 to 1580 with a period of recession at the end of the century in which elementary education suffered. There was a revival after about 1610 which was terminated by the outbreak of the Civil War. Then there was a renewed attack on illiteracy between about 1660 and 1680, but the situation worsened again at the end of the century. By about 1700, Cressy claims,

> educational opportunity was, perhaps more rigidly stratified than it had been since the Reformation. The generous expansion which had characterized the early part of the 'educational revolution' gave way to retrenchment, a closing of doors (which had never been very wide open), and a hardening of class consciousness and snobbery.[9]

For one diocese, Norwich, and working on the depositions of the consistory court, Cressy analyzed no less than eight phases of improvements and setbacks to the development of literacy in the years from 1530 to 1710.

The evidence for one diocese is not of course conclusive for York or Chester or any of the others. There were many variations, not only from time to time, but between one trade and another and between different parts of the country. Town literacy rates were higher than rural ones, and the south was more advanced than the more remote areas of the north and west. In Cressy's view the illiteracy rate among women was about 90% at the time of the Civil War. For men a good deal of evidence is available in the signatures and marks appended to the declarations of the 1640s (the Protestation Oath of 1641, the Vow and Covenant and the Solemn League and Covenant). This sample of about 40,000 men suggests that about 70% of men who were tendered such declarations were unable to sign them. Perhaps a slightly higher proportion could read because writing was the more advanced of the two skills.

The figure of those unable to sign in Yorkshire was higher (74%) than the average, though it is based on only a small number of returns. However a general illiteracy total of 75% for Yorkshire and its neighbouring counties is suggested at the time of the Civil War. By the accession of George I this figure of inability to sign had fallen to 55% for men and 75% for women.[10] Lawrence Stone considered that the male literacy rate in the rural north on the eve of the Civil War was only

15/20%, rising to up to 40% in the countryside near London. In some of the larger towns in the south the literacy rate was as high as 60%.[11] It should be noted that, despite Cressy's arguments about the slow-down in educational progress around 1700, the suggested percentage of literates in Yorkshire was considerably higher in 1714 than it had been at the time of the Civil War.

No attempt has been made in this study to pursue further independent research into literacy levels in 17th and early 18th century Yorkshire. It is sufficient for our purpose to appreciate that those who learned to read and write were a minority – initially a fairly small minority, though one which was steadily growing in size. Not all those who learned these skills necessarily did so at school. Teachers came and went, and a village might enjoy quite good facilities at one period and none at all at another. The next question to ask must be: when there was a school or a schoolmaster, what did he teach and what did the children learn?

In the petty school the children learned their ABC, generally from a sheet of paper mounted in a wooden frame and covered with a sheet of horn, the so-called horn book. They went on to the catechism and the primer, which was both an elementary reader and a handbook of religious instruction. If the master was competent to teach them, they may have done a little writing and accounts, and that is as far as the majority of children went. For the few who entered the grammar school there was a good deal of overlap between the different stages since many grammar schools had a form for the 'petties' taught by the usher or sometimes, as we have seen, by the older grammar school pupils.[12]

Charles Hoole of Rotherham, in his *New Discovery of the old art of teaching School* (1660), began his study by stressing the importance of the elementary teacher and his work.[13] Hoole thought that to learn to read English perfectly required two to three years of study. Children who were going to learn Latin should begin at seven or eight years of age, and those who were not going to do so should go to a writing school. Since petty schoolmasters were poorly paid and enjoyed only low esteem, they should be endowed with a salary of at least £20 a year. Poor boys should be taught free, but others should pay fees. A petty schoolmaster should have some knowledge of Latin, should be able to write well and should have good skills in arithmetic. The school should be divided into four forms. The children should be examined weekly and should learn to say the graces, prayers and psalms. The school day should be similar to, but rather shorter in length than, the grammar school day which has already been explained. Each 40 boys needed a master to teach them. Foster Watson has called Hoole's programme 'the first distinct statement of the curriculum of the three R's for the 'Petty' elementary school by a responsible educationist.'[14]

Hoole's plans for elementary teaching were idealistic at a time when far more attention was concentrated on the grammar schools. Their curriculum will be discussed in more detail later, but before that is done, it is necessary to understand the unique position of strength which they held in the century between 1560 and 1660. Their popularity and success derived from the fact that they succeeded in that period in satisfying three major social pressures – first to acquire more learning, second to achieve higher standards of morality, third to attain higher social status. The late 16th and early 17th centuries were a time when learning, as interpreted by the scholars of the Renaissance, was popular. It promised greater fulfilment to individuals and, more important still, it was in demand as a necessary qualification for the gentleman in Parliament or on his estate, for the clergyman in his pulpit, for the lawyer in his court room, and for the merchant in his counting house. State and society were making greater demands on all these groups, and learning – which meant classical learning as interpreted by the scholars of the Renaissance – was seen as as important tool for enabling these demands to be met.

The objective of the whole process was to achieve higher standards of service in church and state and by doing so to strengthen the existing social fabric. Yet, because education was an important means of bringing forward men who lacked the traditional background of status and high birth, it contained a strong element of radicalism which questioned existing institutions, and which may be linked with the turmoil which eventually erupted into civil war. Certainly many conservatives after 1660 regarded education as a disruptive force which might damage rather than reinforce the stability of the existing social order. The consequences for the schools, and particularly for the grammar schools, of these changes was important. For a century before 1660 they had represented and held in balance the three forces which have been identified – learning, morality, the urge to achieve higher social status. After the Restoration the balance broke down. There was fear of the creation of an over-educated and potentially revolutionary social group. There was a growing conviction that the classical curriculum was not meeting the demands of a changing world which needed more utilitarian types of study. There was a strong desire to train the poor in moral and industrious habits so that they might not be a burden on society as a whole. All these pressures broke up the synthesis which had been created in the two or three generations before the Civil War and produced an entirely new situation.[15]

The classical studies of the grammar school were expounded in the works of John Brinsley, master of the school at Ashby-de-la-Zouch (*Ludus Litterarius*, 1612)[16] and of Charles Hoole, master of the school at Rotherham. Hoole had been a boy at Wakefield under Robert Doughty,[17] and his book, *A New Discovery of the old art of teaching School* (1660) is dedicated to Doughty and to his old Rotherham pupil, Robert Sanderson, the prominent Royalist divine who was bishop of Lincoln 1660–63. Hoole was ejected from Rotherham during the Civil War, and subsequently taught a very successful private school in London. Though his *New Discovery* was not published until 1660, it reflects his Rotherham experience before the Civil War. As he explains in his book, when he came to Rotherham he established his own methods successfully, after which 'I was persuaded to write over what I had done, that I might leave it as a pattern for him that succeeded me; and this was the ground-work of my Discovery.'[18]

Hoole divided his book into four sections. The first of these on the Petty School has already been discussed.[19] Next come the duties of the usher, then the methods to be used by the master, and finally a section on 'Scholastick Discipline: or, The Way of Ordering a Grammar-Schoole'. At the end of the book Hoole added a note on the methods used by Mr Bonner who had been schoolmaster at Rotherham and who had then moved to Chesterfield in Derbyshire. Bonner's programme was in fact very similar to his own.

The usher's duty was to give the boys a thorough grounding in Latin grammar – 'A Plat-forme of teaching Lilie's Grammar' as Hoole called it. To do this with ordinary boys would take three years. They were to begin by learning the accidence or the rudiments of grammar. They were to practise frequent repetition, so that they might become perfect in declining nouns and forming verbs. To learn the first part of the accidence would take half a year, followed by another half year to learn the English rules. At the same time they were to learn the Lord's Prayer, the Creed and the Ten Commandments in English and in Latin. In the second and third forms the boys were to learn the more advanced rules of Latin syntax, to read Aesop's Fables and the Latin Testament and to begin Latin verses. Much use was made of various collections of colloquies which aimed both to teach Latin speech and writing and to frame morals and good manners. Hoole himself had translated Corderius' *Colloquies* in 1657. He says in *A New Discovery* that the boys have these in English and Latin, 'and which they may construe grammatically, and cull the phrases out of it, to make use of them, in common speaking Latine'.[20] On Saturdays the boys were to learn the Assembly's Catechism and 'Perkins' six Principles', a catechism by the Elizabethan divine William Perkins.

In the fourth form the boys came under the master, and they began to study Greek and to use the Greek Testament. They studied Terence, 'the very quintessence of familiar Latine', and practised 'double translations' from Cicero – that is from Latin to English and back into Latin, the method recommended by Roger Ascham. They were to write letters in English and then to turn them into Latin, writing two epistles each week, one in answer to the other. At this stage much attention was given to verse making. They were to compose verses in English using George Herbert and Francis Quarles as their models and, in order to improve their Latin style, they were to spend a year studying Ovid's *Metamorphoses*.[21] In the fifth form the boys were to spend three-quarters of a year on Isocrates 'till they get a perfect knowledge of Etymologie and Syntaxe in Greek'. In Latin they studied Caesar and Virgil, and they wrote weekly themes and verses for which they were to collect material by keeping a commonplace book. Attention was also to be given to verses, to the catechism in Greek and Latin, and to the *Colloquies* of Erasmus which have been called 'the most popular 'reader' of the sixteenth and seventeenth centuries'.[22]

The sixth form was in Hoole's view 'the main credite of a Schoole & the Master commonly delighteth most in teaching it'.[23] He expected that the boys would learn Hebrew and make orations and verses in that language. In Greek they would study Hesiod, Homer, Pindar, Xenophon, Euripides, Sophocles and Aristophanes, in Latin Horace and the other Latin poets, Juvenal, Cicero's orations, Pliny and Quintilian. They made themes and verses, anagrams and epigrams, and gave orations in both Greek and Latin. Foster Watson noted that Hoole made no mention of major Greek authors like Plato and Aristotle, Thucydides and Aeschylus, but he considered that Hoole's expectations of the achievement of his best boys were as high as the levels attained by a student on leaving university in Queen Elizabeth's time.[24]

As far as school organization is concerned, Hoole reiterates what had already been explained in this study. He thought that the most effective school should be very large – at least 500 pupils – though that must have been an aspiration towards an ideal not a statement of reality. Punishments, he thought, should be moderate, and when boys were very troublesome, their parents should be brought in for consultation. He expected that the school would have a writing master who would come in for a month or six weeks in each year, and he mentioned the man who had taught him to write and who came in each year to teach the scholars at Rotherham. The work of writing masters will be referred to later in relation to the development of modern studies.[25]

Hoole urged his fourth formers to 'reap the sweet of their present labours', so that they might 'proceed so chearfully that they will not be sensible of any toil or difficultie'.[26] Perhaps that was a lot to expect from the majority of his boys who were not likely to complete the full classical programme anyway. Yet Hoole was more than a gerund-grinder. He wrote textbooks on the teaching of Latin, like his *Easie Entrance to the Latine Tongue* (1651).[27] He was sufficiently sympathetic to the newer educational movements of his time to translate Comenius' school book *Orbis Sensualium Pictus* in 1659, and he recommended its use in *A New Discovery*.[28] He was anxious that both the master and his pupils should make wide use of supporting literary studies; for example he wanted the scholars to use Erasmus' *De copia verborum*, which is a collection of examples of vocabulary and other illustrative material.[29] In order to make this possible he was anxious that the school should possess a library, both a small collection for each form and a general school library with commentaries and dictionaries and extensive enough for the master to be able to develop his own reading. Were money laid out for the provision of books, Hoole thought, that would offer a great incentive to children to learn.[30]

Hoole was not alone in emphasising the importance of libraries in schools. Wase was interested in the subject and asked a question about it in his enquiry, though in Yorkshire he found very little. At Leeds there was no library. 'Five pounds was once given & layd out for books useful to ye School, but al was lost in ye troublesome times'.[31] A library was later started about 1690.[32] At Halifax, according to Wase, there was 'a thing called a Library' in the parish church... 'ye Roome is very small & incommodious & hath in it but one shelf of Bookes'.[33] At Worsborough a large collection of books – editions of the fathers, the classics and works on medicine – was given by Obadiah Walker, a native of the township, master of University College, Oxford, and a Roman Catholic convert under James II who was displaced from his office at the Revolution of 1689.[34] At Hull a catalogue of 1676 recorded books which were essentially those assembled by John Catlyn.[35] There were 98 of them in all. About a quarter were Greek and Latin texts and commentaries, including grammars, dictionaries and various aids to composition, many of them written by humanists like Erasmus. There were several books on the Bible and on divinity, including two books on Hebrew. Just as Hoole had suggested, there were more general books too which were probably intended for the master's reading – a translation of Thucydides by Hobbes, several scientific works including books on the atomic theory, mathematics and medical botany, a Latin version of Castiglione's *Il Cortegiano*, and a manual on practical teaching method.[36] It is impossible to say how typical such a list is even for the larger and more successful schools, but its contents and Hoole's remarks in his book do suggest a much broader approach to knowledge than that which is presented by the grammar school curriculum studied in isolation.

Hoole's interest in Comenius dates from a period long after he had left Yorkshire. His translation of *Orbis Pictus* was made in 1659. Comenius had started the book in 1653 and published it in 1658.[37] I have found no evidence that the educational reformers of the Commonwealth period like Samuel Hartlib, John Dury and Comenius himself, who was in England in 1641–2, had any direct influence on schools in Yorkshire. They favoured a more practical and utilitarian approach to school studies, and they looked towards a national system of education which would include all children.[38] Their ideas were widely disseminated in the revolutionary years, but they resulted in very little after the Restoration which, in this as in other respects, meant a return to the old order.[39]

In Yorkshire any signs of a move towards a more practically-orientated curriculum do not go much further than a few references to teaching arithmetic and accounts and to writing. One of the nominations for a licence from Scarborough (1664) was in support of a man who had settled in the town to teach English, arithmetic and the rules of navigation.[40] In a port town there would be considerable demand for such instruction. When Dr John Bathurst made statutes in 1659 for schools at Arkengarthdale and at New Forest Helwith he prescribed writing, reading and accounts as well as the rudiments of Latin grammar.[41] Writing was taught separately from reading, and the profession of writing-master was well established. Hoole, as we have seen, mentioned the writing master both at Rotherham and at his own old school at Wakefield.[42] At Hull the bench of aldermen gave permission in 1633 to a writing master, George Wilberforce, to stay in the town, and in 1634 they agreed to pay another man an annual retaining fee in return for which he was to teach the children of burgesses at half his ordinary rate. Later in the century there were many teachers of mathematics in Hull. One of them, Thomas Harrison, taught both writing and mathematics for over 50 years. For many years he taught writing to the boys who sat on one side of the grammar school room and another master taught the boys who sat on the other.[43] In a large port like Hull there was likely to be a much wider demand for such instruction than was provided by the grammar school boys alone.

The growth of private schools for the middle and higher classes will be most conveniently discussed in the chapters on the 18th century when they became very important, though such private education was well established before the Civil War. J.T. Cliffe says that the sons of the Yorkshire gentry in the early Stuart period were often educated at the local grammar school with their more lowly neighbours, but that they were sometimes sent to board with a clergyman or educated in private schools such as that kept by Thomas Smelt in the village of Danby Wiske near Northallerton. Described as 'an excellent grammarian, both of Latin and Greek', Smelt 'taught about three score boys, the greater part of which were gentlemen's sons or sons of the more substantial yeomanry of that part of Yorkshire or the south part of the bishopric of Durham'.[44] The tendency to make such private arrangements was accentuated by the upheavals of the mid-century as first Royalist and then Puritan clergymen, displaced from their posts, sought to earn their livings by teaching school; Charles Hoole was a distinguished member of the group. There is evidence of the existence of a number of such schools in different parts of the country after 1660.[45]

About the education of girls in Yorkshire it is difficult to find much to say with the exception of the work of the Roman Catholic Mary Ward and her sisterhood.[46] Girls of good family were educated at home or in the household of a family of comparable standing – perhaps that of a relative. The account given by Alice Wandesford (later Alice Thornton) is characteristic of the general pattern. She was born in February 1627 at Kirklington near Ripon. Her father, Christopher Wandesford, was a cousin of Thomas Wentworth, Earl of Strafford. He worked with Strafford in Ireland and later himself became Lord Deputy there; he died in December 1640. Alice went to Ireland in 1632 with her mother and two younger brothers. In Ireland she wrote in her autobiography

> I injoyed great eassieness and comfort dureing my honoured father's life, haveing the fortunate opportunity in that time, and affter when I staied there, of the best education that kingdome could afford, haueing the advantage of societie in the sweet and chaste company of the Earle of Strafford's daughter, the most virtuous Lady Anne, and the Lady Arbella Wentworth, learning those qualities with them which my father ordered, namelie, – the French language, to write and speake the same; singeing; danceing; plaeing on the lute and theorboe; learning such other accomplishments of working silkes, gummework, sweetmeats and other suitable huswifery, as, by my mother's vertuous provision and caire, she brought me up in what was fitt for her qualities and my father's childe. But above all things, I accounted it my chiefest happiness wherein I was trained in those pieous, holy, and religious instructions, examples, admonitions, teachings, reproofes, and godly education tending to the welfaire and eternall happinesse and salvation of my poore soule, which I receaved from both my honoured father and mother...[47]

There are a number of points to note about Alice's account. First of all, the emphasis on religious observances and on the active part played by her parents, particularly by her mother in ensuring that she acquired the domestic skills and graces. Secondly, the fact that she was taught in the company of other girls of Strafford's family. Much attention was paid to dancing and learning French, though there is no mention of learning Latin, the central academic discipline of the age. Indeed there was a strongly held view at the time that girls should not learn Latin.[48] Nothing is said about who taught the girls – presumably there were visiting masters and possibly a resident gentlewoman who was able to do some teaching herself and who provided both companionship and religious instruction.

There are references to a number of boarding schools for girls in the London area both before and after the Civil War, and there are a few references to girls attending the lower forms of grammar schools, though they did not progress very far. Dorothy Gardiner says that the first 'public school' for girls of which any record survives was the Ladies' Hall at Deptford. Some of the girls took part in a masque before the Queen and the Court at Greenwich in 1617, and the reference suggests that the school had been started earlier than this.[49] By around 1675 there were the beginnings of a movement towards better education for girls led by a group of middle class women – Mrs. Woolley, Bathsua Makin, Mary Astell – and of these Bathsua Makin had her own school at Tottenham High Cross.[50] There were a few such schools in the provinces too; for example, Mrs. Parnell Amye kept a school in Manchester from 1638 to 1673. Some ten years after she had given up her school, the Leeds antiquary, Ralph Thoresby, rode to Manchester to place his sister at 'Madam Frankland's school'.[51] Celia Fiennes, on her 'great journey to Newcastle and to Cornwall' in 1698, says that there was 'a very fine schoole for young Gentlewomen as good as any in London' at Manchester. She also notes 'a good schoole for young Gentlewomen' in Leeds.[52]

One pioneer figure among Yorkshire women of this time was the Recusant Mary Ward, founder of the Institute of the Blessed Virgin Mary.[53] She was born in

1585 at Old Mulwith manor house near Ripon, and like other Catholic girls who felt themselves called to the religious life, she went overseas, becoming a lay sister with the Poor Clares at St Omer in 1606, though she did not remain long with that order. Gradually she collected a group of women around her, and she opened several schools in Bavaria, where she established a strong link with the ruling family, and in Italy. She and her Institute raised a good deal of opposition. They imitated Jesuit methods; they wore lay habits and they were not enclosed. In 1631 the Institute was suppressed by the Pope, and Mary Ward was imprisoned for a time, though she was soon released and permitted to live in Rome. In 1639 she returned to England where she lived in London and opened a school. She wrote to Rome

> My meaning is to endeavour by prayer and private negotiation that we may have common schools in the great city of London, which will never be without a miracle, but all else will be to little purpose, the ungrateful nature of this people considered.[54]

As the political situation in England grew more tense, she decided to return to Yorkshire, going first (September 1642) to Hutton Rudby near Mount Grace and then in 1644 to Heworth just outside York. She was forced to move into the city during the siege by the Parliamentarians, but she later retired to Heworth where she died in January 1645 and was buried at Osbaldwick.

Her work did not end with her death. Her companions remained at Heworth for some years and then went to Paris. In 1669 Frances Bedingfield opened a school at Hammersmith outside London. Later the sisters went to live at Dolebank near Fountains, and then, in 1686, they were given a site in York just outside Micklegate Bar.[55] The Bar Convent and its school have been there ever since that date, a Roman Catholic community with a remarkable history. The rules of the Institute of the Blessed Virgin Mary were confirmed by Pope Clement XI in 1703, and during the 18th century the order had a number of convents in Germany and Italy.[56]

Only a few of the boys who went to 17th century grammar schools can now be identified; the great majority have left no trace behind them. The most readily traceable are the boys who went to university, a group which was heavily and increasingly dominated by the clergy. The more prominent and successful schools had a permanent link with the universities – generally in Yorkshire with Cambridge – through the award of scholarships and exhibitions.[57] At Beverley, for example, the borough records give the names of boys who went up to St John's in the half-century after 1660. Most of the references relate to the award of exhibitions, but the Corporation occasionally found money from its own resources. In 1660 it was ordered that £5 be paid to Samuel Pearson

> for his present supply at Cambridge, hee being in great want (Doctor Tuckney haveing certified under his hand of the said Samuell Pearson's now residence in St John's Colledge there). And also that the very words of Doctor Metcalfe's will (concerning what he gives for the maintaining of schollers at Cambridge) be sent up to the said Doctor Tuckney. And if upon the same Doctor Tuckney doe certifie that the said Samuell Pearson hath been personally resident in the said Colledge according to the effect of the said will, then the said Samuell Pearson to have thirty three shillings four pence more paid unto him as the rest of his exhibition due the 25th day of March last past.[58]

In 1697 a benefaction of £6 a year left by William Coates was granted to his nephew Richard Coates who was 'in poor estate and desirous of going to the University', though this was not to be a precedent and in future grants were to be made only to students who were actually in residence. When in 1699 Richard Coates was ready to go up to Cambridge, he was given, by the year, £6 of his uncle's money, Dr. Metcalf's exhibition of £6.13.4 and Dr. Lacie's of £8.[59] There are several other examples of two or three exhibitions being awarded to the same man. Like most students in his position Richard Coates took holy orders; he was rector of Saxby (? Lincs.) from 1705 to 1719.[60] Money was occasionally paid to help to meet the expenses of graduation. In 1675 William Ward of St John's had come 'into the country to save charges' because he was in arrears to his tutor, and he asked for his exhibition to be continued. Ward must have found money to return to Cambridge because the following year Mr Johnson, his tutor, was paid £3 when he took his B.A. degree.[61] In 1686 the Metcalf and Lacie exhibitions were awarded to Thomas Elcock, and four years later his father was given £5 towards the expenses of his degree; presumably the father had needed to supplement the income which the son had received from the exhibitions.[62]

One major difficulty in identifying individuals is that very few school registers have survived. The best original example is that of Pocklington School, which covers the years 1626 to 1717 and is especially full for the mastership of Edward Lluellin (1650–57), when 165 names were recorded.[63] Pocklington, particularly under Lluellin, recruited many boys from good county families, though the social range seems also to have been very wide.[64] In addition to the gentry there were the sons of clergymen, lawyers, merchants, farmers and yeomen, and a wide range of tradesmen – shoemakers, butchers, blacksmiths, tanners. As in so many cases, this register records the divisions of the Civil War. Samuel Drake (1635) was ejected from his fellowship at St John's, served in the royal army in garrisons at York and Pontefract, and after the Restoration became vicar of Pontefract and rector of Handsworth. He died in 1678. Joseph Hill (1645) was a pensioner of St John's and then a fellow of Magdalene. Ejected in 1662, he became minister of the Scots congregation at Middelburg in Holland. He was expelled from Holland in 1673 for his political activities, and came into favour with Charles II who offered him a bishopric. He later returned to Holland as minister of the English church at Rotterdam. He died in 1707 aged 83.

James Johnson (1650), whose father was a member of the Westminster Assembly and who became master of Sidney Sussex College, Cambridge 1688–1704, represents the academics, and a few members of other professions are recorded. Robert Freeman (1650) is believed to have gone to India and to have been in the employment of the East India Company at Masulipatam. His contemporary Edward Gower became a lieutenant-colonel and was accused in 1690 of intending to raise a regiment on behalf of King James II. Robert Belt (1652), son of Sir William Belt, recorder of York, was admitted to Gray's Inn in 1655. Benjamin Rouxby (1655) became a London merchant and a governor of Christ's Hospital. Cudworth Johnson (1666), son of a physician at Pontefract, himself became a well-known physician at York. Many of the others in the lists inherited a family estate or continued a family business; they have left no special memorial behind them.

The so-called Sedbergh register is not itself an original source, but for the years up to 1820 a compilation from college registers and other sources.[65] As at Pocklington there were many members of prominent local families like the Lowthers. Gerard Lowther (1550–60) was involved both in the rising of the northern earls and in Norfolk's plot, but he managed to extricate himself from these difficulties. He was a bencher of Lincoln's Inn and High Sheriff of Cumberland in 1592. John Lowther (1662–74) succeeded to the family baronetcy in 1675. He supported William III at the Revolution and was created Baron Lowther and Viscount Lonsdale in 1696. He rebuilt Lowther Hall and the church and rectory at Lowther. Among Sedberghians with Lowther connections was Richard Holme (1662–74) who was rector of the parish from 1694 to 1738. He bequeathed £100 for the maintenance of a poor scholar at Cambridge and he endowed two girls' schools at Lowther. Some of the many clergy in the lists belonged to well-known local families like George Fleming (1680–90), son of Sir Daniel Fleming of Rydal. Fleming was bishop of Carlisle from 1735 to 1747 and himself succeeded to the family baronetcy in 1736. There are a few more bishops and deans and a number of headmasters, including no less than three masters of Pocklington, Rowland Greenwood (1657–64), Miles Farrar (1698–1702), and John Drake (1709–13).

Political and religious divisions can be traced here just as in any other group, but Sedberghians seem to have leant towards the Royalist side. Prominent in that camp was the controversialist and Royalist agent John Barwick (1630–40), dean of St Paul's after the Restoration, who died in 1664. He left £40 to the school to be spent on books and £300 to St John's. One of his friends was John Otway. Ejected from his fellowship at St John's in 1643, he joined the Royalist army. Later he became an M.P., King's Counsel, and Vice-Chancellor of the Duchy of Lancaster. He was knighted in 1673. John Barwick's brother and biographer, Peter, became one of the king's physicians. He wrote a treatise in support of Harvey's theory of the circulation of the blood, and gained much respect because he stayed at his post during the London plague of 1665. Half a century later divergent viewpoints were represented by the non-juror Henry Rishton (1700–06), who was ejected from his fellowship at St John's in 1717 and later became vicar of St James' Barbados, and by Christopher Gibson, curate of St Mary's Lancaster (1713–18) and then vicar of Ormskirk (1718–27).

> While Curate at Lancaster he had to enter the burials in the register – among the rest the names of the Scottish prisoners of 1715 (forty-two of whom were buried at Lancaster). He enters these at first as 'rebel prisoners' but someone (his Jacobite vicar?) seems to have interfered, for afterwards they appear as 'prisoners' only. When he copies the list for the Archdeaconry of Richmond (which the vicar would not see) he calls them all 'rebels'.[66]

There is a fair spread of other occupations in the Sedbergh lists – lawyers and a few doctors, including several members of the Johnston family – Charles, M.B., M.D., 1687, whose father practised at Pontefract, and Pelham, M.D., F.R.C.P., who died at Westminster in 1765. The reference to Pontefract suggests that this must be the same medical family as that to which Cudworth Johnson of Pocklington, whom we have already met, belonged. Among the very few merchants named are William Winder, died 1766, merchant and consul at Barcelona 1723–34; he was also lord of the manor of Dalton in Westmorland. One small sub-group which can be identified consists of several Quakers, for the Sedbergh area was one in which the Friends were strong. James Goad (1680–90) became head of the Friends' school at Swarthmoor in 1697 and later at Mountmellick in Ireland; later he became 'a man of wealth and importance in Low Furness'. Gilbert Thompson, born near Sedbergh in 1658, was head of the Friends' school at Penketh near Warrington; he died in 1719. No list would be complete without its eccentric. Thomas Denny (1700–06) was schoolmaster at Dent, but when he found that this did not suit him, he became a classical itinerant, travelling 'through the counties of Yorkshire Lancashire and Westmorland reciting at the houses of all who had a taste for classics and at various grammar schools. Horace, Virgil and Homer were his chief favourites'.[67]

Both the Pocklington and the Sedbergh lists clearly have many gaps, but they do provide some interesting vignettes of the men trained in two well-known schools in very different areas of the county. A few more boys can be identified, some of whom had careers of great distinction. Of the 29 boys in Robert Pell's return of 1680 at Hull,[68] at least four went to Cambridge and one became an M.D. of Edinburgh. Of the Cambridge men one was the son of a Hull incumbent, another the son of a former headmaster, John Catlyn, the third was the son of a merchant and alderman, mayor in 1681, and the fourth was the son of a grocer, sheriff in 1680. The future M.D. of Edinburgh came from Newcastle, but some of his family were shipwrights in Hull. Other boys whose backgrounds are fairly certain were the sons of master mariners and of a draper, a merchant, a milliner, a surgeon, an inn-keeper and a tobacco cutter.[69]

Among the West Riding schools Bradford produced John Sharp, archbishop of York 1691–1714 and his relative, Abraham the instrument-maker.[70] The most distinguished group, the boys who were at Wakefield in the later 17th century, Radcliffe, Bentley, Bingham and John Potter, have already been mentioned.[71] In the earlier part of the century Wakefield men seem to have been very divided in their opinions. Jeremiah Whitaker, one of the school's earliest pupils, was a Puritan divine and a member of the Westminster Assembly; he died in 1654. Hugh Paulin

Cressy, born in 1605, became chaplain to the Royalist Lord Falkland. He went abroad in 1644, became a Roman Catholic and joined the English Benedictines at Douai. He later became chaplain to Queen Catherine of Braganza and died in England in 1674. Barnabas Oley, who entered the school in 1607, became a fellow of Clare College, Cambridge. At the beginning of the Civil War he successfully evaded a Parliamentarian ambush and brought some of the college plate safely to the King. After the Restoration he became archdeacon of Ely.[72]

Finally something must be said about the education and intellectual interests of the wider community outside the schools and colleges. Two Yorkshire families which produced writers and scholars of repute were the Saviles of Bradley and Methley and the Fairfaxes of Denton. The most distinguished of the Saviles was Sir Henry, provost of Eton, a mathematician and Greek scholar who founded the Savilian chairs of astronomy and geometry at Oxford and who produced an edition of the writings of St John Chrysostom. One of the Fairfaxes, Edward, translated Tasso. Another, Thomas, the Parliamentarian general, was the patron of Roger Dodsworth the antiquary and Andrew Marvell the poet and 'the author of a number of poems and translations as well as of two autobiographical works relating to the Civil War.'[73] The autobiography of Sir John Savile (1546–1607), Baron of the Exchequer, Henry Savile's elder brother, gives a clear picture of his education until he went up to Brasenose College, Oxford in 1561, aged 14/15. John Savile did not go to school, but was educated by a series of private tutors at different places in the Halifax/Huddersfield area. With the important difference that there is no mention of Greek the programme is remarkably similar to that recommended by Charles Hoole 80/90 years later. He studied Aesop's Fables, Castalion's Sacred Dialogues, Cato, Virgil, Terence, Ovid's *Metamorphoses*, Horace, and Eutropius' *History*, which Hoole does not recommend.[74]

Sir George Radcliffe's drafts for his life of Strafford, probably written after the Civil War, take a less academic view of the education of a gentleman than John Savile's autobiography. The boy should learn French from his nurse when the language is easy to acquire. He needs to know Latin and French perfectly, some Greek, logic, rhetoric and philosophy. 'Some of Cicero's Orations and poets Latine and English are recreations rather than study'. Modern history is more useful than ancient, and a man should know some law, that of his own country and, if he is to take any part in government, 'thear wilbe great use of the elements of the Civil and Canon Lawes'. A soldier needs to learn mathematics. 'But it is a great error to propose more than can probably be attained unto. There is a temperance to be used in the studye of knowledge and it is a great fault to be over bookish. Geographie, heraldrie and genealogie are great ornaments and easily attained for so much as is absolutely usefull.'[75]

There were gentry in the county too who were involved in the new mathematical and scientific studies.[76] William Gascoigne (?1612–44) of Middleton near Leeds was a self-taught mathematician who was interested in optics and in improving instruments used for observational work. He was killed at the battle of Marston Moor. His associate Henry Power of New Hall Halifax (1623–68), who was a fellow of the Royal Society, made observations with the microscope, telescope and lodestone, and published his *Experimental Philosophy* in 1663. Of a younger generation was Jeremy Thacker (fl. 1714), an amateur instrument-maker who was interested in the problem of longitude and who designed an instrument for measuring it which he called a 'chronometer'. That word was first used in print in Thacker's pamphlet.[77]

There were also teachers and artificers with similar interests. George Osborne of Hull (fl. 1625–8) was a writing master who could offer the choice of six different hands. He taught mathematics and the art of navigation, and published an almanack in which he mentioned a large number of instruments, 'a list which suggests that he himself had recently spent some time among the mathematical practitioners in London where alone such books and instruments were easily come by'.[78] Abraham Sharp (1651–1742), like his relation Archbishop John Sharp, was an old boy of Bradford grammar school.[79] In the 1680s he worked as assistant to the

Astronomer Royal John Flamsteed at the Royal Observatory. Later he returned to Little Horton near Bradford and made instruments – sundials, sextants, telescopes and way-wisers. When Flamsteed suggested that he should give instruction in their use, Sharp replied that no one in the neighbourhood was interested in such things.[80] Henry Wilson (1673–1741), born at Pickering, taught mathematics and navigation. He wrote a text book, *Navigation New Modell'd* in 1714, and was later at sea with Admiral Byng.[81]

Some evidence has survived about the education and intellectual interests of some yeomen and tradesmen who came from much the same level of society as these teachers and artificers. Adam Eyre of Haslehead near Penistone (1614–61), who had been an officer in the Parliamentary army, kept a diary from 1647 to 1649.[82] Eyre was a great reader, mostly of religious books, though he also mentions Walter Raleigh's *History of the World* and Erasmus' *Praise of Folly*. In his diary he occasionally mentions George Didsbury the master of Penistone school, who was still there after the Restoration, and he notes (Oct. 19 1648): 'This morne I gave 1s. 4d. and promised to find my Godson clothes for this yere to goe to schoole in Leedes, and then to helpe to provide a calling for him'.[83] Eyre and his wife Susannah had no children of their own, so perhaps he had a particular interest in this godson. Eyre's slightly older contemporary John Shaw (b. 1608) came from Bradfield (par. Ecclesfield) in the same south-western corner of the West Riding. Shaw wrote later that his education had been held back because of the want of good schoolmasters so that he was 'tossed from one school to another'. His parents – he was an only child – were anxious that he should stay in his home district, but seeing that he had a great desire for learning, they sent him to Christ's College, Cambridge, where he was admitted as a pensioner at the age of 14/15. He later became vicar of Rotherham and master of the Hull Charterhouse.[84]

Both these examples come from the years before the Civil War. Many years later William Lyster, schoolmaster of Wortley, recorded that in about 1662 he had been sent to learn English with Mr Nicholls who was minister and schoolmaster at

Ilkley. Lyster's account is not entirely clear, but it seems that after Mr Nicholls left Ilkley, he was taught English Latin Greek and Hebrew by Mr Coates who kept a school in his own house. Then, after Mr Coates' death he was removed to Mr Hustler who was schoolmaster and vicar of Ilkley, and he remained with him until he was 17 years old. When Lyster had children of his own, he sent them to Mr Hustler, 'beginning in English which...was never denied to be taught by any of ye schoolmasters of Ilkley School provided they were boys'.[85] That is a puzzling remark; does it imply that Mr Hustler taught girls as well?

The last of these autobiographers is James Fretwell who was born at Thorpe-in-Balne (par. Barnby Dun) near Doncaster in 1699, the son of a timber merchant. He was taught to read by his mother, and when he was five years old, he was sent to school at Kirk Sandal. First of all he walked there every day, but the distance was found to be too great, and he was boarded with a widow, coming home every Saturday. He subsequently went to several schools and was always boarded out, generally with someone who had a connection with his family. From 1709 to 1713 he was sent to the Rev. Samuel Creswick at Stoney Stainton[86] where he began to learn Greek. Creswick was a good schoolmaster, Fretwell recorded, but very severe. After Stoney Stainton he had a year at Doncaster Free School under Mr Edmund Withers, 'a good scholar but was not so diligent as he should have been.'

Fretwell's father then decided that the boy had learned as much Greek and Latin as would be useful to a tradesman and sent him to Joshua Marsden, a Quaker, at Pontefract to learn writing and accounts. 'I went through', he wrote, 'most of the rules of vulgar arithmetick and decimal fractions, with some little of practical geometry'. He was at Pontefract from 1714 to 1715, boarding with Mr John Lapidge a mercer. At the end of that time he was 16 years old, and his father was anxious to put him into business. Since several other possibilities came to nothing, in the end the boy went to work with his father. 'This I've often lamented, for I think they (his parents) did not duly consider which way my genius tended'.[87] James

162

Fretwell lived until 1772. His account of his schooling is a remarkably interesting one. It was not uncommon, as he did, to move from one school to another. His father seems to have been happy for him to follow a classical course until he was about 15. Then, in his final year of formal education he was set to learn writing and accounts as a preparation for business.

Notes Chapter 7

1. Watson F. 1908: 60, 68, 538–9.

2. Cremin, L.A. 1970: 119, 122.

3. Purvis, J.S. 1948: 128; Green, I. 1996.

4. Charlton, K. in Nash, P. (ed.) 1970: 54.

5. *See* pages 130–131.

6. Sheils, W.J. 1977: 55.

7. Purvis, J.S. 1959: 75 (Kirkby Ravensworth); 99 (Kirkburton); 103 (Kirkheaton); 101 (Kirkby Malhamdale).

8. *See* particularly Cressy, D.A. 1973 and 1980, and also his articles: Cressy, 1976: 301–20 and 1977: 1–23. For a brief summary of his argument *see* O'Day, R. 1982: 19–20.

9. Cressy, D.A. 1976: 317.

10. Cressy, D.A. 1980: 72, 75–6, 176.

11. Stone, L. 1969: 101.

12. For the petty school *see* Sylvester, D.W. (ed.) 1970: 78–82; Lawson, J. and Silver, H. 1973: 112; Watson, F. 1908: 36, 163, 165; Baldwin, T.W. 1943: 20–29, 58–9.

13. Hoole, C. 1660/1913: 1–41, 'The Petty-Schoole'; *see also* Vincent, W.A.L. 1950: 92.

14. Watson, F. 1909/1971: 317.

15. For this general argument *see* Wright, L. B. 1935: 43–4, 79–80; Cremin, L.A. 1970: 67, 111; Simon, J. 1966: 296–7; O'Day, R. in O'Day, R. and Heal, F. (eds) 1976: 70–71.

16. For Brinsley *see* Adamson, J.W. 1905: 21–30; Sylvester, D.W. (ed.) 1970: 103–10.

17. *See* page 128.

18. Hoole C. 1660/1913. All the references to Hoole's book are to the 1913 edition by E.T. Campagnac.

19. *See* pages 143–4.

20. Hoole, C. 1913: 51. For the Colloquies of Maturin Cordier (1479–1564) *see* Adamson, J.W. 1922: 167–70.

21. For Hoole on Ovid *see* Ogilvie, R.M. 1964: 11.

22. Bantock, G.H. 1980 vol I: 69.

23. Hoole, C. 1913: 190.

24. Watson, F. 1908: 373. For Hoole's list of authors to be read in each form *see* EYS vol II: 214–18. For a general appreciation *see* Clarke, M.L. 1959: 38–9.

25. *See* pages 149–50.

26. Hoole, C. 1913: 166.

27. Watson, F. 1908: 271–2, 394.

28. Adamson, J.W. 1905: 82, 170–74; Hoole, C. 1913: 6.

29. Hoole, C. 1913: 152; for Erasmus' *De Copia see* Bolgar, R.R. 1963: 273–5.

30. Hoole, C. 1913: 289–92.

31. Oxford, Corpus Christi College: Wase MSS 2: 247.

32. Price, A.C. 1919: 282.

33. Oxford, Corpus Christi College: Wase MSS 2: 243.

34. Wilkinson, J. 1872: 378–9.

35. For John Catlyn *see* pages 73, 124.

36. For a fuller account *see* Lawson, J. 1963; 116–17.

37.   Sadler, J.E. 1966: 268.

38.   *See* Adamson, J.W. 1905 *passim*; Sylvester, D.W. (ed.) 1970: 156–62.

39.   Parker, I. 1914: 42–4.

40.   *See* page 81.

41.   Watson, F. 1909/1971: 305.

42.   *See* pages 147–8.

43.   Lawson, J. 1963: 119–20.

44.   Cliffe, J.T. 1969: 71.

45.   Vincent, W.A.L. 1969: 204–8.

46.   For girls' education generally *see* Gardiner, D. 1929; Notestein, W. in
       Plumb, J.H. (ed.) 1955: 71–107; McMullen, N. 1977: 87–101.

47.   Thornton, A. 1875: 8–9.

48.   Notestein, W. in Plumb, J.H. (ed.) 1955: 82–3.

49.   Gardiner, D. 1929: 209.

50.   *Ibid.*: 222, 224, 244; for these women and their writings *see* Smith, H.L.
       1982; Stone, L. 1977: 201–6, 343–60.

51.   Gardiner, D. 1929: 217–18.

52.   Fiennes, C. 1949: 220, 224.

53.   Chambers, M.C.E. 1882, 1885; Oliver, M. 1960; Aveling, J.C.H. (Hugh)
       1976: 94–8, 101–2.

54.   Chambers, M.C.E. 1885: 467.

55.   Beales, A.C.F. 1963: 226–7.

56.   For the history of the Bar Convent *see* Coleridge, H.J. (ed.) 1887. For the
       history of the school in the 18th century *see* Chapter 13.

57.   For exhibitions at Wakefield *see* Peacock, M.H. 1892: 173–88.

58.   Dennett, J. (ed.) 1932: 121 (21 May 1660). Anthony Tuckney was master of
       St John's from 1653 until he was deprived in 1661.

59.   *Ibid.*: 185, 187 (22 Feb. 1697, 11 Dec. 1699).

60.   Venn, J. 1922–7.

61. Dennett, J. (ed.) 1932: 160–61 (8 April 1675, 25 May 1676).

62. *Ibid.*: 176, 181 (20 Sept. 1686, 29 Dec. 1690).

63. Lawrance, H. 1920: 53–70. All the references to the Pocklington register come from this source.

64. Lawson, J. 1962a: 20.

65. Sedbergh 1909 is the source of what follows about Sedberghians. The entries are arranged in blocks of years and the appropriate year-block is attached for each name cited.

66. Sedbergh 1909: 147.

67. *Ibid.*: 145.

68. *See* page 124.

69. Lawson, J. 1963: 122.

70. *See* pages 160–161 for Abraham Sharp.

71. *See* page 129.

72. For Whitaker, Cressy and Oley *see* Lupton, J.H. 1864: 61–4, 70–74, 75–7.

73. Cliffe, J.T. 1969: 82–3.

74. Clay, J.W. and Lister, J. 1898–9: 420–27.

75. *Wentworth Papers 1597–1628*: 325–6.

76. The following section is based on Taylor, E.G.R. 1954.

77. *Ibid.*: 216–17, 227, 306.

78. *Ibid.*: 210.

79. Hart, A.T. 1949 page 41 says that the exact relationship is unknown. They belonged to the same family and were perhaps cousins.

80. Taylor, E.G.R. 1954: 265–6; 'way-wiser' – 'an instrument for measuring and indicating a distance travelled by road' (OED).

81. Taylor, E.G.R. 1954: 291.

82. For Eyre, John Shaw and James Fretwell *see* Morehouse, J.H. and Jackson, C. (eds) 1877. For Eyre's *Dyurnall see ibid.*: 1–118. There is also a chapter on Eyre in Notestein, W. 1938: 247–69.

83. Morehouse, J.H. and Jackson, C. (eds) 1877: 112.

84. *Ibid.*: 121–62.

85. From a letter dated 5 Jan. 1711: Salmon, N. (n.d.): 15–16.

86. Probably Stainton near Tickhill *see* Hunter J., 1828 vol I: 255.

87. Morehouse, J.H. and Jackson, C. (eds) 1877: 165–243 (Fretwell, J. *A Family History*).

Part Two

The eighteenth century

CHAPTER 8

The Eighteenth Century: Introduction

Education in the 18th century was a major topic of public concern, though the ruling issues were different from those which had predominated under the Tudors and Stuarts. Up to 1660 certainly, and to a considerable extent up to 1714, the debate had centred round religion and questions of church and state which involved the rivalries of Anglican and Puritan, of Protestant and Catholic. After 1700 the focus changes. Education appears as a subject in its own right as opposed to being an ancillary to theology. The leading figure of the new era is John Locke, whose *Some Thoughts Concerning Education* was published in 1693 and went into many later editions. Locke rejected innate principles and emphasized that human beings are to reach their conclusions on the basis of evidence. The mind is freed from authority and is to exercize itself in the real world of things and particulars. Thus the poor are to be trained by learning good habits of order and discipline. At a higher level Locke was interested in scientific studies and he wanted education to produce the man of business rather than the courtier.[1] Later in the century the ideas of Jean Jacques Rousseau had substantial influence in England. He denied the need to create a social nature within which the child might operate, and he was deeply suspicious of the evils of a sophisticated society. The creed of sentiment and sensibility had many followers in England like Thomas Day, the author of *Sandford and Merton*, and R.L. Edgeworth, and it helped to shape the strong 18th century tradition of philanthropy in people like John Howard the prison reformer and

Robert Raikes the pioneer of Sunday schools. Paul Langford calls such people 'truly entrepreneurs of charity, marketing philanthropy as Wedgwood marketed porcelain, Arkwright textiles or Lackington books'.[2]

18th century philanthropy was not only concerned with education. It had other objectives like the foundation of hospitals and of friendly societies for the care of the sick and the elderly. Nor must it be thought that it derived entirely or primarily from the teachings of philosophers like Locke and Rousseau. It inherited a strong tradition of religious action. In the later 17th century the religious feelings which had expressed themselves in bitter doctrinal and sectarian debate were to a great extent diverted into the area of practical charity. An important motive in this was the desire to promote a more Christian style of life among the poor. Their eternal welfare and their temporal interests were to be promoted at the same time and through the same means. Such intentions were not only pious; they were also disciplinary. Men and women who had been schooled in sound religious practice would be sober and orderly, not inclined to riot or dissipation and trained to work hard and to get their own livings. Though the origins of such religious principles were different from those of Lockean empiricism, they frequently led to similar objectives in the lifestyles which they set for the mass of the people.

The promoters of such charity included both laymen and clergymen, but the clergy were particularly important because, through the working of the parochial system, they had a footing in every town and village and their support was vital in promoting every good cause. Voluntary associations for works of piety and charity appear under the Restoration.[3] It is possible that, in a society where religious orthodoxy and uniformity could no longer be taken for granted, voluntary action was both more attractive and more practicable than it had been in early Stuart times when the emphasis lay so heavily on state control. Early examples of the new spirit were religious societies for prayer and private study and the societies for the reformation of manners which campaigned against vice and immorality. Then, at the turn of the century came the two great societies – for Promoting Christian

Knowledge (SPCK) (1699) and for the Propagation of the Gospel (SPG) (1701). SPCK was concerned with the distribution of religious literature and, in its first 40 years, it actively promoted the foundation of charity schools and the advancement of the education of the poor. Its precise role in this area has been questioned by some modern scholars, and its importance can be exaggerated. But much more must be said about it later because it did play an important part in our story of Yorkshire schools.

Then in the middle of the 18th century the voluntaryist movement seems to have faltered. The major religious impulse of the age was the Evangelical Revival and the work of John Wesley and the early Methodists, though in the last two decades of the century the power flowed back into voluntary movements of a type similar to those of the reign of Queen Anne. As at the end of the 17th century there were societies to combat vice and immorality. In the 1780s the Sunday School movement gained strength. Both Anglicans and Dissenters founded missionary societies like the Church Missionary Society (1799). Religious literature was promoted by the Religious Tract Society (1799) and the British and Foreign Bible Society (1804) The problem of mass illiteracy was tackled through the system of mutual instruction pioneered by Joseph Lancaster and Andrew Bell, which led to the creation of the National Society (1811) and of the British and Foreign School Society (1814).

The story of 18th century education is far more complex and diverse than that of the Tudor and Stuart periods which has already been reviewed. The dominance of classical culture was broken down by pressures for newer and more practical studies. The fight to maintain religious uniformity had been lost, and both Roman Catholics and Dissenters set out to establish their own schools. There was a major concern to extend schooling to the mass of the people, some of it linked with the efforts of SPCK, but much of it deriving from the generosity of local benefactors. The century was not a prosperous time for corporate institutions, and both grammar schools and universities suffered decline. Good work was still done in them, but they were much less at the centre of things than they had been in the previous two centuries.

The pattern of schooling in Yorkshire was similar to that in other parts of the country. First of all, the condition of the grammar schools will be examined. In many of them, particularly the smaller schools, the line between classical and elementary education was by no means as sharply drawn as some traditional accounts and legal decisions suggest, and there was not always a clear line of demarcation between them and the elementary and charity schools, the numbers of which increased considerably during the century. Indeed the spread of elementary schools is the most important development of the time, even though many villages did not possess them. The motives behind this expansion were complex. The influence of SPCK was considerable, but it was limited to the larger centres of population like York, Leeds and Sheffield, Hull and Beverley, all of which possessed 'charity schools' of the SPCK type, large institutions which enjoyed substantial incomes, and which in several cases have endured into the 20th century.

But the characteristic elementary school was the creation of a local benefactor or of general village effort, and it owed little or nothing to outside influence of any kind. Some of these local benefactors, like Lady Elizabeth Hastings, were people of considerable wealth and celebrity, others were almost completely unknown to history. In the case of some of the large schools – and here the influence of John Locke is once again important – work as well as instruction was provided for the children. In these cases the story of children's schooling merges with that of the upbringing of children in workhouses and with the training of apprentices, and it is difficult to draw a line between these various themes. Something will be said about work and apprenticeship later, though in the case of the younger children there was not much productive work which they could do.

Whether there was a school in the parish or not, much emphasis was placed throughout the century on the parish clergyman's duty to catechize the children and so to ensure that they were familiar with the basic tenets of Christian belief.

Archbishop Herring, in his visitation questions (1743), asked a question about catechizing, and he commented on the cases where he considered this duty to be neglected. In general it seems to have been done regularly.[4] Perhaps a link may be traced between this traditional feature of parish life and the development during the 1780s of Sunday Schools for imparting religious training and basic skills in literacy both to children who were at work during the week and to those who were likely to get into mischief because they had nothing to do.

The name traditionally linked with the foundation of Sunday Schools is that of Robert Raikes of Gloucester, but there was a good deal of independent activity in Yorkshire, some of it pre-dating Raikes' initiatives, and during the last two decades of the 18th century such schools spread widely throughout the county. They were to be found both in towns and in villages, and they were set up both by Churchmen and by Dissenters. Among the non-Anglicans the Methodists were particularly active. The next stage after the growth of the Sunday Schools was the spread of the day schools promoted by the National and British Societies during the first quarter of the 19th century. This account will end with a brief review of the early days of the societies about the years 1815–20. By that time a new era was beginning with different problems and priorities from those of the 18th century.

A large part of the story of education in 18th century Yorkshire relates to the spread of elementary schooling of the various types outlined above. Many of these schools possessed endowments of their own or, like the town charity schools, were managed by committees of trustees. But many others represented the enterprise of the individual teacher, and the growth of such private schools at all levels, from the village dame school to the expensive boarding academy, was a major development of the 18th century. Among the schools which took older children some specialized in modern languages and mathematics, others ran a classical curriculum similar to that of the grammar schools, many taught a mixture of the two. Though private schools for girls can be traced back to the 17th century, it was during the 18th that they became common. The spread of a more

175

systematized education for girls is indeed an important feature of that time, though girls' schools were always criticized for defective teaching methods and an excessive concentration on showy accomplishments. All these private schools have left few traces behind them, though they were collectively of considerable importance. Often the historian's main source is the newspaper advertisements inserted by their proprietors. By the 1750s the provincial newspapers were an important means of disseminating information.

One distinctive group among private schools was that attached to the various religious bodies. Apart from schools managed and owned by private individuals, Yorkshire possessed several denominational schools: – the Moravian Fulneck (1753), the Quaker Ackworth (1779), the Methodist Woodhouse Grove (1812), the Congregationalist Silcoates (1820/31). The Dissenting Academies often provided a general education for laymen, as well as ministerial training, and Yorkshire, from Richard Frankland at Rathmell to Charles Wellbeloved at York, has a place in their history. Though they lie on the periphery of this book, something will be said about them later.[5] Roman Catholic schools enjoyed much less continuity than those of the Dissenters. The only school with an unbroken history was the girls' school attached to the Bar Convent at York, the origins of which go back to the late 17th century.[6] The English Benedictines, who had to leave their house at Dieulouard in Lorraine in 1793, did not settle at Ampleforth until 1802, and they began a school within the next few years. By 1820 there were 45 boys.[7] These private schools of many different kinds form the final group to be described in this survey, which will end with some general reflection on the changes which occurred when, at the end of the Napoleonic wars, the nation moved into a new age of industrialism and reform.

One of the major changes of the century after 1700 was the great expansion in population over the whole country. The latter part of the 17th century had been a period of stagnation in such growth. In 1700 England and Wales had about 5 million people. In 1801, the year of the first census, this had grown to 9.2 million. It

176

has been estimated that in 1701 Yorkshire had about 430,000 inhabitants, about 240,000 of them in the West Riding.[8] The 1801 census figures are as follows

The whole county	859,133	West Riding	564,593
		East Riding	111,192
		North Riding	158,955
		York and Ainsty	24,393 [9]

The populations of the larger towns (in thousands) were as follows: Bradford, 13; Halifax, 12; Hull, 30; Leeds, 53; Sheffield, 46; Wakefield, 11; York, 17.[10] The preponderance of the West Riding had increased since 1701, and the relative decline in the importance of York is very striking. Leeds and Sheffield had emerged as much the largest towns in the county.

Notes Chapter 8

1. Bantock, G.H. 1980 vol I: 226–46.
2. Langford, P. 1989: 485.
3. Walsh, J. and Taylor, S. in Walsh, J., Haydon, C., Taylor, S. (eds) 1993: 17–18.
4. Herring Returns vol I: xvi (Introduction by Ollard, S.L.); Green, I. 1996.
5. For Richard Frankland *see* page 65; for the academies in general *see* pages 262–3.
6. *See* page 153.
7. McCann, J. and Cary-Elwes, C. (eds) 1952: 202–14, 219.
8. Stephens, J.E. 1977: 60.
9. Hey, D. 1986: 181–2, 246.
10. Mitchell, P.R. and Deane, P. 1962: 24–6.

CHAPTER 9

The Grammar Schools

Though some Yorkshire grammar schools were prosperous and successful during
this period, many others failed to maintain their status as nurseries of the classical
languages and training grounds for the universities. It is clear, from the accounts by
A.F. Leach in the *Victoria County History of Yorkshire*, that by 1800 many of the
smaller schools had become purely elementary.[1] It is not easy to be certain about
the number of grammar schools which had existed in the county during the 17th
century.[2] P.J. Wallis and W.E. Tate calculated that there were over 300 in existence
before 1700, though they emphasized that inclusion in their list did not mean that a
school functioned continuously as a grammar school nor that mentions at different
dates imply a common identity between the schools mentioned. W.A.L. Vincent
thought that between 1600 and 1660 155 such schools existed in Yorkshire.

At the end of our period (1818) the numbers given by Nicholas Carlisle in
his enquiry show a sharp decline from these totals. He listed 52 grammar schools in
the county, 16 of which had sent no answer to his request for information.[3] Of those
which did reply a few were not teaching the classics at all, and in a number of other
cases, though the classics were mentioned, they clearly formed only a minor part of
the total curriculum. At Bedale (NR), for example, 60 parish boys were admitted
and educated in 'Dr. Bell's system' (the mutual system of elementary teaching
promoted by the National Society).[4] At Royston (WR), since there was not a
sufficient number of classical scholars, the trustees permitted the master to teach

English.[5] At Drighlington (WR) the scholars might be taught 'English, writing, arithmetic or *Classics*, according to the ability of the scholar, and the desire of their Parents'.[6] Probably schools largely found their own level according to the desires and needs of their local communities. The number of schools which could maintain the full classical curriculum with strong university links was comparatively small. The rest pursued what might be called a mixed economy, and it is much more difficult to separate grammar from elementary schools than appears at first sight.

Before going on to examine the reasons for this comparative decline of the grammar schools, something must be said about the master's subscription, which had been so important during the 17th century. Grammar schoolmasters still subscribed and took out their licences in the traditional way, but the coercive force of the system had disappeared. Several law cases at the end of the 17th century had limited church control.[7] In Bates' case (1670) it had been decided that the nominee of a founder or of a lay patron could not be ejected by the bishop. In Cox's case (1700) and in Rex v. Douse (1701) ecclesiastical jurisdiction was limited to grammar schools and elementary schools were exempted from it. So Dissenting teachers enjoyed more freedom, though school foundations remained Anglican in character, most grammar schoolmasters were in holy orders, and many elementary schoolmasters were parish clerks. An Act of 1779 provided that no Dissenting minister or layman who was prepared to make a declaration should be prosecuted for teaching as a tutor or schoolmaster, although such persons might not hold the mastership of an endowed college or school unless that school had been founded since 1689 for the benefit of Protestant Dissenters. Similar relief was granted to Roman Catholics in 1790–91. Even after these acts had been passed the hold of the Church of England on educational foundations remained very strong, and this was often the cause of the controversy during the 19th century, when Protestant Dissent had become a very powerful force. The rivalry between Church and Dissent was a major issue in many places for the Schools Inquiry Commission of 1864–8.

The exclusion of Protestant Dissenters from the universities and from public life may have had a harmful effect on the fortunes of the grammar schools generally. There was no formal test to exclude boys from dissenting families from them as there was at Oxford and Cambridge, but the masters were Anglican and the whole atmosphere was permeated by the influence of the established church. The common consensus among all Protestants which had existed before the Civil War had been one cause of the prosperity and success of the grammar schools and universities of that era. After 1660 there was a growth of private schools of all kinds. In the 18th century both the Dissenting Academies and the private schools run by dissenting teachers offered a rival educational system which helped to take boys away from the grammar schools.

The 18th century was a period of stagnation for corporate institutions generally. The extent of this has been exaggerated, but it certainly existed. It has been argued that Georgian society was more static than that of early Stuart times, that it became more difficult for poor men to gain advancement in the church, and that in consequence such men were less likely to offer themselves for education of the traditional kind.[8] If this idea has validity, it certainly fits in well with the fact that the main thrust of the time was towards the foundation of elementary schools not, as had been the case a century earlier, towards expanding the higher levels of education. The story of 18th century elementary schools is generally one of development and progress, that of higher education is rather one of clinging onto old positions with little scope for innovation.

The schools also suffered from financial pressures. R.S. Tompson has argued that fixed endowments and rising prices reduced the real value of endowments and so made it more difficult to finance the full classical curriculum. The wealthier and better known grammar schools were able to maintain their positions; the smaller and poorer dropped out of the race. Some harm may also have been done by the Mortmain Act of 1735 which laid down that a fixed period of time should elapse between the settlement of a donation and the death of the donor.[9] One example of financial pressures on a Yorkshire school is that of Archbishop Holgate's foundation at Old Malton where, in the middle of the century, the bulk of the estates were alienated as fixed rent charges so that subsequent increases in value accrued to the tenants and not to the school.[10]

The major educational issues of the Georgian era revolved, however, not round endowments but round the curriculum. After 1660 the unique authority of the ancient languages broke down. There was growing pressure for the teaching of English at all levels, for modern languages designed for the merchant and for the gentleman who wished to travel, for arithmetic and mathematics for the tradesman and the artificer, the soldier and the sailor. The grammar schools were not equipped to meet these demands, which were satisfied by private schools of various kinds. It would be wrong to think of all private schools as 'modern', for many of them offered classical subjects, but all of them represented something both more eclectic and more flexible than the older schools. Nor must the increasing number of girls' schools be forgotten. Though most of them did not reach a high standard, they concentrated on English subjects, on modern languages and on accomplishments, and, in so far as they had an influence, they reinforced the strength of the modernist movement.

These changes presented the grammar schools with many problems which went largely unresolved. It would be a mistake to think that school curricula remained entirely unchanged, and there are many references to the introduction of modern subjects. At Wakefield, one of the most prestigious schools in the county, a French master was engaged in 1752, and after that there was always a mathematical master.[11] At the less important foundation of Batley the master, Matthew Sedgwick, reported to his governors in 1800 that there were 43 parish boys in the school

> Six are instructed in the Classics, one in the Greek Testament, Xenophon and Virgil, two in Ovid's Epistles and *Selectae e Profanis Scriptoribus Historiae*, one in Cornelius Nepos, one in Lange's Latin Conversations, and one in Latin Grammar. Three of them learn accounts, and all of them

devote part of their time to Writing and English Grammar. Nineteen are instructed in the Bible – twelve of these are also taught English Grammar, and eleven of them Writing. Seven read the Pleasing Instructor, three learn accounts, and all of them Writing. Eleven read the New Testament, and three of them write.[12]

The school was well run and by 1824 there were more than 60 boys. For those which could afford it there was the possibility of legitimizing change by obtaining an act of Parliament, though that was an expensive business. In 1818, for example, the Bradford governors obtained such an act enabling them to sell the old school building and to teach modern languages and other modern subjects.[13]

Such changes often produced severe local tensions with the vicar and schoolmaster, who were sometimes one and the same person, generally supporting the classics and the bulk of the parishioners favouring the English subjects. Several such cases have been quoted by R.S. Tompson. In 1711 George Dawson the vicar and schoolmaster of Ilkley sent a petition to Archbishop Sharp signed by 41 of his parishioners rejecting the suggestion that the parish boys should be instructed in English. At Halifax in 1769 the governors proposed to Archbishop Robert Hay Drummond that the school curriculum should be enlarged to include modern subjects. The master was hostile and the archbishop initially cautious, though he eventually decided that it would not be inconsistent with the charter to implement such changes 'in so flourishing a place of trade'.[14] The later history of Ilkley school shows that the classics did not prosper. In 1818, when a later vicar wrote to the archbishop about appointing a new master, he talked simply about the teaching of reading, writing and arithmetic.[15]

A good deal could be and was done to achieve change through local arrangements, though such changes always faced the threat of legal challenge. At Giggleswick, a comparatively wealthy foundation with an increasing revenue, the governors built a new school in 1790 and announced their plans to employ more assistants to teach new subjects and to award exhibitions either at the universities or

183

while scholars were still at the school. In 1796 the Attorney-General gave an opinion that the granting of exhibitions was *ultra vires* and expressed doubt whether the appointment of a writing master was consistent with the purposes of the foundation, though he did not think a court would censure the governors. The archbishop agreed to an alteration in the statutes which permitted the payment of gratuities to scholars, and in 1798 the governors declared their intention of appointing a mathematical assistant. They further stated that classics, mathematics, writing and accounts were taught in the school ' free of any Expense to any Person in the Kingdom'.[16]

Sometimes local disputes about the efficiency or suitability of individual masters were – in part at least – related to the question of which kind of school the master was to manage. A man who might be very well fitted for one type of school might not meet the demands of another. Something of these issues seems to be mixed up, with other local wrangles, in the history of the small but ancient foundation of Penistone in the south-western corner of the West Riding.[17] John Ramsden, who had been appointed in 1702, had executed a bond with the trustees in which, among other things, he promised to teach his pupils to read English and to allow a salary to an usher who was to teach 'ye said English tongue'.[18] In 1776 Joseph Horsfall was appointed by the only two surviving trustees who had neither filled up the numbers of the trust nor advertized the vacancy. In November 1785 Horsfall was forced to resign when an action in Chancery decided that he had been illegally appointed and that he and his usher had neglected the school for their clerical duties (Horsfall was also curate of Denby in Penistone parish). But there are suggestions in letters of May–June 1785 that part of the case against Horsfall arose from the desire of his opponents that the school should be run as a boarding school. His attorney, William Field of Barnsley, wrote to one of the feoffees, William Spencer-Stanhope (27 May 1785):

From the information I can obtain of the affair, it has arisen in Pique and mistaken hopes that Penistone may be made a Capital City thro' the Intervention of a School that can exist only Chimera (sic).[19]

Moreover Horsfall himself wrote (2 June 1785) that, because of the precarious nature of his nomination, he had been induced

to pay every possible regard to the Education of the Parish Boys without running into an expence of fitting up ye Accommodation for Boarders. And this Conduct has drawn upon me the opposition of a few Individuals who reason upon the ground of it being a great advantage to the Town of Penistone by being made a publick Boarding School.

It is not clear where the group of seven men, who offered (19 June 1785) to contribute towards putting the school and schoolhouse into repair if the problems could be settled without an application to Chancery, stood in the controversy. In December 1784 234 parishioners had already expressed their approval of the management of the school by Horsfall and his usher. Clearly from that evidence he had a lot of local support.

Horsfall's successor, Jonathan Wood, who was a layman, also executed a bond with the trustees in which, against a penalty of £500 for breach of his undertakings, he undertook to teach the children of parishioners 'in the English Language and in the Latin and Greek Classics' without charge and to teach Writing and Mathematics at the rates paid at neighbouring schools.[20] Eventually Wood himself ran into difficulties. 19 years after his appointment the trustees announced that they proposed to hear complaints against him for neglecting to teach the children properly and for not repairing the schoolhouse.[21] It was claimed that he was often absent from the school, that there was no proper discipline, and that Latin grammar was badly taught. In 1814 the curate of the parish, John Haworth, wrote a long letter to Walter Spencer-Stanhope repeating parishioners' complaints.[22] The children were, Haworth claimed, not instructed in geography and grammar at all, not were their copy and sum books properly corrected. If parents complained on behalf of their children, they were told that the master would not 'bring them forward'. Wood's behaviour to the curate himself had been such that, if he were to remain there, Haworth would have no alternative but to leave the parish.

Strong complaints indeed, yet only a year after Haworth's letter, petitions were received from no fewer than 390 inhabitants asking for the continuance of Wood as master of the school 'subject to the conditions first entered into by him with the said Trustees'.[23] In fact Wood remained in office until his death in 1836. The Charity Commissioners' report of 1827 had said that he taught only reading, writing and accounts, and it recommended that his successor should be a man who could maintain the school as a grammar school. So, in the case of both Horsfall and Wood, there is a clear conflict of evidence. Probably Wood was negligent. He remained in office for a very long time, and no doubt he became less effective as he got older. But in the case of both men there is evidence, through the extensively signed petitions, of strong support from local people who were not likely to be deceived about their own schoolmaster. It is at least possible that what both Horsfall and Wood had to offer was acceptable to many of the parishioners, but was not what was wanted by the opponents of Horsfall who favoured a boarding school or by curate Haworth and his friends. The matter is, it is submitted, considerably more complex than the simple issue of the efficiency or inefficiency of the Penistone masters.

Considerable space has been devoted to this Penistone example because it is not well known, and it does bring out very clearly the varied pressures to which the smaller grammar schools were exposed. Sometimes these pressures resulted in expensive litigation. One such case was that of Bingley Grammar School in the West Riding, where the master, Richard Hartley, appointed in 1791, had built up a successful boarding school. The parishioners complained that this had been done to the detriment of the interests of local children, and a Chancery suit began in 1816. In 1821 judgement was found for Hartley and the governors. Like Jonathan Wood,

186

Hartley remained in office for a very long time. By 1827 he had ceased to take boarders and there were only ten free scholars left.[24]

Much the best known example of these legal cases was that of Leeds Grammar School, which became of national importance, though its results have been widely misunderstood by both contemporaries and later historians.[25] The governors of the school, The Committee of Pious Uses, had decided as early as 1777 to appoint masters to teach new subjects, though nothing had been done. The master, Joseph Whiteley (1789–1815), denied the power of the Committee to appoint the new masters, and so a Chancery suit was commenced in 1795. In 1797 a Master in Chancery reported in favour of appointing masters to teach modern languages and mathematics, though he thought that there were already plenty of schools in the town able to teach writing and arithmetic. The master and usher in return protested that the school was a grammar school, that French and German ought not to be part of the institution, and that, if they were not to receive all the income of the endowment, their salaries ought to be augmented.

After further disputes the Lord Chancellor, Lord Eldon, made a ruling in 1805. In this he held that the previous decision of the Court had been wrong because it had not defined the nature of the charity. He found that the school was 'for teaching grammatically the learned languages', though he was not opposed to introducing mathematics and modern languages if, by so doing, more boys were encouraged to attend the school to learn Greek and Latin. And in 1808, after a further application by the governors, he accepted that a mathematics master might be appointed provided that the school remained substantially a grammar school in the traditional sense. After this there were no further legal proceedings. Though there had been frequent discussions about appointing the new master or masters, a mathematics master was not finally appointed until 1818 after Whiteley's death. Essentially Eldon had found that the trust might be modified but that its basic purpose to teach the ancient languages might not be overturned. However, he was

187

widely considered to have made a judgement which prevented all changes in the grammar school curriculum.

The more prominent grammar schools, though their fortunes could fluctuate very much even during the reign of a single master, were still able to attract boys from prominent local families. Beverley, described by Celia Fiennes on her journey of 1697 as 'a very good free schoole for boys, they say the best in England for learning and care',[26] was a successful school throughout the 18th century. In 1710, under Joseph Lambert (1674–1716), there were about 140 pupils, and it was recorded that 'many gentlemen of the best quality send their sons to it from several parts of the kingdom'.[27] A later distinguished master, John Clarke (1736–51) was later headmaster of Wakefield (1751–58). When he died in 1761, 147 of his old scholars erected a monument to his memory. The donors included some prominent Hull merchants, the vicar of Sheffield, country gentlemen like Sir George Cayley of Brompton and Scarborough, Henry Lord Middleton, Sir George Strickland of Boynton, and Sir Alex. Thomson, chief baron of the Exchequer.[28] Though by mid-century there was a growing tendency for prominent local families to send their sons to Eton or Westminster, many of them still made use of local schools with good reputations. One of these was Sedbergh. Though by the early 19th century it was in decline, it produced a number of academics, the most eminent of whom was the geologist Adam Sedgwick, lawyers, clerics and medical men. There were old boys of more unusual mark too, like Christopher Alderson who laid out the gardens at Kew for Queen Charlotte and (probably) James King who was with Captain Cook on *Resolution* in the South Seas.[29] Even much less prominent schools had their successful periods. Richard Hudson went to Hipperholme in the West Riding in 1782. During the 1790s there were 150/200 boys, among them sons of the local gentry like the Armytages and others who became soldiers, clergymen and lawyers. But once again Hudson stayed too long. By 1826 he had ceased to take boarders, and only 20 free places were filled.[30]

Several headmasters stand out from the general mass, though rather confusingly three of them were called Clark or Clarke. John Clarke of Beverley and Wakefield has already been mentioned. He was an excellent teacher of the classics, nicknamed for his own proficiency 'the little Aristophanes', who introduced his pupils to many of the less well-known authors. He spent much time in teaching the Old and New Testaments in Greek and, when his senior boys left the school, he presented them with a small pocket edition of a classical author to encourage them to keep up their reading.[31] John Clarke was also very interested in the school libraries at both Beverley and Wakefield. Under one of his Wakefield predecessors, Thomas Clark (1703–20), a subscription had been raised to build a library there.[32]

The third and most interesting of the namesakes is John Clarke, headmaster of Hull Grammar School (1716–32), though he was not a very successful practical schoolmaster.[33] He became steadily more disillusioned in his school work and finally resigned while he was still in his 40s and died only two years later. Clarke's main objective was to apply the ideas of John Locke to the requirements of the school. He wanted to simplify and rationalize the traditional system, to remove learning by heart as much as possible, and to introduce a simplified grammar in English. He favoured the use of literal translations of the classics, and wanted to place more emphasis on prose and less on poetry. Verse composition he considered 'but a Diversion, a Degree above Fiddling'.[34] He wanted boys to have extensive practice in writing Latin, but he thought that they should only read Greek and not try to write it. Many boys were in his view set to learn Greek before they had sufficient skill in Latin, and this, he thought, was particularly bad for boys who were going to leave school quite young. His list of authors which boys should have read in order to be prepared for 'an Academy' (by which he presumably meant the university) is fairly conventional on the Latin side but rather limited on the Greek – he suggests only the Gospels and the Acts of the Apostles, the 12 books of the Iliad, Theocritus, and the two late classical historians, Herodian and Zosimus.

Clarke also wanted boys to learn geography and 'chronology', both of their own country and of the ancient world. He was anxious to introduce them to newspapers, and he emphasized the value of the *Spectators*. He was opposed to over-severe discipline, and he thought the remedy of the lash a good deal worse than the evils it was meant to cure. Finally he was very concerned about the moral lessons to be taught by schools. The idea of an Almighty Being was to be instilled as the foundation for all religion. Boys were to be taught the arguments for belief in Christianity so that the spread of Deism might be prevented.

Clarke was really an interesting outsider on the 18th century scholastic scene. A layman, he had been a student, though he was not a graduate of the university of Edinburgh, so he did not spring from the close network of Oxford and Cambridge. His own list of the qualifications necessary for a schoolmaster is worth noting. The office should not, he thought, be combined with a cure of souls. The master should have a good knowledge of Latin and should be able to talk it readily, though he did not need such an advanced knowledge of Greek. He should at least in that language be able to read the New Testament, Homer's Iliad and some other easy authors. He should be a philosopher, well read in logic and morality and able to reason well. He should have a good mastery of English, which was necessary to teach Latin well. He should know geography and chronology; history he would have learned from his classical authors. In fact, Clarke thought, there was little encouragement for a man to devote himself to teaching. Rather surprisingly for a grammar schoolmaster, he thought there was a danger of acquiring bad habits in 'public schools'. The best sort of education for a young gentleman would be a private boarding school with about 20 or 30 boys. 'I cannot help thinking', he wrote, 'that a great many young Gentlemen are perfectly thrown away, by being thrown into publick schools, who might be an Ornament and a Security to their Country, if they were otherwise disposed of'.[35]

Clarke's books, particularly his *Introduction to the Making of Latin*, were widely used, but he does not seem to have had any influence on the development of grammar school studies in the ensuing generation. The other two leading heads who have been selected here, Joseph Milner of Hull and James Tate of Richmond, were much more in the central stream of the tradition. Joseph Milner and his better known brother, Isaac, president of Queens' College, Cambridge, were both prominent Evangelicals. The sons of a poor weaver in Leeds, they were both educated at Leeds Grammar School. Isaac wrote long after their schooldays that both he and his brother, Joseph

> ever retained a most grateful remembrance of the advantages which we derived from our education in the said school, and I have no scruple to own that both of us, under a kind Providence, have ever had reason to ascribe all our successes in life to the instructions of the school in Leeds and the liberality of the town and neighbourhood.[36]

Joseph Milner was appointed master of Hull Grammar School in 1767, having previously been an usher in a private school at Thorp Arch near Tadcaster.[37] He died in 1797 just after he had resigned his headship on being appointed vicar of Holy Trinity, Hull. His pupil, the Cambridge political economist George Pryme, gives an attractive picture of the head in his autobiography. The school was, Pryme wrote, 'the great seminary for boys in the East Riding of Yorkshire'.[38] When he was there in the mid-1790s there were about 45 boys. Pryme thought Milner 'a man of *strong* mind, of independent habit of thought and of enlarged views'.[39] He rarely inflicted corporal punishment, preferring other methods of discipline. In school work he was opposed to the learning of quantities of Latin syntax by heart, preferring that the boys should read as much as possible for themselves. He was careful about the correct use of English, and ensured that the boys understood English grammar. The religious training was Evangelical, though the head was tolerant and charitable to those who differed from him. Pryme calls him 'the great Simeonite of that part of the country'[40] [after the Cambridge Evangelical pioneer, Charles Simeon], and his *History of the Church of Christ* was highly thought of by Evangelicals. Apart from his work in school, Milner prepared many young men for

191

ordination, and his religious views had a considerable influence on Hull and its region long after his death.

James Tate of Richmond was much more the pure classical teacher and scholar than Milner. He had himself been a boy at Richmond School under Anthony Temple (1750–95), himself a master of mark. When Temple died, there was an attempt by a party in the town to force into the vacant post another old boy, Caleb Readshaw, of whom many of the parents had a low opinion, but this was resisted by the mayor. Eventually, after an attempt at legal action in the court of King's Bench by Readshaw and his supporters, the matter was remitted by the Lord Chancellor to the diocesan, the Bishop of Chester, whose examiners recommended Tate, who had also been a candidate. During this period of controversy (June 1795–September 1796) the school had been closed.[41] After such an inauspicious beginning, Tate enjoyed a long reign from 1796 to 1833. Though the school was never large – about 50 in the 1820s including 17/18 free scholars – Tate sent up a steady stream of boys to Cambridge, many of whom did very well in the Tripos and became fellows of colleges. Tate was a warm-hearted generous man, keenly interested in his old pupils, and his good qualities stand out clearly in his published letters. After so many years of hard work, he was made canon of St Paul's by Lord Grey in 1833 – a well-endowed ending to a successful professional life.[42]

Successful schools like Beverley and Richmond have to be balanced against the many others which went downhill. Some of the reasons for the decline have already been examined, and the few examples cited here are only a small number among the many which could have been chosen. Hull did not maintain its position as a classical school after Milner's time.[43] There was increasing competition from private schools, and in any event it was becoming more and more difficult to attract boarders to a school in the middle of a large town with all the environmental problems of such a location. In the earlier part of the century Sedbergh had been one of the leading schools in the county. William Stevens in the earlier years of his rule had produced a number of able Cambridge mathematicians. When he died in

1819 he left eight day boys and no boarders. The schoolhouse was closed, and the few boys who remained were taught in the master's own house.[44] The local historian, T.D. Whitaker, himself a Johnian, wrote in 1823 of the school's long connection with St John's College, Cambridge. He would have been glad, he wrote, 'to hail this place as classic ground; but in the taste and fashion of education as well as all other things, there are revolutions, which interest itself cannot control.'[45] A study of the alumni of Sheffield Grammar School shows a steady stream of men going up to the university until about 1750. After that the stream gets very much thinner, and it almost disappears after 1800.[46] At Almondbury near Huddersfield the vicar reported at the archbishop's visitation of 1764 that the master, Samuel Brook, who had been appointed in 1727, was so disabled that no children had been taught for several years. His successor had between 14 and 20 boys during the 70s and 80s.[47] In 1821 an attempt was made to convert the school into an elementary school.[48]

These and many similar cases were largely the result of adverse circumstances and of the illness and old age of a master. There were more serious scandals too which after 1815, when parliamentary sensitivity to such questions was growing, led to the intervention of Parliament. In September 1736 Joseph Taylor, curate and grammar schoolmaster in the remote parish of Bowes on the Co. Durham border, was cited to appear in the Commissary's Court at Richmond. He was charged with allowing his cattle to profane and defile the church porch at Bowes, with failing to read the services on six or seven Sundays, and with absenting himself from the school for five or six weeks. He had taken both the master's and the usher's salaries, but he had not provided an usher to teach the boys during his absence.[49] I do not have any record of the result of the case.

Skipton was a much better known school which suffered serious problems. When Matthew Wilkinson died in 1751, several candidates offered bribes to the electors, who were the vicar and the 11 churchwardens of the parish. Finally two candidates, both of whom had offered bribes, reached a deadlock, and Lincoln

College, Oxford, which had residuary rights of appointment after a certain lapse of time, appointed Samuel Plomer who made good his claim after an initial struggle. When Plomer's successor, Thomas Carr, died in 1792, there were several candidates for the valuable post (the income of the headmaster was over £320 a year). Richard Withnell, who had actively canvassed support among the churchwardens, was elected, but the archbishop (William Markham) insisted on his right to examine Withnell, and a legal contest began in the court of King's Bench. The court found that masters of grammar schools must be licensed by the ordinary, who might examine the applicant as to his learning, morality and religion. Eventually, four years after his appointment, Withnell gave up the struggle, and during the whole of that time the school had been closed. The judgement of the Chief Justice, Lord Kenyon passed an interesting comment on the situation in many schools. Kenyon declared

> Whoever will examine the state of the grammar schools in different parts of this kingdom will see to what a lamentable condition most of them are reduced, and would wish that those who have superintendence or control over them had been as circumspect as the Archbishop of York has been on the present occasion. If other persons had equally done their duty, we should not find, as is now the case empty walls without scholars, and everything neglected but the receipt of the salaries and emoluments. In some instances that have lately come within my knowledge, there was not a single scholar in the schools though there were very large endowments to them.[50]

By the end of the Napoleonic wars Parliament was becoming concerned about the administration of charities, and in 1818 the House of Commons Select Committee on the Education of the Lower Orders reported on the situation at Pocklington school in the East Riding. The school had been ruled from 1754 to 1807 by Kingsman Baskett. This was a very obscure period in its history, apart from the attendance (1771–6) of William Wilberforce who seems to have been treated as a sort of gentleman commoner. Baskett's successor, Thomas Shield, had an almost equally long reign from 1807 to 1848. He devoted much time and trouble to setting aside old leases, and by so doing he greatly increased the school revenues, but he was a very negligent schoolmaster. St John's College, who had made the appointment, did its best over many years to improve the situation, but with little success. The Select Committee in 1818 heard evidence from James Wood, the Master of St John's, and from two fellows, T.W. Hornbuckle and T. Calvert, who had visited the school the previous autumn.[51]

At that time they had found only one boy (October 1817), though the total had subsequently increased to eight. The school was in a dilapidated state. There were two rooms, one above the other. The floor of the lower room was up and the windows were broken. It was claimed, though the visitors did not see this themselves, that the lower room was used as a saw-pit. The master admitted that this room had been used for preparing timber for repairs, though he said that he used another room for school purposes. The visitors understood that when Shield had entered office, there had been 13/14 scholars. Shield testified that 16 free scholars had entered since his residence in 1809 – that is, in a period of 8/9 years, or approximately two per year. When asked if he employed an usher, he said that the usher, Thomas Brown, was competent 'with the exception of an infirmity, that of deafness, under which he has lately laboured'. The parishioners, in their testimony to the visitors, complained about Mr Brown's deafness, and Mr Hornbuckle put the lack of scholars down to this difficulty.

One parishioner said that, when he had been a scholar, the master had not attended regularly, and several people complained that boys had been sent elsewhere who would have attended the school if it had been properly managed. Shield admitted that his many engagements and his absences on law-suits connected with the school property had helped to reduce the number of pupils. One accusation against him was that he had refused to re-admit a boy whose father had taken him away after he had been flogged. It was said that the boy had suffered because his father had complained about the management of the school, but Shield denied this, saying that the boy had been punished for carelessness and idleness.

Wood's somewhat guarded statements to the Select Committee rather suggest that he was unwilling to attribute publicly to the master the blame which he really thought to be justified. He told the committee that he had sent the master a list of proposed regulations which had been observed, and the number of scholars had risen slightly. A competent assistant had been obtained, though there was no power to remove the usher. But in the end the enquiry did no good, and there was no real improvement. Shield held on until 1848 – another 30 years. The Pocklington case must not be taken as typical of Yorkshire grammar schools, but it is no wonder that the Select Committee remarked that its enquiries 'have amply confirmed the opinion which a more limited investigation had led them to form two years ago upon the neglect and abuse of Charitable Funds connected with education'.[52]

Notes Chapter 9

1.   Leach, A.F. 1907: 415–500.
2.   *See* discussion on pages 95–7.
3.   Carlisle, N. 1818 2 vols; the Yorkshire entries are in vol II: 778–920.
4.   *Ibid.* vol II: 782.
5.   *Ibid.* vol II: 891.
6.   *Ibid.* vol II: 799.
7.   For these cases and the acts of Parliament *see* Montmorency, J.E.G. de 1902: 170–78.
8.   Lawson, J. and Silver, H. 1973: 177–80; O'Day, R. 1982: 215–16; and *see also* pages 105–6.
9.   Tompson, R.S. 1971a: 27, 56–7.
10.   Leach, A.F. 1907: 475.
11.   Peacock, M.H. 1892: 145.
12.   Lester, D.N.R. (n.d.): 60, 69–70.

13. Claridge, W. 1882: 44; Leach, A.F. 1907: 473.

14. Tompson, R.S. 1971a: 66–7 (Ilkley); 68–9 (Heath, Halifax).

15. Salmon, N. (n.d.): 19.

16. Bell, E.A. 1912: 91–104.

17. There are two articles about the history of the school in this period: Addy, J. 1958a: 353–63 and 1962: 112–18. These do not discuss the points about the curriculum which are raised here.

18. For John Ramsden *see* page 134.

19. SA: Spencer Stanhope Muniments 60573 cover the following.

20. The bond is dated 1 May 1786 (SA: MD 3348.2).

21. SA: MD 3348.3.

22. SA: Spencer Stanhope Muniments 60573 (2 April 1814).

23. SA: MD 3348.6.

24. Dodd, E.E. 1930: 65–89.

25. *See* Price, A.C. 1919: 134–47; Tompson, R.S. 1971a: 116–24; Tompson, R.S. 1970: 1–6; Roach, J. 1986a: 72–3.

26. Fiennes, C. 1949: 87.

27. *VCH Yorkshire* 1989 East Riding vol VI: 132 (Neave, D. 'Beverley 1700–1815'); Leach, A.F. 1907: 430.

28. Zouch, T. 1820 vol II: 3–31. Zouch himself was one of the subscribers.

29. *See* Sedbergh 1909: 154–214.

30. Facer, P. 1966: 144–5, 167–8.

31. Zouch, T. 1820; Lupton, J.H. 1864: 176–81; Clarke, M.L. 1959: 49–50.

32. Peacock, M.L. 1892: 167–8.

33. Lawson, J. 1963: 150–51, 152–3. For Clarke *see also* Lawson, J. 1962b: 30–38; Clarke, M.L. 1959: 47–8. I have based the following largely on Clarke's own book (Clarke 1740). For his other books *see* British Library catalogue.

34. Clarke, J. 1740: 61.

35. *Ibid.*: 221.

36. Quoted in Price, A.C. 1919: 119.

37. For Thorp Arch *see* page 275.

38. Pryme, G. 1870: 23; for the school at this time *see* Lawson, J. 1963: 171–84.

39. Pryme, G. 1870: 25.

40. *Ibid.*: 26.

41. For the story of the election *see* Wenham, L.P. 1958: 63–6.

42. This account of Tate is taken from Roach, J. 1986a: 78–9. *See also* Wenham, L.P. (ed.) 1965.

43. Lawson, J. 1963: 185–96.

44. Lowther Clarke, H. and Weech, W.N. 1925: 76–9.

45. Whitaker, T.D. 1823 vol. II: 359.

46. Moore Smith, G.C. 1929–37: 145–60.

47. Hinchliffe, G. 1963: 81, 86.

48. Dyson, T. 1926: 25.

49. WYAS: RD/AC/1/7/20 (Articles for Joseph Taylor ... Bowes). Bowes was in the archdeaconry of Richmond and diocese of Chester.

50. Montmorency, J.E.G. de 1902: 180 (Rex v. the Archbishop of York); Gibbon, A.M. 1947: 77–82.

51. For the following *see* Pocklington: *PP* 1818 IV: 146–58; for the general history of the school *see* Sands, P.C. and Haworth, C.M. (?1950): 68–76.

52. Pocklington: *PP* 1818 IV: 60.

CHAPTER 10

Elementary Schooling: the early years

The education of the labouring classes attracted keen interest among the pious and charitable in 18th century England, but there seems to have been little general improvement in overall literacy. Lawrence Stone suggests that, for the labourers, growth had petered out at the end of the 17th century.[1] After Lord Hardwicke's Marriage Act of 1753 the marriage registers reveal how many of those who were married could and could not sign their names. A random sample of 274 parishes from 1754 to 1840 shows that in the middle of the century just over 60% of women could not sign their names. For men the percentage of those unable to sign remained stable at just under 40% until the end of the century.[2] However the rate for women had improved at that point to about 45% literate.[3] Within these general figures there were considerable variations between town and country and between different occupational groups.

No attempt has been made here at detailed investigation into literacy in Yorkshire, but the few studies which have been found suggest either slight improvement or actual regression. The figures have been calculated for 17 rural parishes and chapelries in the East Riding from 1754 to 1800. Such a large number of parishes should help to cancel out the erratic nature of the yearly totals in small rural units.[4] In 1754–60 36% of bridegrooms (121) were illiterate and 61% of brides (208). In 1791–1800 33% of bridegrooms were illiterate (180) and 52% of brides (284). These East Riding figures do bear out the improvement in female literacy by the end of the century which has already been noted.

The background of the other example – the three Wharfedale parishes of Ilkley, Otley and Addingham in the West Riding – is quite different. Otley was a market town with some industry and the centre of a large parish with ten outlying townships; its totals are much larger than those of the other two. Ilkley was a decayed market town. Addingham had a textile industry and, by the end of the century, a water-powered spinning mill. Here in all three parishes the literacy rates actually declined within the period 1754–9 and 1790–99. The literacy rate for men, which at the beginning had been considerably above the national average, had declined to about that average at the end. The literacy figures for women had also got worse, and in all three parishes the percentage of totally illiterate marriages had increased.[5] It must not be argued from this one piece of evidence that such decline was widespread, and the East Riding example cited earlier is more in line with what seems to have been the general picture. The situation will have varied from place to place all over the country, but everywhere, though much had been done, there was still a great deal for the schoolmaster to do.

It was often very difficult, as we have seen, to draw a clear line between classical and elementary education, which frequently went on together in the same school.[6] There was, however, after 1660 an increasing tendency to found schools which were primarily or entirely elementary – parish schools for teaching reading, writing and a little arithmetic.[7] Details about 17th century village schools have already been given in an earlier chapter,[8] and A.F. Leach, in his article on schools in *V.C.H. Yorkshire* vol. I, gives a list of 111 elementary schools founded before 1770. Similar information for the archdeaconry of Richmond can be found in Bishop Gastrell's 'Notitia'. At Patrick Brompton (NR), for example, there was

a little school erected in 1707 by Samuel Atkinson to which he left a close of 20s. per annum at Newton. Given since by Samuel Clark of London £3 p.a. Master nominated by parish. The £3 p.a. was given for teaching 6 poor parish boys. The Curate generally teaches.[9]

It was a school like this in another North Riding village, Great Ayton, endowed in 1704 for eight poor boys, which educated the future Captain James Cook. He left it at the age of 13 or 14, went first to Staithes to work as a shop-boy, and later became a three-year servant to a Quaker family of shipowners at Whitby, working the coal-trade.[10]

The growth of elementary schools throughout the country at this time has long been attributed to the activity of the Society for Promoting Christian Knowledge (SPCK) founded in 1699,[11] which has been seen as the leader of the so-called 'Charity School Movement' which, beginning in London and Westminster, later extended its influence over the whole nation.[12] SPCK was certainly one major expression of the religious and philanthropic impulses of the time, and its concern with the education of the poor can be paralleled by similar movements in France and Germany.[13] The Society's central concern was, it has been said, 'the implementation of a programme of evangelical philanthropy, which would re-assert the spiritual and political primacy of the Church of England in the nation'.[14]

The idea of a 'Charity School Movement' inspired and led by SPCK has been challenged by Joan Simon in her study of schools in Leicestershire.[15] On the basis of that evidence she concluded that the impulse for founding schools at this time was largely inspired by local benefactors who were independent of the Society. The concept of a 'movement' applied only, Mrs Simon argued, to London and Westminster. What the Society did was to try to make education an exclusively Anglican preserve. In Leicestershire it may have had some influence on the squires and the clergy, but the activity of running schools was largely independent of it.

The Yorkshire evidence suggests a larger role for SPCK than Mrs Simon found in Leicestershire. There was in Yorkshire, as we have seen, a strong independent tradition of supporting elementary schooling which began before SPCK

201

was founded and continued long after the days of the Society's major influence on education (1700–1740). On the other hand large charity schools of the kind to be found in the London parishes – supported by subscriptions and providing clothing and sometimes board for the children – did exist in Yorkshire. There is much correspondence about these schools in the Society's records. They were, however, only in the larger towns like York, Leeds, Sheffield, Hull and Beverley, and there is no evidence that the Society had great influence on the mass of rural schools. These, like the Leicestershire schools described by Mrs Simon, were founded by local benefactors and sometimes maintained by local communities. Yet it would be wrong to neglect the penetration of SPCK into Yorkshire. There were strong links between the Society and its local correspondents, and one particular service which the Society offered, and which was not available elsewhere, was that of providing books for the schools. Publishing had close ties with teaching and catechizing.

Before the discussion about elementary schooling in the county is taken any further, the term 'charity school' must be more carefully examined, since it has been widely used both by contemporaries and by modern historians. R.S. Tompson suggested a definition which is appropriate to the large schools in towns like Leeds and York: – 'an elementary school endowed (or supported periodically) by public subscription, in contrast to those endowed by the gift or bequest of a single founder'.[16] In Yorkshire the term seems to have been used in a much more general sense to describe any school which offered an education to the poor financed wholly or partly by gift or endowment. The clergymen who replied to Archbishop Herring's enquiries in his visitation of 1743[17] used the words very broadly. The school for girls endowed by Lady Elizabeth Hastings at Ledsham (WR) was called a charity school, though it was the gift of a single founder in the traditional way.[18] Similarly the Society's own General Board Minutes record the gift in 1706 of £1,000 by Mrs Mary Ingoldsby for a 'charity school' at Ripley.[19] It seems that expressions like 'endowed school' and 'charity school' were much more descriptive than precise in their meaning, and that they were used for institutions of differing kinds.

Yet all these 'charity schools', whatever the precise meaning of the term in different cases, shared one important characteristic. The objective of those who established them was to discipline the poor as much as to educate them. The emphasis on catechizing, the efforts to put poor children to work which will be described later all tended to treat the poor as a distinct social grouping which needed a régime for those destined to be hewers of wood and drawers of water. The grammar schools had always aimed to open access for poor boys to higher things, though it is true that very few such boys were able to take advantage of the opportunities offered. The 'charity school' (whatever the precise meaning of the term) operated within a closed circuit of expectation from which the poor were not to escape. 'The aim of the Grammar Schools', wrote A.E. Dobbs, 'was selective... The aim of the Charity School was disciplinary: to rescue the masses and to ensure their obedience'.[20]

The SPCK *Account of Charity Schools* for 1724 listed 48 such schools in Yorkshire.[21] The information in the Society's archives is very largely to be found in the letters from local correspondents which have been summarized in the Abstract Letter Books.[22] The Society asked their correspondents to meet with the clergy in their own area to encourage one another in the faithful discharge of their pastoral duties and to encourage their parishioners to contribute to the establishment of schools. 'They desire', according to a Circular Letter of February 1700, 'you would from time to time give them information of what progress is made in these matters, and that you would direct your letters to me, whom they have made Secretary of their Society, by whose hands they will communicate what they shall have hereafter to offer you and receive what you shall request from them'.[23]

The Yorkshire correspondents in the early years seem to have been remarkably conscientious in obeying these instructions. Most of what they wrote related to the subscription schools in the larger towns, though they also provided information about a wide variety of schools in the country districts. One stimulus to the activity of these correspondents may have been the concern of Archbishop John Sharp (1691–1714) who himself subscribed to many schools and was much concerned about the schools of which he was visitor.[24] The SPCK Minutes of 5 May 1701 recorded

> that the Arch Bishop of York was very well pleased with the Proceedings of this Society, which he promised to encourage in his Province, & as an earnest of his good will he would send them £10, to be disposed as they should think fit.[25]

The earliest Yorkshire correspondent was Maurice Lisle of Guisborough (NR) who wrote in April 1700 that he hoped 'to obtain something towards the teaching of poor children, but despairs of any fixed settlement for a School; complains of ye neglect of the poor in sending their Children to School where a charitable provision is made for them.'[26] But Lisle appears to have been a controversial figure who was on bad terms with the other clergy in Cleveland who were accused by him of leading irregular lives. John Gibson, a magistrate of Welburn near Kirkby Moorside (NR) whom Lisle had introduced to the Society, wrote in 1701 that he was

> very uneasy in his Ministry, being maligned by his Brethren in Cleveland, who count that Drudgery which he calls Duty. That he ha's Dayly Prayers & Catechising, but doubts whether there are 2 more that do the same.[27]

The importance of books and publishing in the Society's work is illustrated by the references in letters from Lisle and Gibson to the receipt of papers and book parcels,[28] and there are many similar references in the Letter Books. On 4 March 1715, for example, the correspondents at Beverley asked for the following books for their charity school

> 12 Bibles with Comon Prayer claspt as in Nov 1713 & Tate & Brady's Version of Singing Psalms bound therein, if not much dearer. 12 Whole

Duty's of Man bound in Sheep and 12 Osterwald's Grounds & Principles & in sheep, and that they might be directed to Alderman Davies an Apothecary in Beverley nigh Hull and sent by the first Ship that sails from London to Hull with a Bill of the charges that then the money shall be remitted with all convenient speed.[29]

Similar requests also came from country schools like those in the area of the West Riding which benefited from the gifts of Lady Elizabeth Hastings. In February 1737 she asked for a packet of books for herself and another for the school lately set up at Selby. Her parcel cost £10.13.7½, the Selby parcel £2.6.5.[30] In September 1763 Mr Bentham at Aberford reported the death of Mr Potter, the vicar of Collingham, who had been a generous benefactor to the charity school there. '...'tis therefore his humble request that as the Society has all along been so good as to furnish the School with Books on their cheap Terms, they wou'd be pleas'd to continue their kindness, and to favour the School with a Parcel of Books'.[31] Two years after this Dr Kershaw at Leeds was thanking the Society for the present of 40 shillings worth of books for the newly endowed charity school in his parish of Ripley.[32]

The most interesting information in the Letter Books relates to the schools in the larger towns, particularly York, Beverley and Leeds. The progress of the charity school at Leeds, established in 1705, is recorded in letters from the vicar, John Killingbeck. In December 1705 he reported that £160 had been subscribed and that the Corporation of the town had given a house which was sufficient to receive 40 boys. They had been influenced in their plans by the account of a similar foundation already established at York.[33] By May 1706 the subscriptions for the following year amounted to £208, and they were assured of money from other charitable funds and from the church offertory. The school consisted of 28 boys and 12 girls, 'all clothed'.[34] In December 1707 Mr Killingbeck recorded that a merchant had built a 'decent case' for a library, and that this had been furnished with very good books.[35] Later letters detailed a steady stream of benefactions to the school.

Ralph Thoresby, the Leeds antiquary, was a good friend both to the Leeds school and to the Society as a whole, and he put down a good deal about both of them in his diary. On 20 May 1714 he wrote that the annual SPCK feast in London 'seemed to me like the primitive Agapae or Love Feasts, before corrupted'.[36] He became a corresponding member, and there are a number of his letters in the Letter Books. On 1 January 1715 he said that the vicar of Leeds had preached a charity sermon for the children 'whereat there was collected 25^{li} 10^s 9½ ^{d}, which Sum they never reach'd to before'. The constitution of the school was to be changed, so that 100 children would be clothed and taught, of whom 20 would be wholly maintained. The original plan had been to feed, clothe and lodge 40.[37]

In January 1719 Thoresby wrote that the school was in a flourishing condition,[38] but soon afterwards there were difficulties with the master. He had been 'so extravagantly passionate to a poor Boy, as to lose the favour of his Patrons'. Thoresby hoped that the Society might be able to supply them with a master from London.[39] The use by masters of excessive punishments was a common problem, and good men were not easy to find. Nor, despite the hope that the schoolchildren would be able to work and so to cover part of the cost of their keep, was it easy to find work which young children could do. A correspondent wrote to the Society in 1736 that the Leeds schools were flourishing, 'but as to any Constant Work several of the Subscribers are against it, because it crippled the Chil tender limbs and made y^m unfit to Service'.[40] A few years earlier than this, in 1729, it was said that the schools were fully supported without any debt 'notwithstanding the Dearness of provision and deadness of Trade for 2 years past'.[41] In 1763 there were 70 boys and 50 girls from the ages of 8 to 13, so the school's first half century can be reckoned a period of success.[42]

The correspondents from York and Beverley put much more emphasis on the children's work than was the case at Leeds. In both places the civic authorities took an active interest in the establishment of the schools. At York, schools for both boys and girls were opened in 1705. The boys' school, where 40 boys were clothed, fed, lodged and taught, had been supported by the archbishop, the Minster clergy, various townspeople, and the city Corporation which had fitted up the schoolhouse with beds, bedding and other necessary items at a cost of over £100. A correspondent of 1710 gave details of collections made at charity sermons, of subscriptions to buy land to form an endowment, and of legacies. Out of the profits arising from the spinning done by the boys, the governors had founded a 'nursery' for 20 more boys who were to move up into the charity school itself when vacancies occurred. If boys were sick or injured, there were available 'a Physician, a Surgeon & Apothecary who give their Advice, Medicines, Plaisters & Attendance gratis'. The girls' school for 20 children was supported by contributions from ladies of the city. The girls were cared for in the same way as the boys, and were employed in spinning 'Jersey': – 'ye profit of which is a great help to the support of the said School'. Since the boys' school had been established, 20 boys had been put out as apprentices.[43] By 1716 this number had risen to 60.[44] A report of 1707, only two years after the York schools opened, stated that 'the Charity-Children there do almost maintain themselves by their Work'.[45]

When in 1709 the Society was informed about plans for a school at Beverley, the promoters of it asked 'to be advised what employment the Children can be put to, for the best advantage in the School.'[46] The Beverley school for teaching and maintaining 30 children opened in August 1710.[47] By 1714 six boys and two girls had been put out 'Apprentices to Husbandry and Service'; there were 26 boys and four girls in the school. The managers of the school seem to have taken a very wide view of their responsibilities towards the children. In 1711 they reported that, when they were apprenticed, the indentures were to provide that they should come every Sunday to the school to be taught 'that so they may not forget what they have learned'.[48] Two years later the managers expressed their concern that so many children in the town were never taught to say their prayers and, in order to remove this evil, they had been encouraging all the private school teachers to teach their scholars to pray privately every day. The Society strongly supported this action and decided to send down books of prayers to help in the good work.[49] In 1727 the Beverley correspondent asked for help and advice for the newly appointed master of their workhouse,[50] though it is clear from a later letter that the workhouse and the charity school were separate institutions.[51] At Hull in 1712, however, the charity school was a workhouse as well, over 40 children being maintained in it.[52]

Apart from the frequent references to ordering books of various kinds, there is very little in the Letter Books about the curriculum or teaching methods.[53] However, the author of the Society's often reprinted teachers' manual, *The Christian Schoolmaster* (1707), James Talbott, rector of Spofforth, was a Yorkshire incumbent and an interesting and important figure in his own right, apart from the long-lasting influence of his book.[54] Talbott had been a fellow of Trinity College, Cambridge, and was presented by the Duke of Somerset to the rectory of Spofforth in 1700. Much of his energy was occupied with combating the influence of the Roman Catholics who were strong in his parish, but he was also closely concerned with the general concerns of SPCK of which he became a correspondent in 1705. He was keen to promote schools both in his own parish and in the surrounding district, and he encouraged the local clergy to meet for prayer and discussion.

His activities can be traced in the Society's General Board Minutes. In September 1705 he informed the Board that six catechetical schools had been or would be erected within a year in an area of 12 miles from Spofforth. He had printed an exposition of the catechism and established a catechetical lecture every Sunday afternoon. He had obliged his own curate at Wetherby to teach and examine poor children, and had persuaded his parishioners to repair an old schoolhouse. He and they together had asked the Duke of Somerset to pay a schoolmaster, while he also hoped to get a subscription from the Duke of Devonshire at Wetherby.[55] In February 1708 he told the Society that the Duke of Somerset had settled a salary on a schoolmaster to teach ten poor children. He himself was paying for the education of ten children – five at Spofforth and five at Wetherby. He proposed to unite the place of parish clerk with that of schoolmaster, and to require the clerk to teach five children free. He had, with the consent of the parishioners, appropriated the church offertories for the use of all these children, and he hoped to furnish some of them with books and some with clothes. Other schools had been founded in the nearby parishes of Kirk Deighton and Kirkby Overblows.[56] He had also persuaded a merchant at Leeds to find employment for children about 15 years old who could read, write and cipher.[57]

Talbott died in his mid-forties in the autumn of 1708. 'God Almighty fit us all', wrote his friend George Plaxton, 'for that great work, which our good Friend has allmost finished, and I dare tell you with the greatest Joy and Resignac'on'.[58] But Talbott left a lasting memento in his book. In January 1706 the Society had requested him

> to Draw up a small Treatise, Directed to School-masters putting 'em in mind of the great Trust reposed in them with respect to the Christian Education of the Children under their Care &c[59]

The Christian Schoolmaster, published in 1707, was reprinted as late as 1811.[60] The book represents the ideal of elementary education throughout the century, whether provided in schools linked with SPCK or not, and it therefore deserves careful attention here. Talbott begins with the qualifications and duties of the schoolmaster. He must be a member of the Church of England, and must give security to the public that he does not entertain principles inconsistent 'with the Present Establishment in Church and State'.[61] He must be a man of sound morals, fit to give a good example to the children. He must be patient, wise, hard-working and pious, and must be free from covetousness or partiality. So far as learning and knowledge are concerned, he must be able to write a good hand, to understand the principles of arithmetic, and to have a 'good genius for Teaching'.[62] He should not be under 25 years of age, he should have no defect in his speech or person, and he should have the approbation of the parish clergyman.

The minds of the children, wrote Talbott, echoing the ideas of John Locke, were like wax, capable of receiving any impression. For them learning fell into three divisions. The first was religion. Before they could read they were to be taught the Lord's Prayer and the Creed, a morning and an evening prayer, and graces at meat. After they had learned to read they were to be taught the Catechism. They were to learn their duties towards God and the obligations of public worship. Secondly they were to learn their duties towards their neighbour. They must learn such obedience to their schoolmaster as they would later have to pay to their master at work. They must be honest, true to their word, and grateful to those who have been kind to them, avoiding pride, haughtiness and quarrelling. Self-love must be rooted out of their mind very early. Finally they must learn their duties towards themselves – temperance, moderation, chastity, and industry which, next to the service of God, 'is the principal end of all *Education*, and the only Means to Profit under it...'[63]

The last part of the book covers the curriculum and organization of the school. There should be four classes. In the first, children would learn the alphabet and the rudiments of reading; in the second, they would read the Psalter and the New Testament; in the third, they would read the Bible more generally and other useful books and would learn to write; the fourth would concentrate on writing and the first five rules of arithmetic. The reading materials were religious: the catechism, the prayerbook, the psalter and other books of the Bible, though the older children might also read *The Whole Duty of Man* and the younger a 'pleasant but profitable book'.[64] At that time, of course, these religious texts were the principal reading materials which were available. Latin was not to be taught because there would not be time for children to learn enough of the language.

The regulations about school hours and holidays and about church attendance call for no special comment because they are similar to those which have already been explained. Talbott advised against excessive severity and strictness, but he expected that corporal punishments would be used for more serious offences, though care must be taken to avoid anger or revenge towards the children. In the last resort, in cases of real obstinacy or disobedience, the rod must be used 'till the Mind is intirely Master'd and Subdued'.[65] The final responsibility – to God, to the parents and children, to the public – is the master's and this prayer at the end of the book sums up what is expected of him

> Lord, make me diligent and industrious in all Parts of this laborious Employment; that I may give attendance to Reading, to Exhortation, to Doctrine; that I may meditate on these Things, and give myself wholly to them. Possess my Mind with a just and tender Regard for those precious Souls committed to my charge; that I may watch over them, as one that must give an Account, that I may do it with Joy and not with Grief.[66]

From the evidence which has been presented in this chapter it is clear that SPCK had strong links with Yorkshire, but its importance and influence in the county must not be exaggerated. Many of the schools mentioned by the Society's correspondents were largely or entirely independent of it and, though knowledge of the Society's work may have had some influence on local benefactors, they were really continuing a local tradition of founding schools which was quite independent of SPCK. There are many references by correspondents to local schools in the Letter Books. Thus Roger Mitton wrote from Skipton (WR) in March 1710 that there were nine grammar schools within 12 miles of his parish, besides two schools in Skipton itself, 'many of which are free to all Children, come they from what Quarter they will which is the reason that no Charity Schools are erected'.[67] Four years later Mitton reported that John Drake, a Keighley inn-keeper, had left a legacy for teaching the poor children of the parish.[68] A year later a master had been appointed and was teaching 40 children.[69]

At Todmorden on the Lancashire border 'a private person' had built a schoolhouse and given £100, the interest on which was to be paid to the curate for teaching six poor children.[70] Sometimes a number of local landowners were asked

211

for help. When the promoters of a school at Aberford (WR) asked Lady Elizabeth Hastings for assistance, they explained that they were hoping to get help from the archbishop and from Oriel College, Oxford, both of whom had 'Concerns' in the parish. Thus far their chief contributors had been Mr Gascoign and the Lady Dowager Vavasor.[71] In 1737 a school was erected at Scarborough for 20 boys and six girls 'who are cloath'd taught to read and write & put out Apprent. by a Society call'd the Amicable Society.'[72]

The influence of SPCK might be compared with that of a stone thrown into the centre of a pool. In the centre – which in this case would be the large subscription schools in places like Leeds and York – the stone makes large ripples. By the time the movement of the water reaches the edges of the pool – the schools in places like Keighley or Todmorden – the ripples can hardly be observed at all.

Notes Chapter 10

1. Stone, L. 1969: 109, 112.
2. Schofield, R. 1973: 446–50.
3. O'Day, R. 1982: 190.
4. Baker, W.P. 1961: Table II, 12.
5. Smith, D.E. 1992: 58–73, and especially pages 63, 66 which give the tables.
6. *See* pages 179–80.
7. Dobbs, A.E. 1919: 88.
8. *See* the discussion in Chapter 5.
9. *AR*: 83.
10. Crellin, V.H. 1978: 12–19.
11. For its history *see* Lowther Clarke, W.K. 1959; Allen, W.O.B. and McClure, E. 1898.
12. For the development of this view *see* Jones, M.G. 1938/1964.
13. Adamson, J.W. 1905: 203–4.
14. Rose, C. in Walsh, J., Haydon, C., Taylor, S. (eds) 1993: 179–80.

15. Simon, J. in Simon, B. (ed.) 1968: 55–100.

16. Tompson, R.S. 1971a: 1.

17. For Archbishop Herring's visitation *see* pages 218–25.

18. For Lady Elizabeth Hastings *see* pages 227–30.

19. SPCK: G(eneral) B(oard) M(inutes) vol 1 (14 March 1706).

20. Dobbs, A.E. 1919: 91.

21. Jones, M.G. 1938/1964 app I: 371. For charity schools in general, there is useful material in Sylvester, D.W. (ed.) 1970: 170–97.

22. The Abstract Letter Books are referred to as 'ALB'. For a guide to these records I have depended on Tate, W.E. 1955.

23. Allen, W.O.B. and McClure, E. 1898: 51–2.

24. Hart, A. T. 1949: 177–8.

25. McClure, E. 1888: 131–2. There is an interesting picture of Sharp in De la Pryme, Abraham 1870 page 178: 'He is an exceeding strict, religious, and pious man, exceeding humble, affable and kind. He gave us a great deal of most excellent advice, and talked sevearly against drunkeness, loos living, keeping of company, and such like ...' (from Pryme's diary, 6 May 1698).

26. McClure, E. 1888: 286 (9 April 1700).

27. Ibid.: 348; Allen, W.O.B. and McClure, E. 1898: 102.

28. SPCK: GBM vol 1 (1698–1706) (Letters of 2 Nov 1704, 5 Sept 1706, 31 Oct 1706).

29. ALB 5: 4315–7 (10 March 1715); *see* the very similar request, also from Beverley, 10 Nov 1718 (ALB 9: 5799, 27 Nov 1718).

30. ALB 19: 13957 (15 Feb 1737); for Lady Elizabeth Hastings *see* pages 227–30.

31. ALB 24: 25480 (6 Sept 1763).

32. ALB 24: 26098, 26157 (16 April, 4 June 1765).

33. GBM vol 1 (13 Dec 1705).

34. GBM vol 1 (2 May 1706).

35. GBM vols 2–4 (18 Dec 1707).

36.   Thoresby, R. 1830 vol II: 214; and *see also* Thoresby, R. 1816 (2nd edn. by Whitaker, T.D.): 107, 247, Appendix, 119–20.

37.   ALB 5: 4271 (6 Jan 1715); *see also* ALB 5: (23 Dec 1714), ALB 6: 4338 (7 April 1715).

38.   ALB 9: 5895 (22 Jan 1719).

39.   ALB 9: 5972 (19 March 1719).

40.   ALB 19: 13689 (6 July 1736).

41.   ALB 19: 10132 (15 April 1724).

42.   ALB 24: 25295 (8 March 1763).

43.   ALB 2: 2305 (21 Sept 1710).

44.   ALB 6: 4785 (3 May 1716).

45.   GBM vols 2–4 (31 July 1707).

46.   ALB 2: 1969 (2 Feb 1709).

47.   ALB 2: 2242 (31 Aug 1710).

48.   ALB 3: 2824 (18 Oct 1711).

49.   ALB 4: 3584 (11 June 1713).

50.   ALB 14: 9239 (9 May 1727).

51.   ALB 14: 9812 (1 Aug 1728).

52.   ALB 3: 3077 (22 May 1712).

53.   *See* ALB 2: 2032 (23 March 1710). Jo. Moyser at Beverley thanks the Society for information about methods used at St Margaret's Westminster and Stamford.

54.   For Talbott *see* Unwin, R.W. 1982: 9–37 and 1984. The name is spelt both 'Talbot' and 'Talbott'. I have preferred the latter because that spelling appears on the title page of *The Christian Schoolmaster.*

55.   SPCK: GBM vol 1 (20 Sept 1705).

56.   GBM vols 2–4 (5 Feb 1708).

57.   GBM vols 2–4 (18 Dec 1707).

58.   Walker, E.M. 1945: 79 (to Richard Thornton, Recorder of Leeds 15 Nov 1708).

59. GBM vol 1 (31 Jan 1706).

60. Talbott, J. 1707. There are extracts in Sylvester, D.W. (ed.) 1970: 189–97, and *see also* Lowther Clarke, W.K. 1944: 73–5.

61. Talbott, J. 1707: 14.

62. *Ibid.*: 22.

63. *Ibid.*: 76. For a modern account of the curriculum of charity schools *see* Jones, M.G. 1938/1964: 76–84.

64. Talbott, J. 1707: 83.

65. *Ibid.*: 105.

66. *Ibid.*: 118–19.

67. SPCK: ALB 2: 2052 (6 April 1710).

68. ALB 5: 3932 (18 March 1714).

69. ALB 6: 4350 (28 April 1715).

70. ALB 6: 4356 (5 May 1715).

71. ALB 6: 4352 (28 April 1715).

72. ALB 19: 14274 (25 Oct 1737).

CHAPTER 11

Elementary Schooling: the middle years

Some examples of local benefactions for elementary schools during the 18th century have already been given, and for so large a county it is difficult to judge how many more to give. The word 'school' itself can mean many things, and it is certain that the lists – for example those given by A.F. Leach in the *VCH Yorkshire*, vol. I – provide a minimum estimate of those which actually existed at any particular time. Once there was an endowment and a schoolhouse the work of teaching was likely to go on permanently or at least for a very long time. Generally the schoolmaster needed to supplement his basic salary from the fees of the pupils he could attract. The endowment was, so to speak, the 'fall-back', the basic guarantee of the teacher's security. But many teachers had no such guarantee, and many 'schools' were ephemeral only, existing while the master could make a living by his own exertions and coming to an end when he became old or moved away. Perhaps a successor might come to the village and perhaps not.

The fact that the records inevitably concentrate on endowments because they can be easily investigated over-simplifies the position. Much of the teaching done was more irregular and more impermanent than the records suggest. It depended very much on the skill and availability of individuals and on what might be called the state of the market at a particular place and time. Many villages were too small with too few children to provide a regular living for a teacher, and in areas of the county where population was fairly dense, children walked from one village to another to school. Teachers often had to be men of many parts, making up their livelihood through various services to the community of which their teaching role was only one. As soon as the focus of this study moves away from the large town schools on which attention has so far been concentrated, the whole position becomes much more fluid and changeable. There was in one sense more 'education' offered than at first appears. In another sense the provision is more irregular and more fluctuating than we, who are accustomed to large formalized institutions, can easily understand.[1]

Archbishop Thomas Herring's visitation returns of 1743 contain a mass of information about schools in the three-quarters or so of the geographical county contained within the diocese of York.[2] Among the 11 questions which Herring asked his incumbents, two, nos. 3 and 9, deal directly with our subject. The answers to no. 4 on charitable endowments for hospitals, almshouses and the repair of churches occasionally contain information about schools as well. Question no. 9 asked about catechizing. This was in most cases carefully answered, and it is clear that the task was in general thoroughly and conscientiously carried out. Where this was not the case, the archbishop himself sometimes wrote 'bad catechizing' on the paper. Both the presence of the question and the answers to it show that the matter continued to be taken very seriously, not only by the archbishop himself but in the parishes as well. Clearly for our purposes the main interest lies in the answers to question 3, which reads as follows

> Is there any public or Charity School, endow'd, or otherwise maintained in your Parish? What Number of Children are taught in it? And what Care is taken to instruct them in the Principles of the Christian Religion, according to the Doctrine of the Church of England; and to bring them duly to Church, as the Canon requires?[3]

The replies to question 3 do not employ the various terms – 'endowed school', 'charity school', public school', 'private school' – at all consistently, and it seems likely that the various incumbents understood this question in different ways.

One return says clearly that there was no public or private school in the parish.[4] Others took the word 'school' to mean only some kind of endowed school. Some include among the teachers a 'poor man', a 'young man', or as at Marton (NR) a widow who taught a few small children to read in her own house.[5] It seems likely that, whereas some incumbents included these people, others did not. In total there were probably a good many of them, though they would have given only basic instruction. Several returns explain that the numbers catechized in the parish were small because there was no school, which suggests a link between the work of the teacher and catechizing. Several entries of this kind relate to parishes in the East Riding, though I am unable to say whether there is anything significant about this fact.[6]

The statistics of schools and parishes in the Returns as calculated in a recent article are as follows:

	Parishes with schools		Parishes without schools		Total number of Parishes
Riding	Number	% of Parishes	Number	% of Parishes	
East	76	37.8	125	62.2	201
North	77	45.2	93	54.8	170
West	171	59.6	116	40.4	287
Ainsty of York	14	53.8	12	46.2	26
Total	338		346		684
Average		49.4		50.6	

The author estimated that, although 50.6% parishes recorded no schools, only 23% of the population lived in those parishes.[7] In the parishes with schools, there are 226 endowments recorded, a total which does not include cases where the parishioners had built a school, but there was no mention of an endowment in cash or property. These figures need a little further explanation. They include grammar schools, and more will be said about that later. They are a record of 'endowments', and sometimes there was more than one in a parish or chapelry, so that these figures are larger than the number of parishes to which they refer. In a few cases it is difficult to be certain from the return whether a school had an endowment or not. However in broad terms there were about 200 parishes recorded as possessing endowment for a school, and most of these were for elementary education. The SPCK *Account of Charity Schools* for 1724 listed only 48 schools in Yorkshire.[8] The disparity between the two totals shows the strength of the local movement to found elementary schools irrespective of any pressures coming from London.

School incomes varied considerably from place to place. Some, like the 30s. a year left for educating six poor girls in the parish of All Saints' Pavement in the city of York, were very small.[9] At Salton (NR) the endowment was £3 a year, but there was no schoolhouse and the money was given to a crippled man who taught children in another part of the parish 'wch. are sometimes more sometimes less'.[10] In another North Riding parish, Seamer, there was an endowment of £5 and a schoolhouse. 20 children attended 'more or less according to the season of the year'.[11] In the West Riding woollen district the charity school at Huddersfield had an income of £20 per annum and 20 children were taught free.[12] At Hartshead (par. Dewsbury) the charity school had an income of £10 a year. 18 children were provided with books, pens, ink and paper, and were taught English, writing and arithmetic until they were old enough to be apprenticed.[13] At Kirkburton there was an endowment of £22 and 33 poor children were taught.[14] At Coley (par. Halifax) there were two charity schools, one a grammar school and the other an English school with a total of 80 children. In addition there was a small English school endowed with £5 a year, though it had only a few children.[15]

In a few cases the active participation of the clergy is recorded. At Agnes Burton (Burton Agnes (ER)) there were 30 or more children in the schools and, the vicar wrote, 'as the school is at a small distance from the Vicarage House, I frequently repeat, and do expound the Catechism to them'.[16] At Old Byland (NR), where the lord of the manor gave £4 for teaching four poor children, the curate himself taught the charity school.[17] The aristocrat of these village endowments was at Sproatley (ER)[18]

> There is a Benefaction of 56*l̃l.* p annum left for the maintenance of a School-Master and a School Dame to teach so many Boys writing and reading and so many Girls sewing knitting &c and to put poor Children Apprentices, the Minister of Sproatley, the Church-Wardens and Overseers have the direction of it, tis Faithfully Manag'd, and no Fraud, or abuse of any kind has been committed.

In addition to these endowments there were a number of places where the landowner made an allowance during pleasure, though these allowances could be, and sometimes were, withdrawn. In many cases the donor is not named. Among the donors whose names are given are Sir Griffith Boynton (Barmston ER),[19] Lord and Lady Malton (Hutton (Hooton) Roberts WR);[20] (Upper and Nether Hoyland (par. Wath WR));[21] (Swinton (par. Wath WR)),[22] the Duke of Leeds (Harthill WR),[23] and 'Lord Scharborough' (sic) (Maltby WR).[24] The Swinton return says 'this Charity is his free will and w'ch He may withdraw at his pleasure'. At Osbaldwick (NR) there were trustees who paid the master £4 a year, 'but they say it's payable only during their pleasure'.[25] At Sutton upon Darwent (ER) the rector reported that, when he came to the parish, there had been a house and croft given by the Duke of Albemarle, 'but Sir Thos: Clarges Lord of ye Manour has taken in (sic) away, value forty shillings a year, and applys it to his own use.'[26]

Sometimes the return says that the school was maintained by the parishioners.[27] One common form of such support was the erection or repair of the schoolhouse.[28] At Wistow (WR), for instance, the parishioners had built a schoolhouse near the church, which 'is almost in ye Center of four Towns, of wh ye Parish consists'. A master had taught reading and writing for several years. There were about 80 scholars, but 'there is no Salary settled upon ye School'.[29] The foundation of a school might result from a combination of several different kinds of support. At Silkstone (WR) the vicar had obtained subscriptions to build a schoolhouse and had persuaded the Overseers of the Poor to devote the interest of a small legacy to paying a schoolmaster to teach children to read.[30] At Rothwell a small endowment of £3.17.0 a year had been supplemented by annual subscriptions of £20.1.0.

> out of wch sums a Master is allowed £16.0.0 p Ann. for teaching 50 children to read & write; and two widows £1.10 each for instructing 12 of ye smallest children 'till fit to be sent to ye Master.

The children were catechized by the master and by the vicar and the remainder of the money was spent in buying bibles, testaments, psalters '& other small demands'.[31]

Where grammar schools are mentioned in the returns, they normally appear alongside other schools in the parish. At Wakefield, for example, there were 60 boys in the grammar school and 70 boys and girls in the charity school.[32] At Hull, in addition to the grammar school, there was a charity school with 45 children as well as 76 children of various ages in the workhouse.[33] At Bridlington there were 20 scholars in the grammar school and a knitting school where 12 children were taught 'in the art of carding, spinning and knitting in Wool'.[34] At Beverley the grammar school had over 100 boys. In addition, 'we also have Several Masters or Dames that teach Younger Children to read'.[35] Such references both to grammar schools and to what are called at Pontefract 'little schools'[36] are fairly numerous.[37]

Sometimes the grammar school was only one among several endowed schools, for example at Skipton where there were six schools in all,[38] and Birstall where there were three.[39] The parish of Rotherham contained six 'public or charity' schools. One of these was presumably the grammar school, though it is not specifically named. All these schools must have been very small because the total number of children was only about 80.[40] Some of the problems of the grammar schools which have already been discussed appear again here. A few of them taught English subjects as well as 'grammar'.[41] At Overton (NR) the foundation was for a grammar school, '& three Pounds a year is allowed out of the Salary, to teach the children of both sexes till they can read English'.[42] The master of Archbishop Holgate's grammar school at Hemsworth told the archbishop that there was no one 'qualified for Graṁatical Instruction in the Parish'. He had ceased to take boarders and paid half the salary to a man who taught 'the Languages & Accompts'. The other half had been spent on repairs and improvements.[43]

The final group of schools consisted of those which were unendowed and where the teacher was supported by fees paid by the parents. Once again the returns do not follow a systematic pattern, and it is not always entirely clear whether a school should or should not fall under this heading. Sometimes the payment of fees is specifically mentioned. Sometimes the terms 'private' or 'unendowed' are used. If all these examples are included, the number of parishes and chapelries which had some sort of private teaching paid for by fees was 119, which is slightly more than half the number of parishes (about 200) with some kind of school endowment. Much of this 'private' provision was on a very modest scale, but it still represents a substantial slice of the facilities available. The suggested total is likely, if anything, to be an under-estimate because it is likely, as has already been argued, that some respondents did not mention this kind of school at all.

The returns tell us a good deal about the people who ran these unendowed schools. Prominent among them were the parish clerks, who often ran endowed schools as well. In James Talbott's old parish, Spofforth, and its chapelry, Wetherby, there were private unendowed schools taught by the clerk. At Spofforth there were 40/50 English scholars,[44] and at Wetherby about the same number.[45] At Kirkby Sigston (NR) there was no endowment. 'The Clark whose salary is very small teaches the young Children to read for which he is paid by their Parents, he brings them regularly to Church.'[46] There are many references to women: – no

223

school 'but an old woman' (Allerthorpe ER):[47] 'No other School but one where young Children are taught to read by a Mistress' (Darrington WR);[48] 'two poor women' (Bainton ER);[49] 'a poor man and a woman' (Marton on the Forest NR).[50] At Watton (ER) the children were sent to neighbouring villages 'except a poor Woman teach a few children within her own house to read, knit, and sow' (sic).[51] These were dame schools for very young children.

Sometimes private schoolmasters were described in more detail. There were a number of 'young men' and 'poor men'. At Barmby Marsh (par. Howden ER) the master was a Quaker.[52] At Goathland (NR) there was sometimes a private school taught by a weaver.[53] At Cold Kirkby (NR) 'a Neighbour who is out of Business teaches only ye neighbouring Children in winter-time'.[54] The most vivid of these pictures of private school teachers is that of Mr Thomas Preston at Garton-on-the-Wolds (ER)

> formerly Student of Trinity Hall Cambridge...he has about fourteen Scholars who learn to read, & write, he is Carefull to instruct them in the Principles of the Christian Religion, and to bring them duly to Church, his meat from house to house is most he gets for his instruction, he receives very small wages.[55]

It would be interesting to know what had reduced Mr Preston, formerly of Trinity Hall, to accepting such a meagre livelihood.

There are many references to masters – and in one case to a mistress[56] – who were diligent and conscientious and performed their duties well. At Rufforth (WR) the master taught the catechism so carefully to his scholars 'yt. I nevr. meet wth. any yt. say it so well'.[57] The master of the endowed school at Kirkburton, 'a sober, orderly & diligent man', may serve to represent the many who could be cited.[58] Just as typical was the master of the school at Methley (WR) where English and a little Latin were taught and there was a small endowment. 'The Master of it is an honest industrious man, but very poor'.[59] Pupils were not always easy to attract, nor did they attend regularly when they had been enrolled. The return from Featherstone (WR), where there were two unendowed private schools, said that children were sent to school when their parents could spare them from business.[60] At Marton-on-the-Moor (par. Topcliffe NR) the parents usually maintained a school. 'But in ye Time of Harvest they generally give over; & ye Children are sent to Glean in ye Corn-fields'.[61] At Otteringham (ER) 'The Clark undertakes to teach such as come to him, but he is very oft without any Scholars'.[62]

It is remarkable that in nearly 700 returns from Yorkshire parishes there is only a handful of complaints about misused endowments. Where complaint was made, it generally related to some landowner or trustee who refused to disgorge trust property or to pay interest on the money.[63] Elias Harrison, curate of Keighley, complained that one of the trustees had got £42 belonging to the school in his hands, and asked the archbishop to join with him in obtaining a Commission of Pious Uses to look into the matter. 'We've no gentlemen in the Parish to stand up in Behalf of these Charities...' It would be too expensive for him to act on his own.[64] The archbishop also asked the clergy to send him any general comments they might wish to make. Very few took up the suggestion, but one who did was Christopher Coulson, rector of Routh (ER). He asked, in order to propagate knowledge and promote the interest of the church, 'if a way could be found to erect a school in every village, as ye government is said to have done in Scotland...'[65] Coulson had been a student at Glasgow University, but was not a graduate of it. Whether he himself was or was not a Scot, the introduction of the Scottish example is interesting. It was to be a very long time before Coulson's goal was attained in England.

The Herring Returns give a remarkably complete picture of schooling in the county in the middle of the century, though by their nature they do not provide much detail in any particular case. It is appropriate therefore to add to them a more complete picture of some individual benefactors, and three of these have been selected as of particular interest – John Wheelwright, Alderman Cogan of Hull, and

225

Lady Elizabeth Hastings. John Wheelwright of North Shields (d.1724) left an endowment for a school at Rishworth (par. Halifax WR), where 20 boys and girls were to be educated and maintained. He also left a small bequest for teaching boys and girls at Dewsbury.[66] The 20 boys and girls were to be lodged in his own house at Rishworth. There were to be two masters, one of whom was to teach principally reading, writing and arithmetic, and a second who should be able to teach Latin and Greek. The boys were to be paid an apprenticeship premium of £5 at the age of 16, except that one boy who appeared the most capable was to be maintained until the age of 18 and then sent to Oxford or Cambridge. The foundation was wealthy and, although the trust was in Chancery from 1737 to 1780 and another lawsuit began in 1816, the income in 1826 amounted to £1,939 per annum. In 1805 the trustees stated a case for an opinion about the need to raise salaries and to alter the allowances paid to maintain the children. By that time none of them learned Latin nor had been sent to university. A new scheme was not made until 1826. There were to be new buildings at Rishworth and £100 per annum was allowed for maintaining the school at Dewsbury as an elementary school. In 1828 it was decided to run this school on the plan of the National Society. Rishworth was a very wealthy endowment where the educational results hardly justified the money which had been spent. The attempt to combine a charity school with the opportunity for a few boys to go on to the university had not been successful.

The important seaport of Kingston-upon-Hull had several schools for the poor. In the work house, Charity Hall, the children were taught spinning and knitting. They learned to read and write and were then apprenticed. One of the active promotors was Robert Banks, vicar of Holy Trinity, who was an early SPCK correspondent. At the end of the 18th century there were usually about 80 children. The boys were sent to sea, though it was more difficult to place the girls. A later vicar of Holy Trinity who was also an SPCK correspondent, William Mason, promoted in about 1729 a society of tradesmen for the education of poor children. In 1730 the Vicar's School was established. At first there were 20 children. In 1792 the school was rebuilt. 60 boys were then admitted, each of them for three years on the nomination of the vicar. A little earlier in 1787, Trinity House, the corporation which managed the navigation and pilotage of the Humber, opened a marine school for 36 boys who were admitted for three years. At the end of their schooling the boys were apprenticed to ship-masters.[67]

William Cogan, an apothecary by profession, was an alderman of the Corporation and twice mayor of Hull.[68] He had long been interested in the condition of the poor, and had been a governor of Charity Hall since 1726. In 1753 he founded a charity school where 20 poor girls might be taught and clothed. He later added a further endowment for marriage portions, and in 1772, by a codicil to his will, he gave £2,000 to be invested so that boys might be apprenticed to certain trades. He died in 1774. The girls were to remain in the school for three years, after which they were to receive a bible and 20 shillings 'for fitting them with necessities for service'. Their teacher was to be an unmarried woman and was to be paid £14 a year. They were to enter the school at ten years of age. Their parents were to be people of good repute who were not in receipt of parish allowances and who did not allow their children to beg. The girls were trained to be servants, were taught to read, and given a thorough grounding in the catechism and taken regularly to church. After seven years service they could claim a marriage dower of £6. The trades of some of their masters are known. In 1786 girls went to work for a slop man, a broker, a milliner, a whitesmith and a ship broker. The school seems to have done its work well, with the emphasis rather on training for future work than on literary studies. It possessed one unusual distinction in that in 1794 a girl was imprisoned for planning to poison the mistress!

The greatest of Yorkshire benefactors for education during the century was Lady Elizabeth Hastings (1682–1739) of Ledstone Hall, some ten miles east of Leeds. She inherited substantial wealth and lived a life of ordered piety and benevolence. Ralph Thoresby the antiquary, who was a frequent visitor to her house, described the daily religious exercises in her household; he called her 'most pious and excellent...her exemplary piety and charity is above all'.[69] She was a friend of Robert Nelson, the religious writer who was a member of the original SPCK circle, of Archbishop Sharp, and of the saintly Thomas Wilson, bishop of Sodor and Man, who was probably her adviser in her charities.[70] Lady Betty left benefactions to local churches. She established exhibitions of £28 each to be held for five years at Queen's College, Oxford. These were to be awarded to pupils of certain named schools (though the nominated schools could be, and sometimes were, changed if suitable candidates were not forthcoming). Eight of the schools were in Yorkshire and four more in Cumberland and Westmorland. In the five-yearly elections from 1764 to 1859 92 awards were made in total. Among the Yorkshire schools nine each came from Sedbergh and Leeds, eight from Wakefield and seven from Bradford.[71]

The charity estate was vested in the vicars of the three parishes (Ledsham, Thorp Arch and Collingham) of which Lady Betty was patron and in their successors.[72] There were small bequests to various schools, including £20 a year for schools in the Isle of Man, which reflects the friendship with Bishop Wilson. Larger bequests went to the schoolmasters at Collingham and Thorp Arch, and to the master of the boys' school at Ledsham. 20 children were to be instructed in each place,

> and that all be taught to read well and write and cast accounts in such a manner, as may be useful to them if from being Farmers' Servants they should arrive to be Farmers themselves. And be instructed in the Grounds and Principles of the Christian Religion as professed in the Church of England by Law Established and according to ye Tables of Rules given to the Charity School at Ledsham.[73]

There were small additional payments for buying books, and a payment of £9 a year for a youth who was to be trained in the Ledsham school to be a schoolmaster. 'One who has had a proper education so far as a Charity Schoolmaster. One who gives promising hopes of a Genius for teaching and is perfectly sober, of a meek temper and humble behaviour and who has a religious turn of mind'.[74] If in winter children could not come to the school because of bad weather, adults were to be taught to read in their place.

The largest bequest was devoted to the girls' charity school at Ledsham. £82 per annum was to be paid to the mistress for keeping the house and maintaining 20 girls, and there were other provisions for clothing the girls and for buying utensils and beds. The vicar was allowed £5 a year for buying books and medicines, and the Ledsham schoolmaster was allowed 40 shillings for keeping the mistress' accounts. The salary of the mistress was to be £10, there was an allowance of either £4 or £2.10.0 for a serving maid according to experience, and £10 a year for a superannuated mistress if unmarried.

The housekeeper's accounts book survives from the years 1739–40 and an 'Admissions and Goings Out' book from 1771.[75] The account book is purely a record of the housekeeping. In 1739–40 £102.3.4 was received and £101.19.8¾ was spent. £24.15.9½ was laid out on clothing. Thirty years later (1769–70) the receipts were £112.7.0, of which £88.16.10 was cash received from the bailiff. The disbursements were £102.0.11½, the largest items being Butcher's Meat and Fish (£23.5.7), Bread Corn and Meal (£36.0.7) and Gardening and Cow-keeping (£13.8.10). Clothing 20 girls cost £28.19.2, but a profit of £7.16.7½ was made on this item. The bailiff paid £12 for clothing, and £24.15.9½ had been received for spinning, presumably done by the girls themselves. Clothing two out-going girls cost £6. The accounts for 1799–1800 show a substantial deficit of £68.6.5½ which must reflect the very high prices of the 1790s.

The 'Admissions and Goings Out Book' shows that the girls admitted had lost one or both of their parents. There are a few cases where one or other parent was blind, and one where the father had enlisted as a soldier and deserted his family. There are a number of cases where girls were dismissed for disobedience or bad behaviour. One was taken away by 'her termagent mother'; another was 'discharged for having the King's Evil'.[76] When the girls left, they sometimes went

back to their families. Others went into service and their masters are named –
Thomas Pick of Sherburn, farmer, the Rev. Mr Sellon, Mr Pinder of Clubcliff, the
Marquis of Rockingham, an aunt at Sir William Lowther's at Swillington (perhaps
the aunt was the housekeeper). Probably since the girls had been well trained, they
found good places. The Ledsham girls' school, the village charity schools, the
exhibitions at Queen's College, Oxford, all show not only Lady Elizabeth's
generosity, but also the width of her interests and the careful thought which she
devoted to the working out of her projects. She deserves to be remembered as one
of the outstanding Englishwomen of her time.

Notes Chapter 11

1. For the position in the East Riding *see* Lawson, J. 1959.
2. The following is based on the Herring Returns (Ollard, S.L. and Walker,
   P.C. (eds) 1927–31 5 vols). The Yorkshire returns are in vols I–III. Vol IV
   covers the Nottinghamshire parishes. Vol V is appendices and indexes. The
   parish entries are numbered volume by volume and are referred to here in
   this way.
3. The questions are given in Returns vol I: 2-3, together with the archbishop's
   letter, dated 2 May 1743.
4. Herring Returns I: 73 (Bransby NR).
5. *Ibid.* II: 175.
6. *Ibid* I: 206 (North Ferriby); 215 (Fangfoss); II: 114 (Kirk Ella); 181
   (Marfleet).
7. Wilson, R. 1984: 115, 124. An earlier estimate of the number of schools by
   Ollard, S.L. in Introduction to Returns vol I: xi says that of 645 returns for
   Yorkshire parishes, 266 had no school or secular teaching.
8. *See* page203.
9. Herring Returns I: 1.
10. *Ibid* III: 82.

11. *Ibid.* III: 74.

12. *Ibid.* II: 29.

13. *Ibid.* II: 31.

14. *Ibid.* II: 101.

15. *Ibid.* I: 123.

16.. *Ibid.* I: 34.

17. *Ibid.* I: 84.

18. *Ibid.* III: 98.

19. *Ibid.* III: 99.

20. *Ibid.* II: 38.

21. *Ibid.* II: 46.

22. *Ibid.* III: 60.

23. *Ibid.* II: 39.

24. *Ibid.* II. 166.

25. *Ibid.* II: 203.

26. *Ibid.* III: 86.

27. For example, *ibid.* I: 67 (Barnoldswick WR); III: 32 (Rise ER); III: 102 (Swine ER); II: 76 (Sneton (Sneaton) NR).

28. *Ibid.* II: 132 (Luddenden, par. Halifax WR); II: 187 (Normanby near Kirkby Moorside NR); III: 202 (Ormesby NR).

29. *Ibid.* III: 190.

30. *Ibid.* III: 55.

31. *Ibid.* III: 15.

32. *Ibid.* III: 161.

33. *Ibid.* II: 69.

34. *Ibid.* I: 103.

35. *Ibid.* I: 94.

36. *Ibid.* III: 3.

37. For example, *ibid*. Guisborough (II: 8); Mitton WR (II: 161); Pocklington (III:10).

38. *Ibid*. III: 42.

39. *Ibid*. I: 54.

40. *Ibid*. III: 19.

41. For example, Horton in Ribblesdale (II: 26): Haworth (II: 33).

42. *Ibid*. II: 199.

43. *Ibid*. II: 37. The master's name was Thomas Trant. For another reference to Hemsworth grammar school *see* pages 278–9.

44. *Ibid*. III: 38.

45. *Ibid*. III: 157.

46. *Ibid*. III: 84. The many parishes where the parish clerk taught include Lockington ER (Returns II: 143); Skipwith ER (III: 79); Skeckling cum Burstwick ER (III: 101); Thornton ER (III: 149); Wistow WR (III: 172).

47. *Ibid*. I: 37.

48. *Ibid*. I: 156.

49. *Ibid* I: 89.

50. *Ibid*. II: 170.

51. *Ibid*. III: 189.

52. *Ibid*. I: 106.

53. *Ibid*. II: 10.

54. *Ibid*. I: 141.

55. *Ibid*. II: 15.

56. Elizabeth Priest at Penistone WR (Returns III: 5).

57. *Ibid*. III: 13.

58. *Ibid*. II: 99.

59. *Ibid*. II: 162.

60. *Ibid*. I: 193.

61. *Ibid*. III: 139.

62. *Ibid*. II: 207.

63. See Returns I: 164 (Danby NR); II: 35 (Honley, par. Almondbury WR); II: 186 (Nunnington NR).

64. *Ibid.* II: 95.

65. *Ibid.* III: 31.

66. The following is based on Priestley, J.H. (n.d.); *see also* Purvis, J.S. 1959: 23.

67. *VCH Yorkshire* 1969 East Riding vol I: 348–9; Sheahan, J.J. ?1866: 581–2, 591–600.

68. The following is based on Attwood, G.M. 1962: 314–30; *see also* Lawson, J. 1963: 141.

69. Thoresby, R. 1830 vol II: 82.

70. See Medhurst, C.E. 1914; Jones, M.G. 1939–40: 71–90. The contemporary life, by Thomas Barnard, 1742, is simply a panegyric, though it does print some useful material about the benefactions.

71. Medhurst, C.E. 1914: 136–9. The rather remarkable fashion in which the exhibitioners were chosen is set out on pages 108–12.

72. For the trust deed of 1738 *see* Medhurst, C.E. 1914: 142–216.

73. Medhurst, C.E. 1914: 194.

74. Ibid.: 166.

75. YAS: Lady Elizabeth Hastings Trust – Housekeeper's Account Book 1739–1810; Admissions and Goings Out 1771–1831.

76. The 'king's evil' is scrofula, a disease of the lymphatic glands. Dr Samuel Johnson was touched for it by Queen Anne.

CHAPTER 12

Elementary Schooling: the later years

The reformers of the late 17th/early 18th centuries had always seen a close connection between the provision of schooling and the eradication of poverty. First of all, to instruct the children would take them away from idleness and bad company, and would imbue them with sound principles of religion and morality. Then, when they left school, they would be better fitted for labour because they would have gained steady habits of application and self-discipline. The general problem of the poor was always a major issue of national social policy, and there was an overlap between schools and workhouses, in so far as these catered for children, because they were trying to perform similar functions, which were both disciplinary and educative. One question which was often debated was that of children's labour. How far in schools or workhouse was it possible for children to work and earn their own keep? What should be the balance between time spent in such work and time spent in learning to read and write, particularly since many of these young people were not likely to need the skills of literacy in the work which they would do as adults? In 1697 John Locke, in his *Report for the Reform of the Poor Law*, had recommended that working schools should be set up in each parish to which children between the ages of three and 14 years of all those who demanded parish relief should be obliged to come. These children would thus 'from their infancy be inured to work which is of no small consequence to making them sober and industrious all their lives after'.[1]

It is difficult to draw a line between education, which was a private matter dependent on a mixture of endowment, personal giving and the payment of fees, and poor law policy, which was a matter for the state. The objectives of the school and of the workhouse to some extent overlapped. Both forged a link between the worlds of training and of work through the institution of apprenticeship, the system of tutelage through which the young person, usually a boy, passed from childhood to maturity as an adult worker. Apprenticeship was often a private matter involving the master, the parent, the child, and sometimes the school. Examples have already been given and more will be cited later. It was a public matter too since the parishes used it as a means of ending their responsibility for pauper children by passing them on to masters who might often be cruel and violent. This form of apprenticeship was not an educational process at all, and so it does not form part of our subject. But the links between schooling and what may be called 'private' apprenticeship were close, and benefactors often saw the latter as the natural complement to the foundations which had already been laid down in the school-room. The indentures of boys apprenticed to cutlers in 18th century Sheffield sometimes provided that the boys should receive some schooling, generally at a writing school, as part of their training.[2] This happened in only a minority of cases, and it became less common as the century went on, but the fact that it occurred at all does show the link between schooling and the further educative process which apprenticeship represented.

The balance between the different elements – the acquisition of literacy, the enforcement of religious and social discipline, the attempt to cover the cost of maintenance through work – varied from place to place and from time to time. The three elements were found together only in the large subscription schools of the SPCK type and in some of the richer local foundations like Lady Elizabeth Hastings' charity school for girls at Ledsham. The resources of the small village schools, such as the majority of those in the Herring Returns, extended no further than basic religious instruction, reading and some writing. In the early days of SPCK the large London schools spent much of their effort on basic education in literacy, though the desire to set the children to work was also there as well. By the 1720s the balance of interests was changing and the Society itself came under considerable criticism.

It was accused of Jacobite sympathies, and in 1716 the archbishop of Canterbury warned the trustees of schools that teachers and children must not take part in any riots against the government, that catechizing must not introduce dangerous opinions, and that masters and mistresses should sign a solemn declaration acknowledging King George to be the only rightful king.[3] The schools were also attacked for over-educating their charges. In 1723 Bernard Mandeville in *An Essay on Charity and Charity Schools*[4] attacked the motives of those who ran the schools and claimed that the education of the poor was undesirable because it would make them unfit for the hard laborious work which had to be done if the work of the world was to be carried on

> Going to School in Comparison to Working is Idleness, & the longer Boys continue in this easy sort of Life, the more unfit they'll be when grown up for downright Labour...Men who are to remain & end their Days in a Laborious, Tiresome & Painful Station of Life, the sooner they are put upon it at first, the more patiently they'll submit to it ever after.[5]

During the 1720s the policy of the Society moved towards the idea of the working school and of putting children to labour.[6] National policy was moving in a similar direction. The Poor Law Act of 1723 enabled individual parishes to maintain workhouses and within a decade over 100 of these had been set up.[7] Pauper children living in the workhouse were more likely to be put to work than if they and their parents were being relieved at home. The Society's *Account of Several Work-Houses...*, originally published in 1725, contained both recommendations about policy and an account of the institutions which had been set up. It was argued that such workhouses offered the best and most economical way of tackling the problem of poverty and of ensuring that relief was given to the deserving. All orphan children and those whose parents had become a charge on the parish should be sent to the workhouse, educated and set to work at useful tasks. The girls should become 'used to dressing Victuals, Brewing, Baking, Washing and the like'. They should be maintained until they were 12 and the boys until they were 13 after which they were to be put out as apprentices or servants, provided that they were not to be bound, in the case of boys over the age of 22 and of girls over the age of 20 or the time of marriage.[8]

The *Account* gives only two Yorkshire examples. The first was the 'working charity school' at Beverley where the children were employed in spinning yarn. The best spinners, it was explained, could earn 2½ d. a day by spinning five hanks. The Herring Returns later recorded that 12 children were taught spinning, reading, writing and arithmetic.[9] According to the *Account* the parishes of the town had built a workhouse for 100 people. The overseers had announced that allowances for the poor would then cease, but, though 116 had received the allowance, only 26 came into the workhouse and, as most of these were old people or children, there was not much profit from their labour, a complaint which was repeated in many other instances.[10]

At Hull Charity Hall[11] had been built under an Act of 1698 for setting up Guardians of the Poor. For many years this had been a charity school for children while the poor received pensions. In 1728 all weekly pay had been stopped, and thereafter there were about 100 poor in the house. They were chiefly employed in spinning flax and 'jersey' and picking oakum. The children were to go to school up to the age of six and above that age they were to work, 'learning to read or write once a Day'. They were to be washed and dressed to appear at school every morning at 7 or 8 o'clock. For spinning and other work they were allowed to keep 2d. in every shilling earned. As a result of the policy of the guardians the children did not beg and grow up in bad habits 'for want of Instruction or Convenient Labour; such as might enable them to help towards their own Maintenance, and to become in time useful Servants to others.'[12]

The balance between education, work and apprenticeship can be followed in the later part of the century in the histories of several of the larger schools, the three selected for study being York, Leeds and Sheffield. The boys' and girls' schools at York (the Blue Coat and Grey Coat Schools) had been founded in 1705, and enjoyed the active support of the city Corporation.[13] Much emphasis was always laid in both schools on the children's labour. In the Blue Coat School there was originally boarding accommodation for 40 boys between the ages of seven and twelve who were either orphans or the sons of poor freemen with large families. In 1764 there were 45 boys and two girls who did the domestic work.[14] The boys' school seems to have been a successful institution throughout the century, though the girls' school, as we shall see, needed major reforms in the 1780s. A picture of the general working of both of them can be obtained from the Committee minute books of the 1770s and 1780s.[15] These contain a number of references to the collections made at the anniversary meetings at St Michael-le-Belfrey and a few more to collections made at the York theatre. There was a great deal of concern about the children's health. They had to be inoculated against smallpox before they were admitted, and children with various bodily infirmities were often removed. On one occasion (1 May 1778) the treasurer was ordered to pay 20 shillings to buy clothes for a boy who had been turned out 'on account of his being afflicted with incurable Scrhopulous disorder...he being turned out of the school in very bad Cloaths and his Father not being able to find him new ones'.[16] In 1772 the physicians and surgeons were consulted about the children's diet and their recommendations for changes accepted.

The disciplinary regulations were strict. There are several references (2 March 1772; 5 March 1779) to bonds which required a penalty to be paid if children were taken away without the committee's consent – and of the payment being enforced when this had happened. In 1772 a few boys and girls were permitted to eat with their parents on Sundays, though this was not to be allowed if the parents were thought to be 'of indifferent morals'. There are no detailed regulations about

239

manual labour, but plenty of references which show that it was done on a regular basis. In 1775 a girl who had run away was to be chastised and made to spin 'An addition of two Hanks of Worsted a day' until the next committee meeting. The word 'addition' suggests that the girl was spinning regularly in any case. In 1779 Mr Joseph Wolstenholme junior was appointed master of the Blue Coat School at a salary of £25 a year plus another £4 for overlooking the spinning. The year previously (2 January 1778) some of the boys were sent to a toy-making and hardwood factory in Goodramgate in the city during the hours when they would normally have been spinning wool, and a few months later Mr John Lund agreed to take six boys in turning hardwood and making toys. They were to attend from 9 to 12 and from 3 to 6 each work-day, which could not have left them much time for schooling, though the minutes do not say how long this period of labour was to last. In February 1779 Mr Lund asked for two girls; they were to be sent in the hours when they would otherwise have been spinning.

The minutes about the boys' apprenticeships followed a standard form. The lad was bound for seven years. He was to be fitted out 'with the School's allowance'. His master was to teach him the trade, to provide him with 'Cloaths & necessarys' and to give him a new suit of clothes to the value of £4 at least at the end of the term.[17] In a city where there was no dominant industry the boys were apprenticed to a wide variety of occupations. The largest number went into 'husbandry'; a number went to sea – to 'mariners' or to the 'sea service'. Trades which appeared quite frequently were blacksmith, cordwainer and translator (shoe-repairer), carpenter and gardener. There were weavers, tailors, paper stainers, musicians, peruke-makers and hairdressers and barbers, a brush-maker, a breeches-maker, a coach-maker, a brazier and pewterer, a cooper, a cabinet maker. There can have been few trades in the city and its rural hinterland which were not recruited from the boys of the Blue Coat School.

The Committee minutes of the 1780s were much concerned with the problems of the Grey Coat (Girls') School. Its management was put onto a new footing through the intervention of a group of ladies, the most active of whom was Catharine Harrison, who became Catharine Cappe when she married Newcome Cappe, minister of the Dissenting congregation in St Saviourgate, in 1788.[18] Women had been running their own schools since the 17th century and one or two of them like Mary Astell had been active publicists.[19] Women benefactors had exercised a considerable influence for centuries. Lady Elizabeth Hastings is a local example of a type headed in an earlier century by the great Lady Margaret Beaufort. But these York ladies were not individuals of great wealth or powerful influence. They worked as a group in taking up a cause, making changes, and carrying through a new policy. This was something new in English social history, and they must have been among the very first women in the country to attempt anything of the kind. Some of them were Evangelicals who came under the influence of York's pioneer Evangelical clergyman, William Richardson, who became curate of St Michael-le-Belfrey in 1771. Education was only one of the causes in which these people were active. Friendly Societies, the York hospital, anti-slavery, the Bible Society were all subjects of their constant concern.

Mrs Cappe was the publicist of the group, and much of what is known about them comes from her pamphlets and from her autobiography.[20] Her father had been rector of Catterick (NR), and his successor there, Theophilus Lindsey, resigned the living in 1773 because he had adopted Unitarian opinions. Both Lindsey and his wife at Catterick and the future Mrs Cappe at Bedale, where she was then living, had been among the earliest to start Sunday Schools, though she could not persuade anyone in the village to help her with this work. Her defence of Lindsey at the time of his resignation from his living brought her into touch with Newcome Cappe whom she later married, and she herself decided to secede from the Church of England. In 1782 she and her mother settled in York, and she became a friend of Faith Gray (1751–1826), who with her husband William (1751–1845), a lawyer, were members of Richardson's congregation at St Michael-le-Belfrey. William Gray himself was active in good causes, a friend of William Wilberforce and for many years almoner of his charities in Yorkshire.

At the end of 1782 Faith Gray and Catharine Cappe became interested in the bad conditions suffered by the children, and particularly the girls, who were employed in a hemp manufactory. As a result of their intervention the children were taught to read and sew in the evenings after they had finished work. The children were taken to church on Sundays and given religious instruction by ladies who came to help. A few years later a knitting school was started for the children who were too young for the spinning school. The spinning school children were allowed various items of clothing in proportion to their earnings, and they were allowed to keep part of what they had earned at the end of the week. Later in 1798 a house was rented as a permanent home for the spinners and knitters, and the various departments of its management were divided between the lady helpers. In general it was thought that the girls had turned out well, though much more could have been achieved if there had been schools of industry sufficient in number for all those who were in need.[21]

From the spinning school Catharine Cappe and her friends were drawn into the problems of the Grey Coat School, the condition of which was exciting a good deal of concern. The girls were not in good health and many of them did not turn out well, several having become prostitutes. In 1785 Mrs Gray, Catharine Cappe and other ladies were consulted by the trustees about what should be done. The first change made was the appointment of two assistant teachers to control the spinning rooms. It seems from Catharine Cappe's own account that the trustees were initially unwilling to accept the ladies' proposals, but in May 1786 they accepted them for a period of one year,[22] and subsequently they accepted the general guidance of the ladies' committee in the running of the school. The basic changes were two. The master and mistress ceased to receive the allowance for boarding the children and the profit from their labour, and a matron was appointed in their place. The system of apprenticeship was abolished, the girls being retained in the school until they were ready to go out as trained servants.[23]

Mrs Cappe described the new system in two tracts, one published in 1800, the other in 1805. In the first of these she pointed out the success of the girls under the new system

> Some are married, and become the decent industrious Mothers of families; others are in service, many still in the places to which they were at first hired, where they are much valued; and all who left the School for the last few years, shew the greatest attachment to it, and regard the Matron as an affectionate parent, to whom they owe the greatest obligation.[24]

In the same tract she explained the school routine. The numbers had in 1799 been increased to 42. Of these ten at any one time acted as 'servants' to all the rest. These girls had a master three days a week to teach them writing and arithmetic and to improve their reading. The remaining 30 or so were 'scholars'. 20 of these spun wool for the manufacturer and for their own clothing. The remaining spun line, sewed and knitted. All the duties were interchanged at regular intervals, and every girl made her own clothes and stockings. The matron read prayers every morning and evening and the girls were taken to church on Sundays. They were taught the catechism and the collects, and they received the sacrament once or twice before they left school. There is no suggestion that Mrs Cappe, who was a Unitarian, had any difficulty about so strongly Anglican a regime.

In her 1805 tract[25] Mrs Cappe stressed the advantages of bringing up poor children in charity schools rather than in poor houses. There was, she thought, a crucial difference between the position of boys and of girls in relation to apprenticeship because the people who were ready to take girl apprentices were generally unsuitable for such responsibility. There was danger that girls would drift into perilous courses, and she even quoted examples of girls being murdered. At York the girls went out into service at 16 or 17, and ways had been developed for training them after they had received a basic education at the age of 12 or 13. In all this work the help of a ladies' committee had been invaluable, and the ladies were also able to keep an eye on the girls after they had gone into service. Mrs Cappe's charitable interests extended far beyond these York schools. In the same 1805 pamphlet she described the work of the Female Friendly Society established in 1788 for those who had attended the Grey Coat School and the Spinning School. She was also involved in York with the Bible Society, with the County Hospital, with the Savings Bank. She had links with the Ladies' Committee founded in London in 1804 by women connected with the Bettering Society, a national body devoted to good causes.[26] She is a good example of that important 18th century type, the philanthropist.[27] Mrs Cappe and her friends were carrying out a new role for their sex in charitable work and public affairs.

Two more large charity schools were those at Leeds and at Sheffield. The foundation of the Leeds school has already been studied in some detail, so its later history can be treated quite briefly. In the second half of the century the Leeds children, though they were clothed, were not boarded, and since they lived at home, the minute books often record trouble with the parents, for example over the proper custody of the children's clothes. The school orders instructed parents to send their children to school 'clean Washed and Combed', to keep them in good order at home, and to ensure they did not beg or make a riot. Parents were to allow their children to be chastised, and were not to interfere with the master in the performance of his duties. They were to ensure that the children read their bibles, repeated the catechism and said their prayers. If these orders were not obeyed, the children would be expelled. No parent was to put a child out as an apprentice without the consent of the committee of subscribers.[28] The Committee minute books (1750–1800) give much attention to the appointment of successive work-masters, to the purchase of wool and wheels, and to the spinning done by the children.[29] In 1757, for example, it was ordered that two more wheels were to be purchased for 'the working Schollars', who took their turns, 12 boys and 8 girls at a time. Twenty years later it was minuted that boys should leave the school within three months of their 12th birthday and girls after their 13th. (20 June 1777).

It was recorded in the SPCK General Board minutes of 1705 that nearly £50 per annum had been subscribed for a charity school at Sheffield with the hope of more to come, and that this had been achieved largely through the efforts of the vicar, Nathan Drake (1695–1713).[30] Subsequently there are very few references to Sheffield in the letter books; presumably there was no active local correspondent. The first set of accounts (1706–7) of the Sheffield charity school detail subscriptions of £92.14.0, given by 111 donors of whom 96 paid £1 or less, some of them as little as 2s. 6d. or 3s. 0d., which suggests a strong basis of local support.[31] There were 14 subscribers who gave between £1 and £5, including the vicar and his curate at Ecclesall, Robert Turie, each of whom gave £2. The Duke of Norfolk, the lord of the manor, gave £22.10.0 for the last three-quarters of the year. It is clear from the accounts that in the first few years the children, both boys and girls, were clothed, and money was spent on spinning wheels and spindles and on paying a spinning dame who taught the boys to spin.

During the years 1708–10 a schoolhouse was built which cost £275.[32] One donor, Mr Banks, gave £100, Mr Ellis of Brampton, who was a frequent giver to good causes, gave £20, and a subscription in the church collected £20.12.6. By 1712 12 boys were being boarded as well as clothed, though later on there were day scholars as well. In 1776, for example, James Hoole was appointed governor and schoolmaster. He was to be paid £25 for teaching the boys on the foundation plus day scholars who were not to exceed 25 in number. Though there had been girls in the very early years, all those who were boarded were boys. A girls' charity school on an independent foundation was not established until 1786.[33] The number of boys boarded increased steadily during the century. By 1770 there were 31; in 1798 there were 60 (including 6 boys then newly added on a separate endowment). In 1814 the number was increased to 80.[34] By the beginning of the 19th century the school trust had a substantial income (£1,224.0.8¾ in 1810) from investments, the rents of land

and houses and subscriptions. In that year the provisions for the children cost £421.5.6 and their clothing and shoes £202.11.4. The salary of the master and his wife (Mr and Mrs Youle) was £60. 1810 was the year of George III's jubilee; 'Meddles at ye Jubilee' cost £2.12.6.

Detailed information has survived from the 1780s about admissions and about apprenticeships. In 1777 85 parents and guardians had agreed that the boys might be put out apprentice at the option of the trustees.[35] The entry lists record a general pattern of poverty and of large families with many children at home. Many boys were orphans. Some fathers were noted as being soldiers, which presumably meant that they were unable to maintain their families. Other fathers were noted as 'ill', 'supposed to have the evil', vagabond', 'run away'. Mothers are noted as widows, as pregnant, as 'incapable', which presumably meant that they were unable to look after their children. Sometimes other children in the family had 'fits'.[36] The number of admissions in the 1780s and 1790s varied between 10 and 20 a year, the highest total being 1798 with 26 and the lowest 1785 with 6.[37]

It was ordered in 1761 that no boy should be admitted under the age of 7 nor continue over the age of 12.[38] During their time at the school a few boys were removed for misconduct or were taken away by their parents. One or two ran away; a few were removed because they were 'scrophulous', a disease which we have frequently met with before. One wretched child aged 8½ was expelled in December 1798 because he wet his bed.[39] The trades to which the boys were apprenticed were often recorded and sometimes the master's name was given. As might be expected in Sheffield, most boys were apprenticed to cutlers or to related trades – grinder, scissorgrinder, filesmith. A good many boys were apprenticed to their fathers, and one boy in 1783 to his mother who was a widow. It seems to have been not uncommon in 18th century Sheffield for widows to carry on the business of their late husband. Other trades are also mentioned – barber, brusher, tailor, breeches-maker, 'the Workhouse steward', buttonmaker, snuffmaker, combmaker, plasterer.

There is one remarkable difference between the Sheffield school and the similar schools which have already been described. Though in the very early years there are references in the Sheffield accounts to the provision of spinning wheels and to boys learning to spin, these quickly disappear and there are no later references to the boys working. If there had been a systematic work programme as there was in other places, this must have shown up in the accounts. Possibly, though there is no direct evidence of it, there was a conscious decision of policy that the boys should not spin. There is a little evidence from the end of the century about what they learned. A series of annual printed *Reports*, which begins in 1788, contains a section on 'the State of the Children's Improvement'.[40] They were able to read the alphabet, the Testament and Bible, and 'Diction.' (perhaps some kind of word-list which they had learned). They could repeat the catechism and 'Explan.' (presumably an explanation of the catechism), and they wrote on slates and paper. A few boys tackled 'Accompt', which seems to have been simple arithmetic since addition, subtraction, multiplication and division, the rule of three, and extracting square roots are all mentioned. In March 1808, of 60 boys examined, only 11 offered 'Accompts'.

There is a little more information about the curriculum in *The Poor Girls' Primer* by Edward Goodwin, published in 1787 for the use of the girls' charity school which had been founded the previous year.[41] The book contain a series of lessons at different levels of difficulty. The early ones, like this, are very simple

Be kind to the girls who are with you at School

Do all the good you can

Do Harm to none

Do as you would be done by

Do not make a mock of sin

These are followed by a series of stories, most of them on biblical themes, each followed by religious and moral reflections: Joseph, Rebekah, Solomon's Mother,

247

Martha and Mary, Lydia, Tabitha, on Servants. The final and longest story is the tale of Anne Goodwill who becomes a dairymaid, then the housekeeper, and finally marries a farmer on the estate and brings up her family in habits of industry and frugality. The stories are broken up with sets of words for the children to learn. This is the final and most advanced set

Re-pu-ta-ble Ne-ces-sa-ries Fru-ga-li-ty

Af-fec-ti-on In-struc-ti-ons So-ci-e-ty

Ge-ne-ra-ti-on

At the end of the book there is a selection of prayers, hymns and psalms. Goodwin was a clergymen and the *Primer* no doubt reflects his special interests, but its general tone probably represents much of the teaching in girls' charity schools throughout the century.

There were other schools in 18th century Sheffield like the Hollis Charity School and the Free Writing School.[42] Among many similar schools mention may be made of the Clerk's School at Skipton,[43] a 16th century foundation which continued until 1814 when a National School was opened, of the Green Coat School at Wakefield,[44] and of the Hollis School and the Feoffees' Charity School at Rotherham.[45] A more detailed account of the school at Slaithwaite near Huddersfield will serve to represent many others in the smaller towns and villages. The parish school, which had existed in the late 17th century, was endowed by Robert Meeke, curate of Slaithwaite, with £100 in 1721, and there were other benefactions by Thomas Walker and Michael Aneley.[46] The second trust deed of 1731 provided that the master was to be chosen by the original trustees and then by the vicar of Huddersfield and the curates of Slaithwaite and Deanhead. Ten children, both boys and girls, were to be educated. The master was to be a member of the Church of England, able to teach the children to read, to write a good hand, and to understand arithmetic. He was to look after the scholars' behaviour, to teach them the catechism, and to see that they went to church. The children were to be of the poorest sort and chosen from the townships of Slaithwaite and Lingards. The boys were to learn reading, writing and arithmetic 'sufficient to qualify them for common apprentices.' The girls were to be taught only to read and to learn the catechism. If the master had a wife who could teach them to knit and sew, that should be done. The electors were empowered to hold back the master's stipend and to remove him if necessary.

The master of Slaithwaite School from 1738 to 1786 was John Murgatroyd. The son of a blacksmith, he was educated under Mr Wadsworth at Rishworth. He was anxious to become a scholar, though his father was unable to send him to university. After he had been schoolmaster at Slaithwaite for some 15 years, he was ordained deacon and priest, and was, in addition to his school work, for about ten years curate at Almondbury. His commonplace books show an interest in history, poetry and divinity, and some letters record the gratitude of his old pupils. Among his successors in the school were Thomas Gill or Gell (1790–1804), who later became a cotton weaver and then set up a private school, and John Hargreaves (1804–37), who took boarders but at the end of whose time the school sank very low and was suspended by the trustees. Murgatroyd was affected by Evangelical opinions as he grew older, and the same path was followed by a succession of the curates of the chapelry. They may have been influenced by the prominent Evangelical Henry Venn, who was vicar of Huddersfield from 1759–1771, and by the landowner, Lord Dartmouth, who shared the same beliefs.[47] One of these curates, Thomas Wilson (1777–1809), who had been a pupil of Joseph Milner at Hull, was an early supporter of Sunday Schools and of the Church Missionary Society, and Murgatroyd's journal for 1786 records that a Sunday School was started in the parish school in that year. A later curate, Thomas Jackson (1823–39), began a National School in the township in 1835, an act described by the parish historian as 'by far the most important Monument of Mr Jackson's Ministry'.[48]

These initiatives in the village of Slaithwaite were but one example of a national trend. The activity in voluntary organization which had produced the work of SPCK had faltered in the middle of the 18th century, or perhaps it would be truer to say that much of it had flowed into the early stages of the Evangelical Revival. In the latter part of the century voluntary organizations for philanthropic purposes took on a new lease of life. The first expression of this movement was in the Sunday Schools. Later came the missionary societies, the associations for disseminating religious literature like the Religious Tract Society and the Bible Society, and later still the National and British Societies for establishing day schools on the monitorial principle.[49] Much of this activity did not grow to maturity until the 19th century, but its beginnings will be treated briefly here as a conclusion to the story of popular education in the county since the Revolution of 1688–9.

Sunday Schools were a continuation of the long-term movement to christianize and to discipline the poor which had inspired the charity schools of the early years of the century. But full-time schooling was expensive, even when combined with labour, and that combination had proved difficult to bring about. It seemed more productive to concentrate on the proper observance of Sunday, and to try to reach the great number of children who might have many kinds of occupation during the week.[50] Robert Raikes, the Gloucester printer, is often given credit for initiating the movement, but he was one among many who were thinking on similar lines at much the same time. What Raikes did, it has been said, was to give 'the idea the publicity to turn it into a national sensation'.[51] He opened his first Sunday School in 1780. Before that date, as we have seen,[52] Catharine Harrison (Catharine Cappe) had been running a school in her mother's house at Bedale and Theophilus Lindsey and his wife had been teaching children and young men and women in his living at Catterick.

In the 1780s the cause of Sunday Schools made a strong appeal to many of the clergy. An early advocate among the hierarchy was Bishop Porteus of Chester, whose diocese covered much of western and northern Yorkshire. The bishop argued that the depravity and licentiousness of the people could be corrected only by the right kind of education. It had been the intention of the charity schools to offer this, but they had been too expensive to become universal, and the Sunday Schools were a useful appendage to them. Such schools were, Porteus wrote, 'an extension of the principle on which our Charity Schools are founded; an enlargement of that benevolent system of *gratuitous instruction* for the poor...'[53] Sunday Schools were easy to establish and cheap to run. Since the children would be taught only reading and not writing or arithmetic, they would not be made unfitted for laborious employments. They would learn habits of prayer and of regular public worship; they would form associations linked with religion. Already it was clear, the bishop thought, that the schools had had a good effect. The children behaved better and their good habits had influenced the lives of their parents. He had, however, a few reservations. Care must be taken over the conduct of the teachers, and sufficient time must be allowed on Sundays for children to have proper recreation and opportunities for outdoor pleasure and exercise. Porteus' arguments suggest the mind of a humane and well-balanced man.

The case for and against the new developments was argued by local writers as well. Edward Goodwin, one of the assistant ministers of Sheffield parish church, wrote a pamphlet in 1786 addressed to parents, to masters and to the children themselves.[54] He pointed out to parents the religious advantages of sending their children to Sunday Schools. Masters were reminded that they had a religious duty to their servants whose faithfulness and diligence would be increased as a result of their attending school. Children were warned that they must not break the Sabbath nor disobey their parents or their masters. They must behave well at school, go to church on Sundays and continue in the same course for the rest of the week, avoiding the company of bad children. The disciplinary tone of the pamphlet is very strong. Not all those who wrote about Sunday Schools were supporters. The Hull historian George Hadley (1788) attacked the idea of teaching the poor to read and write on lines very similar to those adopted by Bernard Mandeville in the 1720s.[55] He thought that the poor, once educated, would abandon laborious tasks, while itinerant preachers would be encouraged and order and hierarchy broken down. But

Hadley's was probably a minority view; it was more commonly believed that Sunday School instruction would discipline the poor and subordinate the unruly among them.[56]

There is a good deal of evidence about the establishment of Sunday Schools in Yorkshire in the 1780s. John Wesley noted in his journal that before he preached at Bingley Church in 1784, he had a look at the Sunday School: 'Before service I stepped into the Sunday-School, which contained two hundred and forty children, taught every Sunday by several masters and superintended by the curate... I find these schools spinging up wherever I go'.[57] At Rotherham the feoffees' minutes recorded (18 October 1785) that the establishment of Sunday Schools would be of great public utility, and it was agreed to subscribe ten guineas towards carrying such a scheme into execution. In 1788 400 Sunday School children walked in a procession to celebrate the Glorious Revolution and dined at the town hall 'of plumb puddings apple pyes and the broken victuals [from a dinner] which was a truly pleasing sight to see as they all appeared so happy'.[58] At Beverley the corporation subscribed five guineas towards the encouragement of Sunday Schools in 1785.[59] In 1794 the Cutlers' Company of Sheffield gave a like sum to the treasurer of the Sheffield Sunday Schools.[60]

The Sunday School movement affected all the churches. Many of the early schools were inter-denominational, though they later divided on denominational lines. In Charlotte Brontë's *Shirley* (1849), set in the woollen district of the West Riding in 1812, there is a lively description of the clash between the Church scholars and the Dissenting scholars on the feast day as they approach each other from opposite ends of a narrow lane. The forces of the Church, led by their bands, press remorselessly forward and the Dissenters are put to flight.[61] Perhaps a genuine reminiscence which Charlotte had heard from her friends the Taylors at Red House, Gomersal?

At York the Church of England Sunday School Committee had been founded in 1786. There were to be six schools for boys with 50 scholars each and four for girls (three with 50 scholars each and one with 75). Only reading the Old and New Testaments and spelling as a preparation for that were to be taught on Sundays, though week-day instruction was also given which included writing. In January 1828 the Committee had seven schools at which 787 children were present. In 1831, on the occasion of the coronation of King William IV, 918 children assembled and heard a sermon. They were joined by the children of the charity schools and paraded through the streets, each child being presented with a cake.[62]

It has been said that 'the rapidity with which new Methodist Sunday Schools sprang up is the predominant feature of denominational history during the first twenty or thirty years on the nineteenth century.'[63] At York the first Methodist Sunday School was opened in 1791.[64] At Sheffield the Methodist Henry Longden wrote in his diary (11 February 1798)

> This morning we have begun a SUNDAY-SCHOOL. Many brethren and sisters offered their services as teachers, and many children were admitted. The presence of the Lord was eminently among us. Surely this is a good beginning of a great and good work.[65]

The movement expanded rapidly during the early 19th century, and links developed both with day schools and with schools for adults which were promoted by many chapels. According to figures cited by T.W. Laqueur for 1818 6.5% of the population in the West Riding was enrolled in Sunday Schools. In the East Riding the percentage was 4.1 and in the North Riding 1.3.[66] In Sheffield in 1812 all the churches other than the Anglicans and the Unitarians combined to form the Sheffield Sunday School Union. In 1824 the Union had 48 schools with 2,039 teachers and 8,834 pupils.[67] Laqueur argued that, in addition to the clergy and middle class people who promoted the schools, there was an independent working-class tradition of foundation and management represented by men like the Keighley blacksmith Thomas Noble who announced his intention of opening a school on 4 April 1787 'to any person mindfull to have their children tought in the Gospel of Jesus Christ and Fear of God'.[68] As we have seen, pioneers like Bishop Porteus and the York Church of England Committee were anxious to exclude writing from the teaching on the Sabbath day. The local working-class communities often wished to include it. For example, at Sheffield, in the early years of the 19th century, the future Wesleyan leader Jabez Bunting tried to ban writing from the school and the pro-writing faction seceded and founded another.[69] The question of whether or not to teach writing on Sundays remained a matter of controversy for a long time.

The progress from Sunday Schools into full-time education for the children of the poor was facilitated by the introduction of the monitorial system, which allowed large numbers of children to be taught at comparatively small expense. Its pioneers were the Quaker Joseph Lancaster (1778–1838) and the Anglican clergyman Andrew Bell (1753–1832), from whose work developed the two great societies, the Anglican National Society (1811) and the undenominational British and Foreign School Society (1814). The appearance of these national bodies, and on the Anglican side of the diocesan societies which complemented them, put the provision of popular education onto a much more structured basis than had existed before and made it possible to achieve far more than SPCK had accomplished, even in its most active period. The story of the National and British Societies leads on into a period later than that covered by this book, and all that can be done here is to say a little about their early beginnings in Yorkshire.

In York the diocesan society founded two schools in 1812, one for boys at the King's Manor, one for girls in Merchant Taylor's Hall. In 1818–19 they were teaching 460 boys and 240 girls. A girls' school on the Lancasterian system opened in 1813.[70] At Beverley the Corporation decided in the same year to subscribe £20 annually to the 'National Establishment' for the education of the poor, and the school committee later became tenants of a Corporation property.[71] At Sheffield a visit from Joseph Lancaster was followed by the foundation of a boys' school in 1809. National schools for boys and girls followed in 1813.[72] The British school at Halifax, founded in 1813, was established for the children of the poor of all religious denominations. The Bible was taught, but 'particular religious instruction' was left to parents and to ministers of the churches or Sunday Schools to which the children belonged. They were taught reading, writing and arithmetic at the charge of 1d. per week, though in the girls' school 'Writing and Arithmetic have been deemed of secondary importance compared with reading and sewing'. In 1814–15 376 children were in the school, 73 of them Anglicans, the remainder belonging to the various Dissenting bodies.[73]

In 1814–15 the General Committee of the National Society made enquiries from the dioceses about the number of National schools and about the obstacles in the path of setting them up. The York returns made in December 1815 produced replies from 199 places in the archdeaconry of York, from 81 in the archdeaconry of Cleveland and from 161 in the archdeaconry of the East Riding.[74] If the returns from the three archdeaconries are aggregated, the results are as follows

Places with no school, daily or otherwise	43
Places with National schools	31
Places with schools partly on the National plan	33

It was noted in 44 cases that obstacles had been experienced from the age or prejudices of the existing teacher and in 95 cases from want of funds. Information was also given about how schools were maintained. In the three archdeaconries 87 depended on endowments, 153 on subscriptions, and 33 were supported by Dissenters (this final figure covering the archdeaconry of York only). These figures for school endowments should be compared with those which can be derived from the Herring Returns.[75] The grand total of 273 schools must refer to the whole body of schools which had grown up over the previous century or more. In comparison with that number, the newly established National schools had had time to make only a small impact.

Notes Chapter 12

1. Quoted in Pinchbeck, I. and Hewitt, M. 1969 vol I: 309.

2. Binfield, C. and Hey, D. (eds) 1997: 243–4.

3. Allen, W.O.B. and McClure, E. 1898: 145.

4. Appended to his *Fable of the Bees* 2nd edn. 1723.

5. Quoted in Pinchbeck, I. and Hewitt, M. 1969 vol I: 292.

6. Simon, J. 1988: 113–29; Cowie, L.W. 1956: 96–7.

7. Webb, S. and B. 1927: 121; Langford, P. 1989: 133.

8. Workhouses 1732 Preface: viii–x.

9. Herring Returns I: 92 (St Mary in Beverley).

10. Workhouses 1732: 165–71; Jones, M.G. 1938/1964: 93.

11. *See also* page 226.

12. Workhouses 1732; 171–81.

13. For the foundation *see* pages 206–7.

14. *VCH Yorkshire* 1961 The City of York: 443 (Craig, M. 'Schools and Colleges').

15. BIY: Records of the Blue Coat School. Minutes of the monthly meeting of the Committee 1770–80, 1780–9. After 1789 there is a gap in the minutes until 1825.

16. Scrofula – a disease of the lymphatic glands.

17. The example is from the committee minutes of 4 February 1771. The master, Samuel Knowls of Bramham, was a weaver and flax-dresser.

18. For convenience sake her married name will always be used here.

19. *See* page 152.

20. Cappe, C. 1822. For a picture of the whole circle *see* Gray, Mrs Edwin (Almira) 1927.

21. This is Mrs Cappe's account in Gray, Mrs Edwin 1927: 54–9.

22. BIY: Minutes of the School Committee 5 May 1786.

23. Based on Mrs Cappe's account (Gray, Mrs Edwin 1927: 59–66).

24.   Cappe, C. 1800: 51.

25.   Cappe, C. 1805.

26.   Cappe, C. 1822: 341–4.

27.   *See* pages 171–2.

28.   WYAS: Leeds Charity School, 'PIETAS LEODIENSIS'. Sylvester, D.W.
      (ed.) 1970: 187–9 cites other orders for the master and mistress and for the
      children.

29.   WYAS: Leeds Charity School, Minutes and Accounts 1750–1810.

30.   SPCK: General Board Minutes vol 1 (1698–1706), 20 Sept 1705.

31.   SA: Boys' Charity School Account Book 1706–1821 (MD 2079). Most of
      the ensuing material about the school comes from this source.

32.   The very detailed building accounts survive (SA: MD 2079), together with a
      list of subscribers (MD 1103).

33.   Hunter, J. 1869: 322.

34.   *Boys' Charity School Sheffield* (pamphlet) 1905.

35.   SA: Account Book 1706–1821 (MD 2079) 7 Nov 1777.

36.   SA: Boys' Charity School Admission Books (MD 2081).

37.   SA: Admissions 1778–1809 (MD 2080).

38.   SA: Account Book (MD 2079).

39.   The following details come from SA: Admissions 1778–1809 (MD 2080).

40.   Boys' Charity School Sheffield, *Reports* 1788–1821.

41.   Goodwin, E. 1787.

42.   *See* Mercer, M. 1996: 32–42; Matthews, W.G. 1971–9: 280–85.

43.   Gibbon, A.M. 1947 App C: 144–7.

44.   Walker, J.W. 1966: 373–4.

45.   Guest, J. 1879: 417–23, 469–70; Mackenzie, M.H. 1971–9: 350–59.

46.   For Slaithwaite School *see* Morehouse, H.J. 1874; Hulbert, C.A. 1864.

47.   Venn, J. 1904: 77–96.

48.   Hulbert, C.A. 1864: 151.

49. Walsh, J. and Taylor, S. in Walsh, J., Haydon, C. and Taylor, S. (eds) 1993: 17–19.

50. Dobbs, A.E. 1919: 139–41.

51. Langford, P. 1989: 500.

52. *See* page 241 and Cappe, C. 1822: 118–22.

53. Porteus, B. 1786: 8. This paragraph is based on Porteus' *Letter*.

54. Goodwin, E. 1786; *see also* pages 247–8 for Goodwin.

55. Laqueur, T.W. 1976: 125–6; Lawson, J. and Silver, H. 1973: 235. For Mandeville *see* page 237.

56. Langford, P. 1989: 501.

57. 18 July 1784, quoted in Mathews, H.F. 1949: 37; *see also* Dodd, E.E. 1958: 100.

58. Guest, J. 1879: 406–7, 411.

59. Macmahon, K.A. (ed.) 1956: 66.

60. Sheffield, Cutlers' Company, Minutes 28 Nov 1794; for early Sheffield Sunday Schools *see* Mercer, M. 1996: 51–7.

61. Brontë, Charlotte, *Shirley*: ch XVII 'The School-Feast'.

62. Howard, J. 1887.

63. Mathews, H.F. 1949: 40.

64. *Ibid.*: 62.

65. Longden, H. 1865: 109.

66. Laqueur, T.W. 1976: 49.

67. Salt, J. 1964–9: 179–84.

68. Laqueur, T.W. 1976: 29.

69. *Ibid.*: 144.

70. Benson, E. 1932: 87, 91.

71. Macmahon, K.A. (ed.) 1956: 109, 110, 112, 132, 133.

72. Mercer, M. 1996: 68–70.

73. For the Halifax school *see* Unwin, R.W. and Stephens, W.B. (eds) 1976: 52.

74. National Society, *5th Annual Report*: 160–67. The York return is on page 167. I have in the figures cited excluded the archdeaconry of Nottingham. The original returns for the archdeaconry of York are in the Borthwick Institute. There are extracts in Unwin, R.W. and Stephens, W.B. (eds) 1976: 46–7.

75. *See* pages 219–20.

CHAPTER 13

Denominational Schools

All the schools which have been so far described, from the most prestigious grammar school to the smallest village school, were 'public' in the sense that they were open to all comers. Many of them depended on some form of endowment, though in almost all cases endowment income needed to be supplemented by fees if the master was to make a decent living. The final group of schools to be considered is that which by contrast may be called 'private' in the sense that these schools were limited to particular groups of people. Some of them catered for Dissenters or Roman Catholics, and were one expression of the religious divisions which had grown up since the Reformation. The majority were private ventures undertaken by a master or mistress. They appealed to a particular clientele, often to one particular class or social group. They were not, like the schools already described, established for the whole community. Since they had no endowments, they were generally short-lived. They depended entirely on the skills and talents of individual teachers, and, like any other business, they were highly vulnerable to economic conditions. Men and women grow old; fashions in schools, as in other things, change; the margin between success and failure was often very narrow. Yet many of these private venture schools prospered, and they fill an important place in the story of 18th century education, not least because of their large numbers and the varied types of provision which they offered.

The first group of 'private' schools (using that term in the sense here defined) were those run by Dissenters, who had been driven out of the Established Church by the legislation of the Clarendon Code in the 1660s. Though Dissenters were not allowed by statute law to teach school until 1779, and even then were subjected to considerable restrictions, they had in fact begun to set up their own schools in the Restoration period. Roman Catholics suffered under even greater disadvantages, and they did not receive statutory freedom to teach until 1790-91.[1] The most celebrated and the most interesting group of institutions founded by the Dissenters were the Dissenting Academies, though, since their primary purpose was to train men for the ministry of the churches, they lie largely outside the scope of this book. However they did provide a general education for many laymen in addition to their commitment to ministerial training.

One of the pioneers of the Academy movement was Richard Frankland, who opened his academy at Rathmell near Giggleswick in 1669-70 and was forced to move several times to keep out of the clutches of the law.[2] He returned to Rathmell in 1689 and died in 1698. It has been calculated that the total number of his students (ministerial and lay) was 304, which included 'the majority of the Nonconformist ministers of the North'.[3] One of his pupils was Timothy Jollie who conducted an academy at Attercliffe, Sheffield, from about 1690 until his death in 1714. His work was continued for some years by his successors in the pastorate of Upper Chapel, Sheffield. Jollie's teaching was criticized; for example, one of his students, the future archbishop, Thomas Secker, complained that only 'the old philosophy of the schools' was taught, and that he had forgotten much of his Latin and Greek while he was under Jollie's tuition.[4] One of the outstanding Dissenters of the century, Joseph Priestley, was born at Birstall in the West Riding and was probably educated at Batley Grammar School 1744-6,[5] though his teaching work was all done outside the county, for example at Warrington Academy in the 1760s.[6] Priestley was a Radical who became a Unitarian. A more orthodox tradition within Dissent was represented by later academies at Heckmondwike and Idle and at

Rotherham (from 1795), where the course included some natural philosophy supported by a collection of scientific instruments.[7]

The liberal tradition of Warrington was continued by the college at Manchester (1786–1803) which moved to York in 1803 in order to secure the services of Charles Wellbeloved as theological tutor. Manchester College remained at York until 1840. Wellbeloved, who succeeded Newcome Cappe, Catharine Cappe's husband, as minister of St Saviourgate chapel, played a prominent part in the life of the city and became an authority on the history of Roman York. The college divinity course lasted five years, the lay course three years. 235 students passed through between 1803 and 1840, about half of whom followed lay careers. They were to be found in professions like the law, medicine, engineering and journalism. Many of the leading Unitarian families like the Fieldens, the Ashtons and the Strutts sent their sons to York at a time when it was very difficult for them to obtain a university education, and it has been claimed that the college kept alive an ideal of social and educational progress which was in danger of being lost.[8]

Dissenters also played a part in establishing charity schools, interesting examples of such foundations being the Hollis schools at Sheffield and Rotherham.[9] Among the various bodies the Quakers were particularly active. The Epistle issued by the Yearly Meeting of 1695 instructed Friends to ensure

> that schools, and schoolmasters (and mistresses, 1691), who are faithful Friends, and well-qualified, be placed in all counties...and that such schoolmasters sometimes correspond with one another for their improvement in such good methods as are agreeable to the truth and the children's advantage and benefit: and that care be taken that poor Friends' children may freely partake of such education, in order to apprenticeship.[10]

There were several Friends' schools in Yorkshire in the 18th century, among them a school at Skipton kept for over 30 years by David Hall. In 1760 a special committee set up by the Meeting for Sufferings reported that there were 21 boarding schools throughout the whole country as well as many day schools. There were not enough of them and the staffs were poorly paid. Local aid, it was suggested, might be provided by the quarterly and monthly meetings.[11]

This report drew the attention of Friends to educational matters, but nothing more happened until the Yearly Meeting of 1777 moved that action be taken to provide boarding school education for the children of Friends 'not in affluent circumstances'. A group led by the physician Dr John Fothergill, which also included the banker David Barclay and the York merchant William Tuke, led a movement to purchase the buildings and estate vacated by the London Foundling Hospital at Ackworth (WR), and a boarding school for boys and girls was opened there in 1779.[12] In terms of numbers the school was an immediate success. In 1784 there were 326 boys and girls.[13] Since the school had been founded for poor children, the original curriculum was limited in scope. In the early years the boys were taught reading, spelling and English grammar, writing, arithmetic and accounts. The girls learned sewing, reading, knitting and spinning. At first they were taught writing and arithmetic by the masters, but later the women teachers took over this work themselves.[14] In the early 19th century grammar was taught from the book written by the American Friend Lindley Murray who had settled in York. His *Reader* also provided an introduction to English literature and to some of the classical legends. In 1825 it was arranged that Latin should be taught to 20 of the most advanced scholars (who were all boys).[15]

The foundation of Ackworth did not remove the need for other Quaker private schools. At York Esther Tuke started a girls' school in 1785 which lasted until 1814. It was for this school that Lindley Murray wrote his grammar, and this is probably the 'York School' described by Sarah Grubb. The house could accommodate about 30 girls. They were taught reading, writing, arithmetic, English grammar, history and geography. They learned needlework and knitting, but everything purely ornamental was discouraged.[16] In 1831 the York Quarterly Meeting founded a girls' school which was later to become the well known girls' public school, The Mount. A few years earlier the Quarterly Meeting had taken over responsibility for an existing boys' school, which was later to become Bootham. Bootham and The Mount offered a wider curriculum for a higher social class than Ackworth.[17]

The Moravian Church, revived in the early 18th century by Count Zinzendorf in Germany, set up its English headquarters in London in 1738. They soon established links with Yorkshire, and in 1743 Zinzendorf chose Fulneck near Pudsey in the West Riding as the location of their settlement. It was to be a centre for preaching, a place both of education and of refuge, and a training ground for candidates for the ministry. In the ensuing years a group of buildings were built on the Fulneck hillside.[18] In 1753 the boys' school, established in London in 1741, moved to Fulneck, followed two years later by the girls' school. Later (1768, 1775) day schools for both boys and girls were founded.[19]

In the early years the place was more like an asylum or an orphanage than a school of the normal type. The boys came very young, sometimes at the age of three, and they stayed for ten years without leaving and with very little contact with their parents. The food was very plain and the masters and the boys did all the domestic work. About the girls very little information has survived; they seem to have followed a curriculum very similar to that of the girls at Ackworth. Initially the boys learned only the 3Rs and some music, but the curriculum later expanded. Details have survived about the public examination of the boys held in 1795.[20] This covered, in addition to the basic subjects and the Church of England catechism, French (a dialogue on the utility of the French language), Latin (Corderius' dialogues, the historian Quintus Curtius and some Virgil), Greek (part of St Matthew's Gospel), geography, history, and 'Natural History' (another long dialogue on various scientific subjects). After 1782 boys from non-Moravian families were admitted, and the place became more like a normal school. The small children disappeared and the boys stayed longer. By 1818 there were more than 200 children in the two schools – 120 of them boys – though after 1820 there were troubles with discipline and numbers fell considerably.

Two of the other major denominations, the Wesleyan Methodists and the Congregationalists, opened schools for the sons of their ministers in Yorkshire in the early 19th century. The Methodists had maintained Kingswood near Bristol for this purpose since the days of John Wesley, but there was a need for a second such school, and Conference, meeting at Sheffield in 1811, decided to purchase Woodhouse Grove at Apperley Bridge near Bradford. The choice was strongly supported by Jabez Bunting, who was to become the leading figure in the connexion, and it was the largest financial undertaking which Conference had accepted up to that date. The school opened early in 1812 with 27 boys. The first headmaster, Joseph Fennell, was the uncle of Maria Branwell, and it was from the school that she married Patrick Brontë, so it has a place in the history of the Brontë family.[21] The Congregationalist school at Silcoates Hall near Wakefield developed out of a Dissenters' grammar school established in the same place in 1820. This school came to an end about 1830, and George Rawson of Leeds, who had been a member of its committee, led a movement to found a school for the sons of Independent ministers. Opened in 1831, the new school, named 'the Northern Congregational School' the following year, had 69 pupils in 1836.[22]

The years after 1689 were a period of stagnation and decline for the Roman Catholic community.[23] Many of the leading families conformed in the 18th century, and by 1800 only a few prominent landowners remained loyal to the faith.[24] Catholics themselves talked in pessimistic terms about the religious condition of their poor. In 1772 the Benedictine John Fisher spoke of a rural flock 'mean and indigent as to worldly substance, illiterate and ignorant as to Religion notwithstanding the pains taken by my predecessor...Such as I found them such I believe I shall leave them.'[25] There is evidence of schools in some places. In the North Riding there were schools at Brandsby (1722), Dalby (1724) and Scarborough (1735).[26] In the East Riding there was a mixed school kept in a private house at Burstwick in 1735, and later in the century the Constable family maintained schools at Everingham and Marton and the Langdales at Sancton.[27] The Franciscans ran a school in their house at Osmotherley (NR) from about 1700 to 1723, when it was moved to the Midlands. This school had been intended to supply vocations to the order, but in 1713–15 it was described as a preparatory school for lay boys before they went abroad to the Jesuits at St Omer or to the Benedictines at Douai. A similar preparatory school was started at Ugthorpe (NR) by the missioner the Rev. Monoux Hervey ('John Rivett') in about 1737. The school is mentioned in the Herring Returns, and in 1745 'Rivett' was said to have about ten pupils. The school was broken up when he was arrested and taken to York Castle in December 1745. He remained a prisoner there until June 1747.[28]

All these schools were short-lived and obscure. The only Roman Catholic school with a continuous history was the school of the Bar Convent in York, the origins of which have already been described.[29] During the 18th century the sisters of Mary Ward's Institute of the Blessed Virgin Mary lived together simply as a community of ladies. They dispensed with the externals of religious life. They did not adopt the religious habit until 1790, nor begin to keep enclosure to the house and grounds until the early 19th century. They received friends in the house and went out to return visits and to care for the poor. When a new novice made her vows, this was kept secret. But they managed to hold on. They had periods of difficulty with the authorities – for example in the 1690s and in 1748–51 when the reverend mother was cited to appear in the spiritual court, though the case was eventually withdrawn. The convent was referred to somewhat obliquely in the Herring Returns under the York parish of Holy Trinity Micklegate: 'there is a Boarding House call'd the Nunnery, wherein Girls are educated; at present there are about thirty. It is the same House Mass is performed in...'[30] As late as 1788, the centenary of the Glorious Revolution, there was a threat of an attack on the convent, though this was prevented by the activity of the lord mayor and other gentlemen of the city.[31]

The code of rules for the school, drawn up in their original form about 1690, direct that each nun should perfect herself in writing, casting accounts, orthography, and in reading English and Latin.[32] A draft statement prepared in about 1780 says that the girls were taught reading, writing, accounts, geography, French, needlework, music, drawing and dancing. There was a resident chaplain who instructed them in their religion.[33] In the 18th century there were no regular vacations, though there were days of recreation at Christmas and at other times. Numbers increased after the middle of the century; about 1820 there were about 80 children in the school.[34] The boarding school was not the only school run by the sisters. From about 1700 they ran a day school as well. The statement of 1780 already cited says that the day school for poor Catholics had its own mistresses 'separated from the School of the Young Ladies Pensioners, though under the same roof'. At the end of the century the day school taught the elementary subjects and plain needlework; there were about 20 pupils.[35]

The boarding school was attended by the daughters both of the Catholic gentry and of substantial tradesmen in the city. Some recorded parental occupations among the latter group include a merchant tailor, an upholsterer and undertaker, a haberdasher and leatherseller, and Thomas Kerrigan who built the first York theatre. The pupils of the day school did not all come from very poor families. Two of them, Anne and Elizabeth Bolland, were the sisters of Thomas Bolland who set up the Roman Catholic charity school in 1785–6, probably at the instigation of the priest of the chapel in Blake Street. Bolland was something of an entrepreneur since he also ran a printing, publishing and book-selling business, and sold tea and coffee. In 1819 there was a Roman Catholic school with about 40 scholars in Castlegate.[36] The major gap in what was offered to York's Roman Catholics was that there was no provision for the more advanced education of boys.

In 1777 a celebratory ode, written for the jubilee of Mother Anne Aspinal of the Bar Convent looked forward to a bright future.

Still spreading virtue's rich perfume,

This Garden of the North shall bloom,

And raise its plants to Heaven.[37]

In fact the closing years of the century did bring a new era for English Roman Catholics and their education. The Relief Acts of 1778 and 1791 improved their legal position. Before 1789 many English boys and girls had been sent for their education to English religious houses abroad. As the pace of revolution accelerated in France and the Low Countries in the early 1790s these communities found their position intolerable and returned to England, hoping to maintain there the conventual life and educational work which they had practised abroad ever since the days of the first Elizabeth. They settled at Ware, at Ushaw, at Stonyhurst, and one group, the Benedictines who had been at Dieulouard in Lorraine since 1608, came to Yorkshire.

The Dieulouard house had experienced increasing problems, first with the French anti-clerical legislation and then as a result of the outbreak of war with England.[38] In October 1793 the monks had to leave Dieulouard and they spent Christmas of that year at Acton Burnell in Shropshire, moving to other places until the chance came for a more permanent settlement. Fr Anselm Bolton, a member of the community at Dieulouard, had been chaplain to Lord Fairfax at Gilling Castle and had acquired Ampleforth Lodge, not far from Gilling East and some 20 miles north of York. In 1802 Fr Bolton handed over the Ampleforth Lodge property to the community who made it their permanent home. Boys came from other places at first, and the school developed quickly. At first its primary purpose had been to train boys for the religious life, but later the emphasis turned towards educating lay boys. In 1820 there were 45 pupils, and thus began what was eventually to become one of the leading English Roman Catholic public schools.

Notes Chapter 13

1. Watson, F. 1916: 82–3.
2. For Frankland *see also* page 65.
3. Matthews, A.G. 1934: 211; Ashley Smith, J.W. 1954: 17–21; McLachlan, H. 1931: 63–8.
4. Ashley Smith, J.W. 1954: 109–11; for Secker's comments *see* Adamson, J.W. 1922: 193.
5. Lester, D.N.R. (n.d.): 48–51.
6. See Turner, W. 1813–15/1957.
7. Beckwith, F. in Popham, F.S. (ed.) 1954: 88; Ashley Smith, J.W. 1954: 187–8; McLachlan, H. 1931: 201–8.
8. Wykes, D.L. 1991: 207–18; *see also* McLachlan, H. 1931: 262; Seed, J. 1982: 9–17.
9. Mercer, M. 1983: 68–81; Blazeby, W. 1906: 100–106.
10. Allott, W. in Popham, F.S. (ed.) 1954: 104.
11. Campbell Stewart, W.A. 1953: 47–8.
12. *Ibid.*: 48; Thompson, H. 1879: 26–36; for the Foundling Hospital *see* Scott, B. 1989: 155–72.
13. Thompson, H. 1879: 70.
14. *Ibid.*: 40; Grubb, S. 1837: 231.
15. Campbell Stewart, W.A. 1953: 112, 114; Thompson, H. 1879: 104, 173.
16. Grubb, S. 1837: 243–5.
17. Campbell Stewart, W.A. 1953: 65–6.
18. Hutton, J.E. 1895: 197.
19. For the following *see* Waugh, W.T. 1909; Lewis, A.J. in Popham, F.S. (ed.) 1954: 124–32; Hutton, R.B.M. 1953.
20. Hutton, R.B.M. 1953: 19–20.
21. Pritchard, F.C. 1949: 79–82; Towlson, C. W. in Popham, F.S. (ed.) 1954: 146.

22. Oakley, H.H. 1920: 4–7.

23. For Roman Catholic schools in the 17th century *see* page 62.

24. Roebuck, P. 1980: 57–8.

25. Quoted in Bossy, J. 1975: 275; *see also* Aveling, J.C.H. (Hugh) 1976: 299–300.

26. Kitching, C.J. 1959: 290.

27. Lawson, J. 1959: 18.

28. Herring Returns vol II: 157 (Hervey is referred to as 'John Rivett'); vol IV App A (Ollard, S.L. 'Roman Catholics'): 196, 209; Aveling J.C.H. (Hugh) 1966: 385.

29. *See* page 153.

30. Herring Returns III: 16.

31. This is all based on Coleridge, H.J. (ed.) 1887.

32. Kitching, C.J. 1959: 291–4.

33. Coleridge, H.J. (ed.) 1887: 224–5.

34. *Ibid.*: 292.

35. Kitching, C.J. 1959: 294–5.

36. This information about York tradespeople is taken from Aveling J.C.H. (Hugh) 1970, especially pages 145, 146–9, 355, 360, 367, 378, 379.

37. Coleridge, H.J. (ed.) 1887: 215.

38. The following is based on Mc Cann, J. and Cary-Elwes, C. (eds) 1952.

CHAPTER 14

Private Venture Schools

Much more numerous than the religious schools dealt with in the last chapter were the schools run by individuals for private profit which became steadily more important during the 18th century. These private venture schools attracted many boys who in an earlier generation would have been sent to the local grammar school. They also provided wider opportunities for the education of girls than had existed in earlier times. Many such private schools had already existed in the 17th century.[1] Sir John Reresby of Thrybergh, for instance, born in 1634, had a childhood much affected by the Civil War. His father died in 1646 after he had been taken prisoner by the Parliamentarians. John Reresby was educated at home by a tutor until he was nearly 15, and then his mother took him to London. He was sent for six months to a school in Whitefriars and then for two years to another in Enfield Chace 'where we were instructed in Latin, French, writing and dancing'. After this he went home for a few months and was then admitted to Gray's Inn.[2] When he became a parent himself, he was attracted to the London area for the schooling of his own sons. In September 1681 he recorded that he went to Newmarket, taking his two eldest sons with him, 'intending to put them to school in the South, finding they improved but little in the country'. Four years later the boys were transferred from one school at Kensington to another in the same place. Later they were sent to Eton.[3]

Such schools as those at Enfield Chace and Kensington increased in number during the 18th century. As the classical curriculum of the grammar schools became less attractive to many parents, there was a demand for more modern studies to meet the needs of a more utilitarian age – mathematics, modern languages, practical skills like surveying and navigation. Such subjects as these provided an appropriate training for boys who were to follow careers in the army and navy, in business and overseas commerce, and later in industry. Something of the prestige of the classics was lost as more and more works of scholarship appeared in English and in French. According to Daniel Defoe, 'you can be a gentleman of learning, and yet reading in English may do all you want'.[4]

Reformers like Joseph Priestley, writing in 1765, argued that school programmes should change as 'the course of reading, thinking and conversation' had changed.[5] He did not advocate the entire removal of Latin, but he emphasized the value of subjects like natural history, natural philosophy, history, law, French and mathematics. Even a grammar schoolmaster like John Clarke of Hull was critical of the intellectual fare offered in schools like his own. Moreover he feared that bad habits were acquired in 'public schools', and he thought that the best sort of education for a young gentleman was a private boarding school with about 20 or 30 boys.[6]

It would be wrong to think that such schools always offered a modern curriculum of the kind suggested by Priestley. Many of them concentrated on the classics, and many others tried to combine the old and the new in quantities varying according to the interests of the schoolmaster and the demands of his clientele. The great advantage offered by all these private schools was that their arrangements were flexible and could be adapted quite easily to whatever demands were made upon them. Finally J.H. Plumb has argued that during the 18th century a new attitude developed towards children. They were treated with more liberality and kindness. There were more toys for them to play with and books for them to read.[7] The private schools were able to adapt to these changes far more easily than the traditional grammar schools, and that fact may help to explain their growing popularity.

By the end of the century the larger towns had a number of schools offering a commercial education for future clerks and warehousemen.[8] At a higher level there were many boarding schools which generally seem to have charged £15/20 a year, though it is difficult to compute a total fee since different subjects were often charged separately, and there were often extras to inflate the bill. Some examples of school fees are given in the advertisements of the *Leeds Mercury* to be cited later.[9] In 1788 Mr Ephraim Sanderson of Aberford charged £12 to 15 guineas according to age. Latin was half a guinea a quarter extra.[10] About a decade after that Mr Simpson's Academy, Wodencroft Lodge, Greta Bridge, charged 16/17 guineas, according to age, for board and instruction 'in the English, Latin and Greek languages, writing, arithmetic, Merchants' Accounts and the most useful branches of the Mathematics'. French, taught by a native, was one guinea a year extra.[11] Mr Simpson explained in his advertisement that he was in London and could be met at the Saracen's Head in Snow Hill. The reader may perhaps be inclined to look ahead 40 years to Dickens' Yorkshire schools. Greta Bridge is in the right part of the county, and Mr Squeers was also to be contacted at the Saracen's Head in Snow Hill.[12]

The principal modern account of private schooling is contained in Nicolas Hans' book, *New Trends in Education in the Eighteenth Century* (1951). Hans names a number of schoolmasters in Yorkshire, though he does not distinguish very clearly between the masters of private and of grammar schools.[13] Most of those named in his list of classical schoolmasters who kept private schools and sent students to Oxford and Cambridge were clergymen who combined school-keeping with the care of a parish. One of them, Christopher Atkinson, vicar of Thorp Arch near Tadcaster (b. 1713), had as an assistant Joseph Milner, later the well-known head of Hull Grammar School.[14] Other parson-schoolmasters from different parts of the county were Robert Dent, vicar of North Otterington near Northallerton from

1732, Francis Haigh, curate of Midhope, who kept a school there in the 30s and 40s, Thomas Murgatroyd, curate of Kirkleatham 1727–32 and rector of Lofthouse-in-Cleveland 1732–80, and Charles Zouch, vicar of Sandal Magna near Wakefield 1719–54.

Information has survived about a number of mathematical teachers. Among them were Thomas Baxter, who published *The Circle Squared* in 1732 and who kept a school at Crathorne near Yarm (NR), and Robert Pulman, land-surveyor and writing-master, who kept schools at Leeds and at Halifax in the 1760s and 1770s.[15] The professions of land-surveying and school-keeping were also combined by the elder and the younger William Fairbank of Sheffield.[16] One of Pulman's assistants at Leeds was Henry Clarke (1743–1818) who later published *The Seaman's Desiderata*, containing new rules for finding both latitude and longitude, and who became professor of history, geography and natural philosophy at Sandhurst.[17] Another author whose mathematical text-books were widely used was William Emerson (1701–82) of Hurworth near Darlington on the Yorkshire-Co. Durham border, though he claimed that the teacher of mathematics received little encouragement. Emerson's books were particularly designed for the self-educated mechanic.[18]

Though information about private schools is scanty, something has survived about schools in the major centres. At York Joseph Randall, whose academy at Heath near Wakefield will be studied in more detail later,[19] opened a commercial school in the Thursday Market Hall in 1756. He retired from actively conducting the school in 1776, but continued to give private lessons in his own house. The subjects taught in Randall's school were 'Latin, Greek, French, the best English authors, Writing, Arithmetic, the Italian Method of Book-Keeping, the Terrestrial Globe considered as a Map of the World, with the Astronomical Parts of Geography.' Randall's assistant George Brown opened his own school in Spurriergate in 1776, and other schools at that time were taught by George Haigh in Micklegate, by Simon Raper in Precentor's Lane, and by the Rev. J. Parker in

Davygate.[20] There was a succession of French teachers in the city during the century, one of whom, M. Des Nesles, taught at the girls' school in the King's Manor.[21]

Newspaper advertisements are a valuable source of information about these schools because by this time the provincial press was becoming steadily more important. Newspaper publishing began in Leeds in 1718 and in York in 1719, and by the end of the century both towns had more than one paper.[22] A selection of advertisements in the *Leeds Mercury* around the year 1770 shows what was being offered at that time in Leeds and its neighbouring areas. Robert Pulman, whose academy has already been mentioned, advertised a curriculum with a strong mathematical emphasis.[23] The boys were taught English, Latin, French and most of the modern languages, penmanship, arithmetic, merchants' accounts, mensuration and gauging, Euclid's Geometry, algebra, mechanics, trigonometry, navigation, astronomy and geography. Board and lodging were £12 per annum, and the parts of the curriculum were charged separately.

All proper Regard will be paid to the Morals and Behaviour of the Pupils. Such as are modest and diffident will be treated with Tenderness and Indulgence; those who, by an honest ambition strive to excell in every Thing that is excellent and praise-worthy will be regarded with peculiar Marks of Favour and Esteem; and such as are rebellious, obstinate or incorrigible, must be removed from the Academy.

Mr Townshend, in his academy near the church in Doncaster, offered classics, modern languages and several branches of science. His charges were similar to Pulman's and to those of the other schools cited earlier. Board and lodging (including English, writing and arithmetic) were 14 guineas a year when a bed was shared with another boy. For a single bed the fee was 20 guineas. Like Pulman, Townshend stressed morality and comfort. 'He will treat his Pupils with

Tenderness, and be always ready to submit their Morals and Attainments to the Opinion of any Impartial Judge.'[24]

Mr J. Malham, at his country boarding school at Long Preston near Settle, set out a programme similar to Pulman's, but with an added grandiloquence designed to woo the prospective parent.[25] English was to be taught 'grammatically, after a Method most easy and familiar, whereby the Young Scholars may learn to write as true English as those who have attained a Classical Education'. Arithmetic 'both Vulgar and Decimal' would be 'digested into the most competent form to render that invaluable art worthy the Attention of all Mankind'. Algebra and fluxions included 'the Improvements of the present Age'. Mensuration and gauging appear again, and this time they include 'Geodesia', or 'the Theory and Practice of Surveying and Mapping Estates etc.' Trigonometry was to include 'many Properties of a Triangle never yet publickly known' and astronomy 'the Flamstedian Method of projecting a Solar Eclipse according to the Improvements of the Present Time'. Merchants accompts would qualify 'a Person for any public Business', while mechanics taught the 'Application of the Mechanic Powers, and many useful Problems in Natural Philosophy'. About morals and conduct Mr Malham is surprisingly brief: 'Due Regard paid to Morals and Religion'. He cites no fees for this pedagogical banquet. This kind of over-writing was to be common in private school prospectuses, and it would be interesting to know what the parents really got for their money!

A few among these advertisements relate to grammar schools. The master of Archbishop Holgate's grammar school at Hemsworth had reported at the time of the Herring visitation that there was no one qualified for classical instruction in the parish.[26] In March 1774 the Rev. Richard Garthwaite advertised that young gentlemen were 'genteely boarded' in the school and taught classics and English, writing and accounts, mensuration, surveying and the Italian method of book-keeping.

Mr Garthwaite, having been at a very great Expence in repairing and improving the School and School-house, has made it as complete a Spot as most; and for a fine air and healthy situation, it is inferior to none in the North.[27]

What Mr Garthwaite was attempting, and other grammar schoolmasters did the same, was to try to increase his income by grafting his own private school onto the old grammar school foundation.

The four masters already cited (Pulman, Townshend, Malham, Garthwaite) were all aiming at a fairly select sector of the market, but there were advertisements too for schools of a more modest kind. Messrs. Crookes and Bean, in their school in Briggate, Leeds, taught penmanship, arithmetic, the Italian method of book-keeping, merchants' and company accounts, geography, trigonometry and algebra with the usual applications to mensuration and land surveying. Astronomy and geography included the use of the globes, 'the Projection of the Analema, and others of the sphere, with many Branches too tedious to mention'. The pupils, in order to prepare themselves for real business, would be taught to draw bills on one another, and a master had been engaged to teach French. 'Also at proper seasons the boys will be taken out into the Fields, and other suitable Places, there to be taught the practical part of Land-Surveying, Timber-Measuring, Heights and Distances accessible and inaccessible, Gauging &c'. Since instruments for this kind of work were expensive, the boys would be taught to make 'such Instruments, at a trifling Expence, as will be sufficiently accurate for the Purpose'.[28]

Probably at a lower level again than Messrs. Crookes and Bean was the academy opened on 19 April 1773 'in Mr. Barker's yard, the end of Boar Lane, in Briggate, Leeds' by W. Squire from London, who described himself as 'Writing-Master, Accomptant, Teacher of the Mathematics', and author of several text-books.[29] 'Young gentlemen will be carefully and expeditiously instructed in every branch of genteel literature, necessary for Trade, the Merchant's Compting-House, the Public Offices, and the Sea'. In addition, the advertisement explains, 'Young

279

Ladies are taught in a separate Apartment, Writing, Arithmetic etc.' Perhaps that task was undertaken by Mrs Squire.

This selection of advertisements from around 1770 tells us something about the boys' private schools available in and around one commercial centre, Leeds. At Hull, another such centre, middle class private schools increased in number after the 1790s and offered serious competition to the town's grammar school.[30] Benjamin Snowden's Mercantile Academy in Blanket Row was thriving in 1790 and lasted for half a century. A classical academy, which endured for 25 years, was opened in 1800 by George Lee, minister of Bowlalley Lane Chapel. Schoolmastering was a common occupation of Dissenting ministers, as of the Anglican clergy.[31] In the early years of the 19th century Doncaster, with excellent communications along the Great North Road, was a centre for boarding schools. In 1812 there were 11 large boarding schools for boys and girls, as well as smaller ones. Some were kept by laymen, some by clergy. Among the former was Robert Graham who opened his first school in 1809, and 20 years later moved to Prospect House Academy on the edge of the town. The Rev. Peter Inchbald had six pupils in January 1803. By 1814, in much larger premises, he had 35 pupils, 'many from the most respectable families', some of whom went on to the English and Scottish universities. Finally, after many years teaching in the town, both masters met unsuccessful ends. Graham left Doncaster; Inchbald died after a spell in the Fleet Prison.[32] Private school teaching was always a perilous occupation, very susceptible to changing fashions and to fluctuating economic circumstances.

Joseph Randall's commercial academy in the Thursday Market Hall at York has already been mentioned. His earlier academy at Heath near Wakefield (1740–54), which failed financially, was a much more ambitious venture, and his account of it is the most complete description known to me of such a private boarding school. As such it makes an appropriate conclusion to this survey of boys' schools, though the reader may wonder, as he reads it, how much of what Randall was describing was aspiration and how much fact.[33] According to the *Account* the teaching accommodation at Heath consisted of three rooms in which classics were taught, a large school for mathematics and studies preparing for business, a building for music, dancing and fencing where the pupils also dined together, a large library room containing 1,500 volumes, and apparatus for experiments in astronomy and natural philosophy, which included an orrery.[34] There was accommodation for 170 boys, including 30 out-boarders in the village. In general, the boarders slept two in a bed, though there were a few private rooms for those who were prepared to pay extra for them.

There was a staff of ten masters and assistants. The teaching hours were from 7 a.m. to 5 p.m., Wednesday and Saturday afternoons excepted when there were lectures and experiments in astronomy and natural philosophy. The pupils, whose ages ranged 'from Man's Estate to eight years of age' were allowed time for walks and 'manly diversions', and every evening there was reading time under a master. The boys were required to give an account in writing, or for the younger pupils by telling a story, of what they had read. Wednesday mornings were set aside for discipline, complaints and public declamations. The power of the rod was preserved, but it was to be used sparingly.

Emphasis was placed in the school course on English language and history as foundation subjects. In Latin the boys learned the prose writers before the poets, and they began Greek after they had studied Ovid and Virgil. Abler boys who were intended for business could learn Latin and Greek, and still find time for other studies, though the particular course followed should be adapted to boys' individual abilities, and they should not be forced into Latin if they had no ability for it. The boarding fee was ten guineas per annum, about the normal figure for schools of this kind at that time. Four basic courses were offered, for which separate fees were charged. The University course included Latin, Greek and French, as well as mathematics and natural philosophy. The Business course included Latin and French, together with book-keeping, mensuration and surveying. The Army and Navy course covered French and the classics, together with geometry, trigonometry and navigation, fortification and gunnery. The fourth course – for a Gentleman – was presumably meant to offer a general education. It took in classics and French, some science, ethics, logic and metaphysics. In the same year as his *Account* appeared, Randall published his lectures to his pupils in geography, astronomy, chronology and pneumatics (the study of the air and atmosphere). Unless the air were preserved in its present condition, he wrote, mankind would immediately perish: 'and this cannot fail to engage our grateful acknowledgement to the Divine Being, for such express marks of Care and Goodness to his needy creatures'.[35]

With this conclusion very typical of its time we must leave Joseph Randall. Elaborate programmes of studies such as these need always to be taken with a pinch of salt. They were after all advertisements written in order to attract pupils. But at least they do tell us something, both about the aims of a private school of that time and about the methods used to achieve those aims. Randall's ideas should be compared with those of John Clarke of Hull which have already been explained.[36] Though there were many differences between these masters of a grammar school and of a private academy, there are resemblances too. Both were anxious that boys should not be forced to learn subjects for which they had no aptitude. Both were opposed to over-severe discipline. Both were interested in subjects like chronology and geography. Both were concerned about the moral lessons of education. Perhaps Randall was the more effective schoolmaster of the two because, although the academy at Heath failed, he went on to run a successful school at York.

There was much discussion throughout the century about the education of girls. The charity schools educated girls as well as boys, and boarding schools, which went back to the 17th century, grew in number.[37] Yet the assessments made by contemporaries were curiously mixed. There was a sense that women's education had advanced. Johnson spoke of 'the amazing progress made in late years in literature by the women'. He remembered 'when a woman who could spell a common letter was regarded as all accomplished, but now they vie with the men in everything'.[38] On the other hand there was widespread criticism, and there was no consensus about the objectives to be attained. Girls were generally taught religious knowledge, some English and some French, together with needlework and domestic skills. Opinions were divided about whether they should learn Latin. Much time – an excessive amount in the view of the critics – was devoted to accomplishments like drawing, music and dancing.

Writers like Hannah More at the end of the century thought that much of what was offered was too superficial, and that girls needed to develop real intellectual interests and to think for themselves.[39] At the other extreme from Hannah More's position there were those who thought that too much was being attempted already. Girls' schools were criticized for endangering the fabric of society by offering to girls from modest backgrounds an education which was appropriate only for their superiors in rank.[40] There was a fear too that women might demand as rights what had been ceded to them as privileges. James Fordyce, in his *Sermons to Young Women* (1765) denounced

> the dangers of boarding-school education, the folly of extravagant dress, the damage done by novel-reading and play-going. Primacy was accorded to domestic economics, scriptural support being cited for the moral value of needlework.[41]

No doubt these matters were debated at many Yorkshire firesides, but they do not appear in the record. Information – rather scanty in the present state of knowledge – has to be put together piece by piece about what was available to girls in the county. One early example of a girls' school was that kept in the King's Manor at York from the end of the 17th century. There Mrs Lumley (1693–1703) taught 'all sorts of work in their Perfection, in the pattern of the London schools'.[42] Ralph Thoresby the Leeds antiquary recorded in his diary (17 July 1710) that he had taken his daughter to 'Mr Lumley's, at the Manor House', and then the following day: 'Walked to the Manor to see my poor daughter, and discourse Mr. Lumley;

looked at a variety of ingenious books; pitched upon some needlework embroidery, and some cross-stitch worsted for chairs'.[43]

The Manor House school had a long life. An author of 1818 referred to a 'well-known and highly respectable Boarding School for young ladies' which had been carried on 'for several successive generations by the ancestors of Mr. and Miss Tate, the present occupiers', and had been 'long patronized by some of the principal families in York and in its opulent and extensive county'.[44] Hans refers to a school in the Manor House kept by Mrs Forster (?1760–85). She was said to be 'incapable of proper superintendence' and nothing was to be learned at the school.[45] Perhaps Mrs Forster was an ancestor of the Tates of 1818.

Apart from the school in the King's Manor and the Bar Convent which has already been described, there are other references to schools in York during the century. Catharine Cappe the philanthropist, born in 1744, was sent in her 13th year to a boarding school in York. She does not name it, though she says that a great deal of emphasis was placed on appearance and on the possession of money. Later she was taught dancing, arithmetic and French, though she says the French teacher gave her no help with the grammar of the language. Since these lessons are mentioned separately from the account of the boarding school, it is possible that she was, after she had left the school, boarded with a family and taught by individual masters.[46] In the 1770s there are references to a 'French' boarding school, the principal subjects of study being music, dancing and French, kept by Ann Hill (d. 1776) and to Mr and Mrs Thienot's French and Italian boarding school for young ladies at Monk Bar.[47] Until 1791 a small boarding school for girls was run by Mrs Silburn, who may have been the Catholic widow of a wine-cooper.[48] This evidence about York schools is fragmentary, but it does suggest a continuous record of activity in girls' education throughout the century.

At Leeds the selection of advertisements of the *Leeds Mercury* around 1770, which has already been used for boys' schools, also provides some useful information about girls' schools as well. This second group of advertisements shares some things in common. There is a general stress on personal comfort and on the careful supervision of morals. Among the subjects taught much stress is laid on needlework, and much of the teaching is to be provided by visiting masters. Mrs Dawson, whose boarding school was in Boar Lane, Leeds, advertised on several occasions.[49] Her pupils were 'genteely boarded' and instructed in all kinds of needlework. They were taught English and French, writing, arithmetic, modern geography and the use of the globes 'by Mr Pulman and his assistants' – presumably the Robert Pulman whose boys' school has already been mentioned.[50]

> Mrs. Dawson takes this opportunity to return her sincere Thanks to those Gentlemen and Ladies, who have been pleased to favour her with the Care of their Children; and begs them and the Public to be assured, that due Regard will be paid to the Health, Morals and Behaviour of all such Young Ladies as may be intrusted to her Care.

'Able Masters' were employed to teach drawing, music and dancing. In June 1774 Mrs Dawson announced that her school would be opened on the 13th of the month and that Mr Hadwin had been engaged as dancing master. He would teach on Mondays, Tuesdays and Wednesdays in every week 'till his Ball'.

There were other advertisements for girls' schools over a wide area of the West Riding. Mrs Moorhouse at Skipton explained that she proposed to open her school at the end of June 1774, thanked her friends for their past favours, and hoped to earn their further approbation 'by an unwearied Attention to the Morals and Improvement of the Young Ladies committed to her care...' 'Reading, Writing, Dancing, Music &c taught by the usual Masters'.[51] A year earlier than this Miss Watson had announced that she proposed to open a boarding school at Pindar-Oaks near Barnsley.[52] The young ladies were to be taught needlework, and 'every branch of useful Knowledge'. The subjects offered – much the same as those already mentioned – would be taught by assistants from the academy at Barnsley. There would also be a master to teach music. At Northowram near Halifax the Misses Hesketh informed their readers that they proposed to carry on their boarding school in the same manner as when their father, the Rev. Mr Hesketh, had been living.[53] Their advertisement does not mention any visiting masters. Since the academic curriculum offered was restricted in scope – only writing, arithmetic and reading English grammatically – perhaps the sisters could teach it themselves. But needlework was covered in great detail: 'Plain Work, Dresden, Tambour, Tent and Cross Stitch &c'.

> The House and School are large and commodious, the Air good and healthful, the situation agreeable, and well suited for the same purpose.

No doubt the Misses Hesketh looked after their pupils well, but they probably did not teach them very much. The girls' schools mentioned here seem to have been boarding establishments. There is nothing in this group of advertisements similar to the more modest boys' day schools which educated clerks and warehousemen.

Around 1800 the information about girls' schools becomes more abundant. At Hull there were four such schools in the 1790s, and in 1810 a Roman Catholic school for young ladies was opened.[54] At Doncaster five boarding schools opened between 1795 and 1805. One of them, kept by the Misses Baker, educated the daughters of the Marquis of Tweeddale. Elizabeth Armstrong, who had been a teacher at Esther Tuke's school at York, educated the children of some well-known Quaker families. She was described as a capital teacher for an English education. Several schools were kept by women whose husbands were also teachers, like Mrs Ann Haugh whose husband was an artist and drawing master. She started her school in 1797 and ran it into the 1840s. She published an outline of ancient history for her pupils called *A Few Slight Sketches of History etc. Intended as Hints for Future Study.*[55]

One headmistress who is remembered for a popular school book is Richmal Mangnall whose *Historical and Miscellaneous Questions for the use of young people* went through many editions after its first anonymous publication in 1798.[56] Miss Mangnall was born in 1769 and died in 1820. She went to Crofton Old Hall near Wakefield as a pupil, became an assistant there, and finally headmistress in about 1808 when there were some 70 girls in the school. The *Questions* may have been a response to the demands of her own teaching. One of her pupils, Elizabeth Firth, left a journal for the years 1812–13, which gives a unique picture of the life in a girls' boarding school of that time.[57] Elizabeth was 16 when she left Crofton, though the diary reads like the work of a much younger person. 'My governess' (Miss Mangnall) is an active presence in the life of 'the ladies'. They were regularly 'looked over' (perhaps an inspection of their dress). 'My governess' showed them 'a beautiful Bible of hers with Ripon Minster on the edge'. In March 1813 she read Walter Scott's *Rokeby* to them; it had been published only a few months earlier. She 'called out' to a man who came to rob the pigeon house. She gave Elizabeth an inkstand and Miss Lockwood a silver knife 'for answering well at geography'.

Geography, together with history and 'dictionary' (perhaps some method of learning words and definitions) loomed large in Elizabeth's entries about her school work. In May 1813 she recorded 'a brain-day in Geography. I had 7 mistakes which was the least of anyone'. The girls had their pleasures too. There were whole holidays – with apples or 'preserves to supper'. On another day, when they lay in in the morning and had preserves to supper, 'I was sick'. They had a concert, attended by 30 to 40 ladies and gentlemen: 'The schoolroom was lighted up with 68 candles. I played a trio and a glee'. In September 1812 they danced 'hands forty in honour of a great victory in Spain'. Sometimes they misbehaved; they wrote on the desks and two girls had a fight. Many punishments are recorded. Several girls were whipped. Others 'had the cap on', or were 'sent to Coventry', which seems to have been an official punishment. 'Ippertinence' (sic) was a frequent source of trouble. Girls were sent to bed for spelling mistakes or punished because they had not learned their catechism. One 'lady' had 'her dirty clothes pinned to her back for having them under her bed'. There were tasks and impositions too. Elizabeth got verses 'for throwing a blackboard down', and for a 'slop at breakfast'. In November 1812 she had ten 'words of dictionary' for 'poking' (not walking erect), a punishment shared on that day by a number of other girls. Miss Mangnall's regime was severe, but Elizabeth does not sound unhappy.

A final picture of girls' schools in the county can be taken from Edward Baines's *History, Directory and Gazetteer of the County of York*, which was published in 1822/3.[58] The entries for all the larger towns list the schools and academies, though many of these are likely to have been no more than common day schools. But girls' boarding schools are generally noted, and others are described as 'ladies' school' or 'ladies' day school', which presumably means that they served the middle class clientele which is being discussed here. The numbers of boarding and superior day schools in a selection of towns throughout the county are as follows:

West Riding	Leeds	8
	Bradford	6
	Wakefield	6
	Ripon	2
East Riding	Hull	7
	Beverley	6
North Riding	Scarborough	3
	Richmond	3
	Northallerton	3

It would be a mistake to put too much weight on these figures. They tell us nothing about the numbers of pupils in the schools, nor do they provide any precise information about the standard of the work. But they do make it clear that by about 1820, which is the approximate end of this study, girls' boarding schools and superior day schools were numerous in all parts of the county. That marked a considerable advance over the position a century earlier.

Notes Chapter 14

1. *See* pages 150–51.
2. Reresby, Sir J. 1936: 2–3.
3. *Ibid.*: 230, 363, 428.
4. Quoted in Pinchbeck, I. and Hewitt, M. 1969 vol I: 283.
5. *An Essay on a course of liberal education for civil and active life* (1765), quoted in Tompson, R.S. 1971a: 48.
6. *See* pages 189–90 for John Clarke's ideas.
7. Plumb, J.H. 1975: 64–95.
8. For the position in Sheffield *see* Mercer, M. 1996: 79–80.
9. *See* page 277.
10. Sylvester, D.W. (ed.) 1970: 252–3 (from the *Leeds Intelligencer*, 1 January 1788).
11. Bayne-Powell, R. 1939: 85–6; *see also* estimates of the cost of schooling given in novels of the time (Langford, P. 1989: 86–7).
12. Dickens, Charles *Nicholas Nickleby* ch III.
13. For a criticism of Hans' book *see* Simon, J. 1979: 179–91.
14. For the list of classical schoolmasters *see* Hans, N. 1951 App 1. For Joseph Milner *see* pages 191–2.
15. Hans, N. 1951: 95, 112; Taylor, E.G.R. 1966: 270. For Pulman *see also* page 277.
16. The younger William Fairbank died in 1801; *see* Hall, T.W. 1932: 5–8 and 1937: 209–15.
17. Taylor, E.G.R. 1966: 257–8.
18. *Ibid.*: 157.
19. *See* pages 280–82.
20. Knight, C.B. 1944: 531, 537; Benson, E. 1932: 50–57.
21. Aveling, J.C.H. (Hugh) 1970: 139, 146.

22. Looney, J. Jefferson in Beier, A.L., Cannadine, D. and Rosenheim, J. (eds) 1989: 487.

23. *LM* 16 Jan 1770; this is reproduced in Sylvester, D.W. (ed.) 1970: 250–51.

24. *LM* 14 March 1769.

25. *LM* 24 Jan 1769.

26. *See* page 223 for the entry in the Herring Returns.

27. *LM* 29 Nov 1774.

28. *LM* 2 Jan 1770. 'Analemma' – a projection of the sphere made on the plane of the meridian or a gnomon or astrolabe having the projection on a plate of wood or brass (OED).

29. *LM* 20 April 1773.

30. Lawson, J. 1963: 188.

31. *VCH Yorkshire* 1969 East Riding vol I: 350.

32. For schools in Doncaster *see* Harrison, J.A. 1958, 1960.

33. Randall, J. 1750a. For Joseph Randall *see also* Tompson, R.S. 1971a: 39–40. Hans, N. 1951 calls him John Randall (pages 94–5). Randall's colleague, George Gargrave, wrote (5 Dec 1754) after the failure of the academy: 'Mr Randall is broke, fled, and left all his poor Masters to shift for themselves' (quoted in Unwin, R.W. and Stephens, W.B. (eds) 1976: 26.

34. 'Orrery' – a piece of mechanism devised to represent the motion of the planets about the sun by means of clockwork (OED).

35. Randall J. 1750b: 123–4.

36. For John Clarke *see* pages 189–90.

37. On the 16th and 17th centuries *see* Charlton, K. 1981: 3–18.

38. Quoted in Rogers, K.M. 1982: 28.

39. *Ibid.*: 29, 209–10.

40. Miller, P.J. 1972: 302–14; McDermid, J. 1989: 309–22.

41. Quoted in Langford, P. 1989: 606.

42. Gardiner, D. 1929: 341 n 2.

43. Thoresby, R. 1830: 61–2.

44. Knight, C.B. 1944: 531.

45. Hans, N. 1951: 196.

46. Cappe, C. 1822: 45–51.

47. Knight, C.B. 1944: 557; Benson, E. 1932: 50–57.

48. Aveling, J.C.H. (Hugh) 1970: 147.

49. *LM* 21 March, 11 April 1769, 7 June 1774.

50. For Robert Pulman *see* page 277.

51. *LM* 31 May, 7 June 1774.

52. *LM* 30 March 1773.

53. *LM* 15 Feb 1774.

54. *VCH Yorkshire* 1969 East Riding vol I: 350–51.

55. Harrison, J.A. 1960: 51–5.

56. *See* Roach, J. 1986b. References are included there.

57. This account of Elizabeth Firth's journal is in *ibid.*: 157.

58. I have used the 1969 reprint (2 vols).

CHAPTER 15

Conclusion

The history of some individuals at different levels of society throws a more individual spotlight on the general story of education in 18th century Yorkshire. The aristocracy and the richer gentry and merchants tended, as time went on, to send their sons to the 'great schools' outside the county like Eton and Westminster. The Hothams of Scorborough and South Dalton in the East Riding had, in the 17th century, educated their boys at home and at Sedbergh. Sir Charles Hotham (1735–67), who succeeded to the baronetcy at the age of two, was sent to Westminster and then on a grand tour which took him to France, Switzerland, Italy, Russia, Denmark, Sweden, Prussia and most of the German states.[1] Such grand tours, planned and organized on whatever scale the family means allowed, were regarded as the final stage in the education of a young man of family.[2] Some of the richer merchants also sent their sons to schools outside the county. William Milner of Leeds, who died in 1740, had himself been educated locally. He sent his son, the first baronet, to Eton, Cambridge and the Middle Temple. The son, after the father's death, settled permanently on his country estate, leaving the family business to a cousin.[3]

Modern studies of the mercantile communities in both Leeds and Hull show that merchants' sons were still usually sent to the town's grammar school, though private schools were patronized as well.[4] At Leeds the grammar school lost prestige at the end of the century,[5] and boys were sometimes sent to neighbouring grammar schools at Bradford and Wakefield. At the beginning of the 19th century Benjamin Gott (1762–1840), the pioneer factory owner, who had himself been educated at Bingley Grammar School, sent his sons, Benjamin and John, to James Tate at Richmond for two years, then to a private school at Dumfries, and finally to attend lectures for two sessions at Edinburgh University.[6] At Hull George Pryme, born in 1781, was a day-boy at an academy in Nottingham, then a private pupil with the vicar of Bunny (Notts.), and then he went aged 14 to Joseph Milner at Hull Grammar School. Pryme greatly admired Milner, and he remained at the school until Milner died in 1797. He then read at home for two years with occasional help from the vicar of Sculcoates, and, after passing the summer of 1799 with the famous mathematical coach John Dawson at Sedbergh, he entered Trinity College, Cambridge the same year.[7] Pryme became a fellow of Trinity and ultimately professor of political economy in the university. He was one of the many men from mercantile backgrounds in towns like Hull and Leeds who went into the professions, especially into the church.

Several diaries and autobiographies written by tradesmen and professional men have survived which show an interest in schools and schooling. The education of James Fretwell, born at Thorpe-in-Balne near Doncaster in 1699, has already been studied.[8] In adult life he lived in Pontefract. He looked after and taught three of his nephews. One of them, James, was with him for nearly four years, but, Fretwell wrote (13 May 1756)

> tho' I took great pains in teaching him, he did not improve so fast (as) I could have wished; and I was in hopes that he would have improved more in a school amongst other boys, so his father put him to one Mr. Bowzer, a very good school-master in Doncaster. But alas! he made but small proficiency under him. I had brought (him) to read in his bible, and he never got any further.[9]

Fretwell was also a benefactor to the school at Thorpe, his birthplace, the first stone of which was laid on 14 August 1749. He contributed towards purchasing an annuity for the school, having earlier given money for teaching children to read, 'but (he writes) the parents took 'em away before they could read'. In his will (1751) he left an annuity for a sermon, for buying bibles for two poor children who could read, and for teaching others who could not.

> And as it was from a principle of Christian love that I have made this small provision for the benefit of my poor Christian brethren, so I desire and hope that my trustees and their successors will, from the said benevolent principles, see that it may be employed to the uses designed by me: and for their encouragement in so doing, they have the best assurance of being requited by Him from whom every man shall receive his own reward, according to his own labour: and I pray God to give a blessing to this small beginning, and to raise up benefactors to this poor village, who are of abilities and dispositions to do more than is in my power to do for it.[10]

A similar interest in a village school is recorded in the journal (1754–6) of Ralph Ward, a cattledealer and money-lender in the Guisborough area of the North Riding. At the end of the year the entries and departures of the children are noted along with Ward's other business – 'Dec.3 1754 Ralph Jackson went away but intended to lie at Yarm the night, the School Dame came when was entered 8 children into the Charity School and others their time was expired. Ralph Jackson did not go away till next morning.'[11]

Another kind of intellectual activity can be traced in the diary of the Presbyterian apothecary Arthur Jessop (1682–1751) of New Mill near Huddersfield, who wrote a good deal, during the 1730s and 1740s, about the book-club which he had helped to found. In 1741 there were 21 members, each of whom paid 3/- for the books which they had obtained from John Swale, a book-seller in Leeds. Eventually the books were sold to the members. Jessop puts down the admission of new members, the fines levied for being absent from meetings, and for swearing! Perhaps that last forfeit is linked with the fact that the club seems to have had a strong social side. The books which Jessop mentioned were, however, serious fare – Tacitus' *Annals*, Tillotson's *Sermons*, Pope's edition of Homer, the life of Lady Betty Hastings by Thomas Barnard, Burnet's *History* (either of the Reformation or of his own time), a History of the Conquest of Mexico, and works now forgotten like 'An Enquiry into the Natural Rights of Mankind to debate freely concerning Religion, by a Gentleman of Lincoln's Inn' (1737). Perhaps the last has some links with Jessop's Presbyterian opinions. Some of the members paid 1/- for the 'magazine' (4 April 1745), which may have been either *The Gentleman's Magazine* or *The London Magazine,*[12] so there was clearly an interest among the group in the contemporary scene.

Later in the century Methodist and Evangelical influences had a strong effect on family life and on the upbringing of children. Sometimes the discipline was severe. The Sheffield Methodist Henry Longden (1754–1812) wrote in his memoir that, because his own parents had spoiled him, he had set to work to extirpate stubbornness in his own children and to teach them instant obedience. To ensure regular habits of discipline, 'he met his family stately once a week in the form of a class meeting'. Because he wished to avoid the errors of over-leniency, 'he ran, perhaps, at first into the opposite extreme, viz. too frequent and severe correction', though as the children grew older, he adopted gentler methods, 'labouring to render the path of duty pleasant and easy'.[13] Somehow the picture is not an attractive one, however excellent Longden's intentions may have been.

A happier environment is suggested in the account of the family life of the York attorney William Gray (1751–1845) and his wife Faith Hopwood (1751–1826).[14] As we have seen, the Grays were closely involved with the philanthropic circle to which Catharine Cappe belonged, and they were active in all kinds of good works in the city of York. They also had connections with the highest Evangelical circles. William Gray was a friend of William Wilberforce, and he and his wife visited both Mrs Trimmer and Hannah More and her sisters. Faith Gray's diary tells us something about the education of their children and grand-children. Their daughter Lucy had a strong desire for self-improvement and was sent at the age of

16 to Mrs Wyatt's school at Bellefield near Birmingham where she was taught French, Drawing, Music and Ornamental Work. Lucy died young in 1813.[15] Their son Edmund was sent to the Rev. Mr Fawcett at Stanwix near Carlisle. He was then apprenticed to a land-agent near Leeds, but eventually in 1814 went back to Mr Fawcett to be prepared to enter the ministry.[16] It was common at that time for clergymen to train young men for ordination in this way.

William and Faith's son, Jonathan (1779–1837) was also an attorney and continued in the same religious tradition as his parents. Jonathan's son, William, aged about four, was sent to school with Mrs Richardson, a protégée of Mrs Cappe's, who had been educated at the Grey Coat School and had then become a domestic servant. Presumably Mrs Richardson's was a dame school. Later William went to school with the Rev. James Simpson at Brantingham near South Cave in the East Riding.[17] William's sister, Margaret, born in 1808, died at the age of 18. Her 'plan for the employment of time', drawn up for the winter of 1825–6, has survived. On each week-day she gave herself a full programme. She read the Psalms regularly, on Wednesday evenings she went to church, and on Saturday mornings she collected for the Church Missionary Society. She practised music for at least one hour a day and singing for about half-an-hour. On most days she took a walk. She studied French, Italian and drawing. She read books like Watts' *Improvement*, Jowett's *Researches in Syria*, and Thomas à Kempis in French. For ornamental reading, she remarked, 'one has always both time and inclination'. In addition to all this, she had prescribed hours for meditation and devotion.[18] It was an intense régime for an adolescent girl, but typical of the more severe members of the circle in which she grew up. There is no information about her school or whether she went to school at all. Where the schools of the Gray boys are mentioned, these are private establishments, probably kept by people who shared the religious sympathies of the family. The Evangelical experience was a somewhat enclosed one.

This brief survey of personal interests and family life has provided some glimpses of the aristocracy, the town merchants, the rural middle class and the

Evangelicals, and has taken the story in time up to about 1820 at which point this study concludes. It does not end with any revolutionary event which provides an obvious finale, but, in a broader, more evolutionary sense, the years 1815–20 do mark the watershed to a new era. After about 1815, as the country moved slowly into an age of reform, the emphasis changed towards a much firmer central direction in which opinion was more and more formed at the centre and mediated down to the localities. The enquiry into Pocklington School by the Select Committee of 1818 heralded the move towards regulating educational endowments which reached its climax in the Taunton Commission of 1864–8 and the Endowed Schools Act of 1869. The foundation of the National and British Societies began the national promotion and regulation of elementary education which was eventually to lead to the Forster Act of 1870 and the creation of a national system. The new societies exerted much more power than SPCK had ever possessed, and controls over the local school were to grow closer and closer as time went on. Finally, as political Radicalism developed, education was seen by many people as an important element in a national reforming programme of social and political change, a major issue in the debate of a more democratic age. As all these changes took place, regional autonomy was to break down more and more,

The major themes which have been studied over the three centuries after 1500 include the effects of the Reformation, the growth of the grammar schools, the attempts of both church and state to regulate schools and schoolmasters, the dissemination of elementary schooling, and the development of private schools for both boys and girls. The question remains whether, in attempting such a survey of Yorkshire, a case has been successfully made out for a regional approach to the history of education as suggested at the beginning of the book. Does such a regional study show that there were distinctive features about the area, and how great were the contrasts between this and other regions? One difficulty about this approach is that there are not many comparable studies which can be used to answer these questions. One such recent book, Nicholas Orme's valuable work on education in the west of England 1066–1548,[19] only overlaps with the early part of *Yorkshire Schools*. Though Orme concentrated on the secular schools, he provided a great deal of information about the religious houses and friaries, including their contribution to higher education, about which very little has been said here. There are also other works to supply useful comparisons, particularly Joan Simon's research on Leicestershire, and use will be made of these later.

All through the three centuries from 1500 to 1800 national standards and pressures were important, particularly in the post-Reformation and early Stuart period when control over the schools was seen as an important part of exerting a national discipline in church and state. Yet it is always misleading to look at the story entirely or primarily from the point of view of London and Westminster. The episcopal licensing of schoolmasters was an important plank of national policy, yet, as we have seen, it was only partially effective in the dioceses. The history of elementary education in the early 18th century has largely been told in terms of the activities of SPCK, yet it is clear that what happened in the large charity schools of the capital was often quite different from what happened in the counties, especially those which were a long way from London.

Yorkshire is the largest of English counties, and there were considerable differences between the Ridings or indeed within the Ridings themselves. In the West Riding the industrial regions were always very different from the remote districts of Craven and Garsdale. Hull and Holderness in the east were very different from Swaledale and Wensleydale in the north. Yet there was always a real sense of continuity within diversity. Tudor Yorkshire was a disorderly place a long way from London, and that common sense of remoteness was something which endured right down to the 19th century. York was in a sense the capital of the north of England. Until the Civil War it was the seat of the Council of the North. It remained the ecclesiastical capital of the northern province and the diocesan centre round which the church life of the greater part of the county revolved. In the 16th and 17th centuries Roman Catholicism, the old faith, was strong in some districts, and although fractured and interrupted, a tradition of Catholic schools and schooling did survive in the county, its most remarkable example being the schools of the Bar Convent at York with a continuous history dating from 1676. It would be interesting to compare the Yorkshire story with that of even more strongly Catholic Lancashire. If the Roman Catholic tradition was one landmark of Yorkshire particularity, it was soon to be joined by Puritanism which was strong in the industrial districts of the West Riding and in the East Riding. Yorkshire was the home of one of the first of the Dissenting Academies taught by Richard Frankland. Within its bounds the Quakers established Ackworth and the Moravians Fulneck, while the county was a strong centre of Methodism. It had a Nonconformist as well as a Roman Catholic tradition of education, and Nonconformity gained greatly in strength as the 19th century went on.

A great deal of educational history, particularly of the Tudor and Stuart era, had always been written in terms of individual founders, successors on a narrower stage of William of Wykeham and King Henry VI. W.K. Jordan wrote much of his history of charities in terms of benevolent individuals, London merchants giving their wealth to the towns and villages where they had been born. Yorkshire too had its great founders like the two archbishops of York, Thomas Rotherham and Robert Holgate, and later, in the 18th century, Lady Elizabeth Hastings. Yet the distinctive feature of Yorkshire education in the three centuries under review was not the gifts of the rich benefactors but the communal action of men and women in their local communities, some richer, some poorer, but all alike joining together in group activity to found grammar schools in the 16th century and parish and charity schools in the 18th. This is true both of the towns and of remote villages in the north and west of the county.

This strong and continuing sense of local collective action is the most remarkable feature of our story, and it would be very interesting to know how far the same is true of other counties and communities, though, if it is, little notice seems to have been taken of that fact by the history books. It has already been suggested that one of the few regional studies which can be compared with this book is the volume of essays on *Education in Leicestershire 1540–1940*, edited by Brian Simon (1968). Part I of this consists of three essays by Joan Simon, which cover a period of time similar to that considered here.[20] Though Mrs Simon's interpretation of the Leicestershire evidence is in some ways different from what seems to have happened in Yorkshire, there are strong similarities too. She also emphasized the strength of group activity, led in many cases by people of middling wealth and purely local importance rather than by rich and outstanding individuals.

The argument has been put forward that the chantry legislation of King Edward VI's reign was intended to lay the basis for a national system of education. Whatever the intentions may have been, events in Yorkshire show no sign of such a plan being implemented. The fate of schools seems to have depended very much on chance – particularly the chance of finding powerful supporters at the crucial moment. What is especially interesting about the Reformation changes in Yorkshire is the frequent concealment of chantry properties and the long struggle to preserve them for local purposes, among which education ranked high. Mrs Simon suggests that something of the same happened in Leicestershire,[21] and it would be interesting to know how far these attempts at concealment, which were often successful, went on in other parts of the country. They were, of course, another aspect of the group activity and anxiety to defend local interests which have already been noted as characteristic of Yorkshire people. The tendency of recent historical writing has been to argue that the dissolution of the chantries did little lasting damage to English education, and that it was more than made good by the flood of benefactions after 1560. It is at least worth asking the question how much of the older endowments was preserved through the activity of local people in hiding them from a remote and distrusted central government.

Some scholars have argued that the Reformation changes marked a move towards lay control of schools and towards the transformation of the schoolmaster into a professional person in his own right instead of his being simply one member of the clerical order. In the Yorkshire of the 16th, 17th and 18th centuries the influence of the church remained very strong at all levels of schooling from the grammar schoolmaster to the parish clerk who taught the village children. The central point of church influence lay in the episcopal licensing of schoolmasters, a complex and difficult subject on which much work remains to be done, while the records are bulky and difficult to use. In this book some of the diocesan records of York and Chester have been studied, and there are a few references to those of London and Norwich and of Coventry and Lichfield.[22] All of these show that the system was only partially effective, but much more research would need to be done to show exactly how effective it was, and how far its rigour varied from time to time and from diocese to diocese.

Apart from the rather legalistic question of how many schoolmasters were and were not licensed, there is the wider issue of how much can be learned, through the study of the licensing system, about the actual working of parish life and about the expectations which local people formed of their schoolmasters. The York diocesan records, through the series of nominations and testimonials, do provide a lot of information of this kind – what might be called licensing from the bottom upwards instead of, as it is usually seen, from the top downwards as the bishop and his officials operated the system. If material similar to these testimonials and nominations survives for other dioceses, this would provide valuable information about schools and their communities in different parts of the country, and indeed about parish life in general.

One important point about the nominations and testimonials is that they come from a very wide range of towns and villages, some large, some small, scattered over a very wide geographical area. This wide scatter is very important. It is worth noting that many of the best known grammar schools like Richmond, Giggleswick and Sedbergh had been established early on in quite remote places. By about 1700 the grammar schools were declining in relative importance and the parish schools were increasing. Though there were many villages with no school at all, it is noteworthy how many schools there were, and how many of them were to be found in remote areas where an interest in education might not have been expected. This wide diffusion of schooling is a striking conclusion which emerges from all the sources and in particular from the Herring Returns. It is likely, indeed, that those returns underestimated the number of teachers because many of them, teaching a few children simply for the fees paid by the parents, will not have been named by the incumbents who answered the questions. It would be interesting indeed to know how far this situation was peculiar to Yorkshire, or whether this widespread diffusion of schooling was common in other counties.

This question of the diffusion of primary schooling after 1700 is closely bound up with the further question how far it was the result of the work of SPCK during the early part of the 18th century. The standard accounts, particularly that of M.G. Jones, have propounded the idea of a 'Charity School Movement', led by SPCK, an idea which has been strongly challenged by Joan Simon in her studies of schools in Leicestershire.[23] The Yorkshire evidence about the work of SPCK has been carefully examined in Chapter 10 of this book. It was suggested there that SPCK did have a substantial influence, particularly on the subscription schools in the larger towns, but that the general movement to extend popular education was largely independent of the Society. This argument fits in, of course, with the strong sense of local collective action which has been called the central theme of the Yorkshire story.

Once again it would be valuable to have studies of other counties or regions because the influence of SPCK may have varied a good deal from area to area. In his study of 18th century Cheshire Derek Robson reached conclusions rather similar to those put here for Yorkshire. He found that only five schools were established in Cheshire using the method of subscription promoted by SPCK and that the response to their initiative was weaker in the country districts.[24] The whole subject of 18th century popular schooling, approached from the regional standpoint, deserves a great deal more study.

The remoteness of Yorkshire from the centre has already been stressed, and some of the educational movements which attracted attention in the capital raised few responses so far afield. In the 17th century there is no evidence that the plans of the circle around Comenius, Dury and Hartlib made any impact. Charles Hoole did indeed translate Comenius' *Orbis Sensualium Pictus*, but that was long after he left Yorkshire. Celia Fiennes mentions a girls' school at Leeds in 1698, but I have found no trace of any links with the London women educators of the time like Bathsua Makin and Mary Astell. After 1700 provincial differences appear to diminish. Derek Robson's picture of 18th century Cheshire is similar in many ways to the picture painted here of 18th century Yorkshire. The growth of the private schools, an important new development of the century, seems to have been remarkably uniform everywhere. R.S. Tompson, in his study of grammar schools, points out the same tendency to diversify the curriculum in many schools which has been noted for Yorkshire. The 18th century grammar school was by no means so entirely devoted to the study of Greek and Latin as has been conventionally believed.

There remain areas for further study which have been only briefly touched on here. Much more could be done to explore the links between schooling and apprenticeship, the poor law and work, which have been tentatively sketched in Chapter 12. Here the focus moves from education into issues of public policy for the relief of poverty. And, as far as sources are concerned, no use has been made in this book of parish records which might fill in the picture a good deal. In these and in other ways much remains to be done, but it is submitted that, on the basis of what we already know, a strong case can be made for more such regional studies. For Yorkshire distinctive points of interest have been found in the events of the Reformation, the working of the system of licensing, and the development of the parish schools, particularly in relation to the work of SPCK. Finally the whole story is bound together by the strong sense of local co-operative effort. Other regional studies might test these, and other ideas, against what was happening in various parts of the country. It might in addition be possible to look at some particular places, to compare ports like Bristol and Hull, textile and mercantile towns like Leeds and Manchester, manufacturing centres like Sheffield and Birmingham. The results of such studies might considerably modify the accepted story and lend a new depth to some familiar themes. Moreover more would thus be learned about the lives of local communities since the schools had close ties with local people and with other local institutions. In this way an important contribution might be made to local history in general.

Notes Chapter 15

1.   Roebuck, P. 1980: 101.
2.   Bloy, M. 1995: 22–34 gives a very interesting account of the young Rockingham's grand tour.
3.   Roebuck, P. 1980: 26; Wilson, R.G. 1971: 209.
4.   Wilson, R.G. 1971: 208–11; Jackson, G. 1972: 275–7.
5.   For Leeds Grammar School *see* pages 187–8.
6.   Wilson, R.G. 1971: 210, 243–4.
7.   Pryme, G. 1870: 10–37; for Joseph Milner *see* pages 191–2; for John Dawson *see* Lowther Clarke, H. and Weech, W.N. 1925: 132–3.
8.   Morehouse, H.J. and Jackson, C. (eds) 1877: 165–243; *see also* pages 162–3.
9.   Morehouse, H.J. and Jackson, C. (eds) 1877: 239–40.
10.   *Ibid.*: 449.
11.   Whiting, C.E. (ed.) 1951: 146.
12.   *Ibid.*: 25–108 (Arthur Jessop's diary); for the 'magazine' *see* pages 87, 98.
13.   Longden, H. 1865: 152–65; for Longden *see also* page 253.
14.   The following is taken from Gray, Mrs Edwin (Almira) 1927; *see also* pages 241–2 for Mrs Cappe and her circle.
15.   Gray, Mrs Edwin 1927: 105, 201.
16.   *Ibid.*: 104, 230.

17. *Ibid.*: 195, 237.

18. *Ibid.*: 257–8.

19. Orme, N. 1976: 1–34.

20. Simon, J. in Simon, B. (ed.) 1968: 3–100. The three essays are called:
     'Town Estates and Schools in the Sixteenth and Early Seventeenth
     Centuries', 'Post-Reformation Developments: Schools in the County 1660–
     1700', 'Was there a Charity School Movement? The Leicestershire
     Evidence'.

21. *Ibid.*: 6–7.

22. *See* page 57.

23. *See* page 201.

24. Robson, D. 1966: 23.

MAPS 1–3

Location of schools in the East, West and North Ridings

Map 1 Location of schools in the East Riding

Map 2 Location of schools in the West Riding

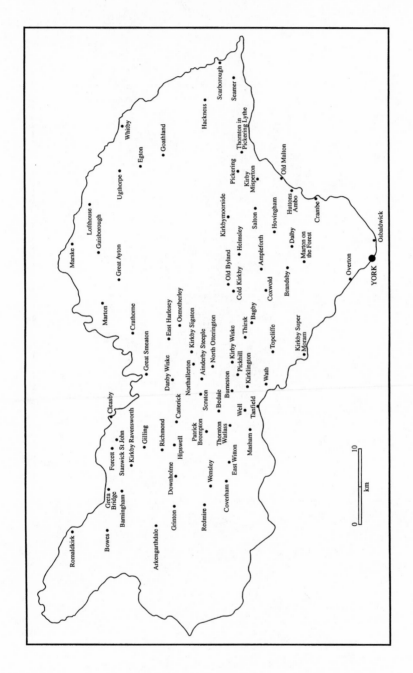

Map 3 Location of schools in the North Riding

BIBLIOGRAPHY

(*All books are published in London unless another place of publication is cited*)

Manuscript sources

Leeds, West Yorkshire Archives

(Archdeaconry of Richmond)

Cause Papers (RD/AC/1/5)

Richmond Churchwardens' Presentments (RD/CB/8/1)

Comperta Books (RD/C 2)

Articles for Joseph Taylor Schoolmaster of Free Grammar School of Bowes (RD/AC/1/7/20)

(Leeds Charity School)

Minutes and Accounts 1750–1810 (DB 196/1 A)

'PIETAS LEODIENSIS, or An Account of the Benefactors, Gifts, Collections, Legacies &c to the Charity School in Leedes' (1735 and later) (DB 196/1)

Leeds, Yorkshire Archaeological Society

Lady Elizabeth Hastings Trust (DD 112): Housekeeper's Account Book 1739–1810; Admissions and Goings-Out 1771–1831

London, Society for Promoting Christian Knowledge

General Board Minutes 1, 2–4 (1698–1709)

Abstract Letter Books 2, 3, 4, 5, 6, 9, 14, 19, 24 (1709–70)

Oxford, Corpus Christi College

Wase School Collection (MSS 390/1, 2, 3)

Sheffield, Sheffield Archives

(Boys' Charity School, Blue Coat School)

'The acc^{ts} for Building the Charity School-house' (1708–10) (MD 2079)

Account Book 1706–1821 (MD 2079)

Admissions Books 1778–1847 (MD 2080–3)

Visitors' Book of Accounts 1795–1827 (MD 2084)

List of subscribers towards building a Charity School 1708 (MD 1103)

(Penistone Grammar School)

Papers relating to Mr Jonathan Wood 1785–1836 (MD 3348, 1–7)

Letters and Papers concerning a dispute over the Headmaster of Penistone Free Grammar School 1784–1833 (Spencer Stanhope Muniments 60573)

Sheffield Cutlers' Company

Minutes of the Company 28 November 1794

York, Borthwick Institute of Historical Research

(Diocesan Records)

Schoolmasters Nominations (Nom SM) 1607–1714

Schoolmasters Nominations, Dean and Chapter of York 1663–1707

Subscriptions Books 1606–27, 1679–1712

(Blue Coat School)

Minutes of the monthly meeting of the Committee 1770–80, 1780–9

(BCS 6, 7)

(Grey Coat School)

Minute Books of the Ladies' Committee 1789–1815, 1815–71 (GCS 1, 2)

York Minster Library

Subscription Book 1660–1726 (S3 (4) e)

Theses

Benson, E. (1932) 'A History of Education in York 1780–1902'. Ph.D. London

Cressey, D.A. (1973) 'Education and Literacy in London and East Anglia 1580–1700' (2 vols). Ph.D. Cambridge

Facer, P. (1966) 'A History of Hipperholme School from 1660 to 1914 with a Biography of its Founder, Matthew Brodley (1586–1648)'. M.A. London

Kitching, C.J. (1970) 'Studies in the Redistribution of Collegiate and Chantry Property in the Diocese and County of York at the Dissolution'. Ph.D. Durham

Stephens, J.E. (1975) 'Yorkshire Schools and Schoolmasters 1600–1700; Aspects of the Control of Education'. Ph.D. Leeds

Books and articles

Adamson, J.W. (1905) *Pioneers of Modern Education 1600–1700.* Cambridge, Cambridge University Press

Adamson, J.W. (1922) *A Short History of Education.* Cambridge, Cambridge University Press

Addy, J. (1958a) 'Penistone Grammar School in the eighteenth century' *Yorkshire Archaeological Journal* vol 39: 356–63

Addy, J. (1958b) 'Penistone Grammar School 1329–1700' *Yorkshire Archaeological Journal* vol 39: 508–14

Addy, J. (1962) 'Penistone Grammar School in the nineteenth century' *Yorkshire Archaeological Journal* vol 40: 112–18

Allen, W.O.B. and McClure, E. (1898) *Two Hundred Years 1698–1898. The History of the Society for Promoting Christian Knowledge* SPCK

Allott, W. (1954) 'The Society of Friends in Yorkshire' in Popham (ed.) *A History of Christianity in Yorkshire* (Wallington, The Religious Education Press)

Armytage, W.H.G. (1964) *Four Hundred Years of English Education* Cambridge, Cambridge University Press

Ashley Smith, J.W. (1954) *The Birth of Modern Education. The contribution of the Dissenting Academies 1660–1800* Independent Press Ltd

Attwood, G.M. (1962) 'Alderman William Cogan and the establishment of his Charity School for Girls, Hull' *Studies in Education* (University of Hull Institute of Education) vol III: 314–30

Aveling, J.C.H. (Hugh) (1960) *Post-Reformation Catholicism in East Yorkshire 1558–1790* East Yorkshire Local History Society–Local History Series no 11

Aveling, J.C.H. (Hugh) (1963) 'The Catholic Recusants of the West Riding of Yorkshire 1558–1790' *Proceedings of the Leeds Philosophical and Literary Society: Literary and Historical Section* vol X, vi: 191–306

Aveling, J.C.H. (Hugh) (1966) *Northern Catholics. The Catholic Recusants of the North Riding of Yorkshire 1558–1790* Geoffrey Chapman

Aveling, J.C.H. (Hugh) (1970) *Catholic Recusancy in the City of York 1558–1791* Catholic Record Society Publications (Monograph series) vol 2

Aveling, J.C.H. (Hugh) (1976) *The Handle and the Axe* Blond and Briggs

Aylmer, G.E. and Cant, R. (eds) (1977) *A History of York Minster* Oxford, Clarendon Press

Baines, E. (1822–3/1969) *History, Directory & Gazetteer of the County of York* David & Charles/S.R. Publishers (reprinted) 2 vols

Baines, T. (n.d.) *Yorkshire Past and Present: A History and a Description of the three Ridings of the great County of York from the earliest ages to the year 1870* 2 vols in 4 parts (William Mackenzie)

Baker, W.P. (1961) *Parish Registers and Illiteracy in East Yorkshire* East Yorkshire Local History Society – Local History Series no 13

Baldwin, T.W. (1943) *William Shakspere's Petty School* Urbana, University of Illinois Press

Baldwin, T.W. (1944) *William Shakspere's Small Latin and Less Greek* 2 vols. Urbana, University of Illinois Press

Bantock, G.H. (1980) *Studies in the History of Educational Theory*, vol I *Artifice and Nature 1350–1765* George Allen and Unwin

Barnard, T. (1742) *An Historical Character relating to the holy and exemplary LIFE of the Right Honourable the Lady Elizabeth Hastings* (Leeds, James Lister for John Swale)

Bayne-Powell, R. (1939) *The English Child in the eighteenth century* (John Murray)

Beales, A.C.F. (1963) *Education under Penalty. English Catholic Education from the Reformation to the fall of James II 1547–1689* (Athlone Press)

Beckwith, F. (1954) 'The Old Dissent' in Popham (ed.) *A History of Christianity in Yorkshire* (Wallington, The Religious Education Press)

Beier, A.L., Cannadine, D. and Rosenheim, J.M., (eds) (1989) *The First Modern Society. Essays in English History in honour of Lawrence Stone* Past and Present Publications (Cambridge, Cambridge University Press). *See* Looney, J.J. (1989)

Bell, E.A. (1912) *A History of Giggleswick School from its foundation 1499 to 1912* (Leeds, Richard Jackson)

Benson, G. (1925/1968) *An Account of the City and County of the City of York...* vol III (East Ardsley, S.R. Publishers, reprinted)

Binfield, C. and Hey, D. (eds) (1997) *Mesters to Masters. A History of the Company of Cutlers in Hallamshire* (Oxford, Oxford University Press)

Blazeby, W. (1906) *Rotherham: The Old Meeting-house and its ministers* (Rotherham, H. Garnett)

Bloy, M. (1995) 'The Early Life of Charles Watson-Wentworth, the North's forgotten Prime Minister' *Transactions of the Hunter Archaeological Society* vol 18: 22–34

Bolgar, R.R. (1963) *The Classical Heritage and its Beneficiaries* (Cambridge, Cambridge University Press)

Bossy, J. (1975) *The English Catholic Community 1570–1850* (Darton, Longman and Todd)

(Boys' Charity School Sheffield) *Reports 1788–1821: An Account of the Rents of the Lands and Tenements belonging to the Charity School for POOR BOYS in Sheffield; together with the Annual Subscriptions; the Treasurer's Accompts...and a State of the Children's Improvement*

Boys' Charity School Sheffield (1905) *Bi-centenary 1706–1906. History of the Institution*

Brook, R. (1968) *The Story of Huddersfield* (Macgibbon and Kee)

Brown, J. H. (1933) *Elizabethan Schooldays* (Oxford, Blackwell)

Butler, L.A.S., ed. (1986/1990) *The Archdeaconry of Richmond in the eighteenth century. Bishop Gastrell's 'Notitia'. The Yorkshire Parishes 1714–25* Yorkshire Archaeological Record Series vol CXLVI

Campbell Stewart, W.A. (1953) *Quakers and Education. As seen in their Schools in England* (Epworth Press)

Cappe, C. (1800) *An Account of two Charity Schools for the Education of Girls: and of a Female Friendly Society in York: interspersed with reflections on*

Charity Schools and Friendly Societies in general (York, William Blanchard)

Cappe, C. (1805) *Observations on Charity Schools, Female Friendly Societies, and other subjects connected with the views of the Ladies' Committee* (York, William Blanchard)

Cappe, C. (1822) *Memoirs of the Life of the late Mrs ... written by herself* (Longman)

Cardwell, E. (1844/1966) *Documentary Annals of the Reformed Church of England; being a Collection of Injunctions, Declarations, Orders, Articles of Inquiry, &c from the year 1546 to the year 1716; with notes historical and explanatory* 2 vols (New edn, Ridgewood, NJ, The Gregg Press)

Carlisle, N. (1818/1972) *A Concise Description of the Endowed Grammar Schools in England and Wales* 2 vols (Baldwin, Cradock, and Joy. New edn, Richmond Publishing Co.)

Chambers, M.C.E. (1882, 1885) *The Life of Mary Ward 1585–1645* 2 vols, H.J. Coleridge (ed.) (Burns and Oates)

Chaplin, W.N. (1962-3) 'A.F. Leach: A Re-appraisal' *British Journal of Educational Studies* vol XI: 99–124

Chaplin, W.N. (1963–4) 'A.F. Leach: Agreement and Difference' *British Journal of Educational Studies* vol XII: 173–83

Charlton, K. (1965) *Education in Renaissance England* (Routledge and Kegan Paul)

Charlton, K. (1981) '"Tak the to thi distaff...": the education of girls and women in early modern England' *Westminster Studies in Education* vol 4: 3–18

Charlton, K. (1970) 'The Teaching Profession in sixteenth and seventeenth century England' in Nash, P. (ed.) *History and Education. The educational uses of the past* (New York, Random House)

Claridge, W. (1882) *Origin and History of the Bradford Grammar School from its foundation to Christmas 1882* (Bradford, J. Green)

Clarke, J. (1740) *An Essay upon the Education of Youth in Grammar-Schools* 3rd edn (Charles Hitch)

Clarke, M.L. (1945) *Greek Studies in England 1700–1830* (Cambridge, Cambridge University Press)

Clarke, M.L. (1959) *Classical Education in Britain 1500–1900* (Cambridge, Cambridge University Press)

Clay, J.W. and Lister, J. (1898–9) 'Autobiography of Sir John Savile of Methley, Knight, Baron of the Exchequer, 1546–1607' *Yorkshire Archaeological Journal* vol XV: 420–27

Cliffe, J.T. (1969) *The Yorkshire Gentry. From the Reformation to the Civil War* (Athlone Press)

Cobley, F. (1923) *Chronicles of the Free Grammar School of Prince Henry at Otley* (Otley, William Walker)

Coleridge, H.J., ed. (1887) *St. Mary's Convent Micklegate Bar York 1686–1887* (Burns and Oates)

Costin, W.C. and Watson, J. S. (1952) *The Law and Working of the Constitution. Documents 1660–1914* 2 vols (A. and C. Black)

Cowie, L. W. (1956) *Henry Newman. An American in London 1708–43* (SPCK for the Church Historical Society)

Cox, T. (1879) *A Popular History of the Grammar School of Queen Elizabeth at Heath, near Halifax* (Halifax, F. King)

Crellin, V.H. (1978) 'Education and Social Mobility in the 18th Century: The Schooling of Captain James Cook' *Journal of Educational Administration and History* vol X: 12–19

Cremin, L. A. (1970) *American Education. The Colonial Experience 1607–1783* (New York, Harper Torchbooks)

Cressy, D.A. (1976) 'Educational Opportunity in Tudor and Stuart England' *History of Education Quarterly* vol 16: 301–20

Cressy, D.A. (1977) 'Levels of Illiteracy in England 1530–1730' *Historical Journal* vol 20: 1–23

Cressy, D.A. (1980) *Literacy and the Social Order. Reading and Writing in Tudor and Stuart England* (Cambridge, Cambridge University Press)

Curtis, M.H. (1962) 'The alienated intellectuals of early Stuart England' *Past and Present* no 23: 25–43

Curtis S.J. (1951) 'Ripon Grammar School' *Researches and Studies* (University of Leeds Institute of Education) no 4: 73–80

Curtis, S.J. (1952) 'Tadcaster Grammmar School' *Researches and Studies* no 6: 69–81

Curtis, S.J. (1953, 1954) 'The Ancient Schools of Yorkshire' *Researches and Studies* no 8: 25–39; no 9: 13–19

De la Pryme, A. (The Yorkshire Antiquary) (1870) *The Diary of...* (Surtees Society Publications vol LIV)

Dennett, J., ed. (1932) *Beverley Borough Records 1575–1821* (Yorkshire Archaeological Society Record Series vol LXXXIV)

Dickens, A.G. (1937) 'The Marriage and Character of Archbishop Holgate' *English Historical Review* vol LII: 428–42

Dickens, A.G. (1939) 'Some Popular Reactions to the Edwardian Reformation in Yorkshire' *Yorkshire Archaeological Journal* vol 34: 151–69

Dickens, A.G. (1941) 'Archbishop Holgate's Apology' *English Historical Review* vol LVI: 450–59

Dickens, A.G. (1947a) 'A Municipal Dissolution of Chantries at York, 1536' *Yorkshire Archaeological Journal* vol 36: 164–73

Dickens, A.G. (1947b) 'Robert Parkyn's Narrative of the Reformation' *English Historical Review* vol LXII: 58–83

Dickens, A.G. (1957) *The Marian Reaction in the Diocese of York* Part I, *The Clergy*; Part II, *The Laity* (London and York, St Anthony's Press)

Dickens, A.G., ed. (1959) *Tudor Treatises* (Sherbrook, Michael 'The Fall of Religious Houses') (Yorkshire Archaeological Society Record Series vol CXXV)

Dickens, A.G. (1959) *Lollards and Protestants in the Diocese of York 1509–1558* (Oxford University Press for the University of Hull)

Dickens, A.G. (1981) *The English Reformation* (Fontana edn)

Dobbs, A.E. (1919) *Education and Social Movements 1700–1850* (Longmans Green)

Dodd, E.E. (1930) *A History of the Bingley Grammar School 1529–1929* (Bradford, Percy Lund, Humphries)

Dodd, E.E. (1958) *Bingley. A Yorkshire Town through nine centuries* (Bingley, Harrison and Sons)

Dodd, E.E. (1962) 'Bingley Chantry Endowments' *The Bradford Antiquary* new series, vol VIII: 92–9

Dransfield, J.N. (1906) *A History of the Parish of Penistone* (Penistone, James H. Wood, The Don Press)

Duffy, E. (1992) *The Stripping of the Altars. Traditional Religion in England 1400–1580* (New Haven and London, Yale University Press)

Dyson, T. (1926) *Almondbury and its Ancient School. Being the History of King James' Grammar School, Almondbury, with incidental chapters on the History of the District and its inhabitants* (Huddersfield, Advertiser Press)

Edmonds, E.L. (1958) 'The S.P.C.K. and early inspection in Anglican Charity Schools' *Studies in Education* (University of Hull Institute of Education) vol III: 50–59

Edwards, K. (1967) *The English Secular Cathedrals in the Middle Ages* 2nd edn (Manchester, Manchester University Press)

Feingold, M. (1979) 'Jordan Revisited: Patterns of charitable giving in sixteenth and seventeenth century England' *History of Education* vol 8: 257–73

Fiennes, C. (1949) *The Journeys of...* C. Morris (ed.) (The Cresset Press)

Fox, L. (1984) *The Early History of King Edward VI School Stratford-upon-Avon* (Oxford) Dugdale Society Occasional Papers no 29

Frere, W.H., ed. (1910a) *Visitation Articles and Injunctions of the period of the Reformation* vol I (Historical Introduction and Index) Alcuin Club Collections XIV (Longmans Green)

Frere, W.H. and Kennedy, W.M. (eds) (1910) *Visitation Articles and Injunctions of the period of the Reformation* vol II (1536–1558) Alcuin Club Collections XV (Longmans Green)

Frere, W.H., ed. (1910b) *Visitation Articles and Injunctions of the period of the Reformation* vol III (1559–1575) Alcuin Club Collections XVI (Longmans Green)

Gardiner, D. (1929) *English Girlhood at School. A Study of Women's Education through twelve centuries* (Oxford University Press)

Gee, H. and Hardy, W.J. (eds) (1896) *Documents illustrative of English Church History* (Macmillan)

Gibbon, A.M. (1947) *The Ancient Free Grammar School of Skipton in Craven. A Study in Local History* (Liverpool, Liverpool University Press)

Goodwin, E. (1786) *An Address to Parents, Masters and Poor Children relative to Sunday Schools* (Sheffield, W. Ward)

Goodwin, E. (1787) *The Poor Girls' Primer. For the use of the Charity School, in Sheffield* (Sheffield, W. Ward)

Gray, Mrs Edwin [Almira] (1927) *Papers and Diaries of a York Family 1764–1839* (The Sheldon Press)

Greaves, R.L. (1969) *The Puritan Revolution and Educational Thought. Background to Reform* (New Brunswick, NJ, Rutgers University Press)

Green, I. (1996) *The Christian's ABC. Catechism and Catechizing in England c.1530–1740* (Oxford, Clarendon Press)

Grubb, S. (1837) *Some Account of the Life and Religious Labours of...With an Appendix, containing an account of the Schools at Ackworth and York, Observations on Christian Discipline, and extracts from many of her letters* 3rd edn (Belfast, William Robinson)

Guest, J. (1876) *Rotherham Ancient College and Grammar School. A Paper read before the Rotherham Literary and Scientific Society on December 20th 1875* (Rotherham, W. Wightman)

Guest, J. (1879) *Historic Notices of Rotherham: Ecclesiastical, Collegiate and Civil* (Worksop, Robert White)

Hall, T.W. (1932) *The Fairbanks of Sheffield 1688 to 1848* (Sheffield, J.W. Northend)

Hall, T.W. (1937) *Incunabula of Sheffield History* (Sheffield, J.W. Northend)

Hamilton, D.H., ed. (1977) *A History of St. Peter's School* (York) (Typescript, York Minster Library)

Hans, N. (1951) *New Trends in Education in the eighteenth century* (Routledge and Kegan Paul)

Harrison, J.A. (1958, 1960) *Private Schools in Doncaster in the nineteenth century* Parts I and II (Doncaster Museum Publications)

Hart, A.T. (1949) *The Life and Times of John Sharp Archbishop of York* (SPCK)

Heal, F. and O'Day, R., eds (1977) *Church and Society in England: Henry VIII to James I* (Macmillan). *See* Kitching, C.J. (1977)

Herring Returns. *See* Ollard, S.L. and Walker, P.C., eds *Archbishop Herring's Visitation Returns*

Hexter, J.H. (1961) 'The Education of the Aristocracy in the Renaissance' *Reappraisals in History* (Evanston, Ill., Northwestern University Press)

Hey, D. (1986) *Yorkshire from A D 1000* (Longman): A Regional History of England (Cunliffe, B. and Hey, D. eds)

Hinchcliffe, G. (1963) *A History of King James's Grammar School in Almondbury* (Huddersfield, Advertiser Press)

Hoole, C. (1660/1913) *A New Discovery of the old art of teaching School in four small treatises* Campagnac, E.T. (ed.) (Liverpool, Liverpool University Press; London, Constable)

Houlbrooke, R. (1976) 'The Decline of Ecclesiastical Jurisdiction under the Tudors' in O'Day, R. and Heal, F. (eds) *Continuity and Change. Personnel and*

Administration of the Church in England 1500–1642 (Leicester, Leicester University Press)

Howard, J. (1887) *Historical Sketch of the origin and work of the York Incorporated (Church of England) Sunday School Committee, instituted 1786* (York, John Sampson)

Hulbert, C.A. (1864) *Annals of the Church in Slaithwaite...from 1593 to 1864 in Five Lectures* (Longman)

Hulbert, C.A. (1882) *Annals of the Church and Parish of Almondbury Yorkshire* (Longmans Green)

Hull, J. (1984) 'The Role of the Commissioners for ejecting scandalous, ignorant and insufficient Ministers and Schoolmasters appointed under the Ordinance of 28 August 1654' *Aspects of Education* (University of Hull Institute of Education) no 31: 45–65 ('Aspects of Education 1600–1750' J.E. Stephens, ed.)

Hunter, J. (1828, 1831) *South Yorkshire. The History and Topography of the Deanery of Doncaster in the Diocese and County of York* 2 vols (J.B. Nichols. Reprinted 1974, East Ardsley, E.P. Publishing)

Hunter, J. (1869) *Hallamshire. The History and Topography of the Parish of Sheffield in the County of York* A. Gatty (ed.) (Sheffield, Pawson and Brailsford)

Hutton, J.E. (1895) *A Short History of the Moravian Church* (Moravian Publication Office)

Hutton, R.B.M. (1953) *Through Two Centuries. An account of the origin and growth of Fulneck School 1753–1953* (Fulneck School Bicentenary Memorial Committee)

Jackson, C. and Margerison, S., eds (1886) *Yorkshire Diaries and Autobiographies in the seventeenth and eighteenth centuries* (Surtees Society vol LXXVII) 'The Note Book of Sir Walter Calverley, Bart'

Jackson, G. (1972) *Hull in the Eighteenth Century. A Study in Economic and Social History* (Oxford University Press for the University of Hull)

James, M. (1930) *Social Problems and Policy during the Puritan Revolution 1640–1660* (Routledge)

Jewell, H.M. (1982) "'The Bringing up of Children in Good Learning and Manners": a survey of secular educational provision in the North of England, c.1350–1550' *Northern History* vol XVIII: 1–25

Jewels, E.N. (1963) *A History of Archbishop Holgate's Grammar School York 1546–1946* (Foundation Governors of the School)

Jones, M.G. (1938/1964) *The Charity School Movement. A Study of eighteenth century Puritanism in action* (Cambridge, Cambridge University Press, reprinted Frank Cass)

Jones, M.G. (1939–40) 'Lady Elizabeth Hastings' *Church Quarterly Review* vol CXXIX: 71–90

Jordan, W.K. (1959) *Philanthropy in England 1480–1660. A study of the changing pattern of English social aspirations* (Allen and Unwin)

Jordan, W.K. (1960) *The Charities of London 1480–1660. The aspirations and achievements of the urban society* (Allen and Unwin)

Jordan, W.K. (1961) *The Charities of Rural England 1480–1660. The aspirations and achievements of the rural society* (Allen and Unwin)

Jordan, W.K. (1962) *The Social Institutions of Lancashire. A study of the changing patterns of aspiration in Lancashire 1480–1660* (Chetham Society vol XI 3rd series)

Jordan, W.K. (1968) *Edward VI: the Young King* (Allen and Unwin)

Jordan, W.K. (1970) *Edward VI: The Threshold of Power* (Allen and Unwin)

Kennedy, W.P.M. (1924) *Elizabethan Episcopal Administration. An essay in Sociology and Politics* vols I; II (Visitation Articles and Injunctions 1575–82); vol III (Visitation Articles and Injunctions 1583–1603) Alcuin Club Collections vols XXV, XXVI, XXVII (A.R. Mowbray)

Kitching, C.J. (1958, 1959) 'Catholic Education in the North and East Ridings of Yorkshire and the City of York during Penal Times': Part I: 1571 to 1700; Part II: 1700–1778 *Durham Research Review* vol II: 193–207, 287–98

Kitching, C.J. (1972) 'The Chantries of the East Riding of Yorkshire at the Dissolution in 1548' *Yorkshire Archaeological Journal* vol 44: 178–94

Kitching, C.J. (1977) 'The Disposal of Monastic and Chantry Lands' in Heal, F. and O'Day, R. (eds) *Church and Society in England: Henry VIII to James I* (Macmillan)

Knight, C.B. (1944) *A History of the City of York from the foundation of the Roman Fortress of Eboracum A.D.71 to the close of the Reign of Queen Victoria A.D.1901* (London and York, Herald Printing Works)

Kreider, A. (1979) *English Chantries. The Road to Dissolution* (Cambridge, Mass., Harvard University Press) Harvard Historical Series XCVII

Lahey, P. (1982) 'The Qualifications of Schoolmasters in the Diocese of York' *Journal of Educational Administration and History* vol XIV: 1–6

Lahey, P. (1984) 'Schoolmasters in the York Subscription Books' *Aspects of Education no* 31: 20–44

Langford, P. (1989) *A Polite and Commmercial People. England 1727–1783* (Oxford, Clarendon Press) New Oxford History of England

Laqueur, T.W. (1976) *Religion and Respectibility. Sunday Schools and Working Class Culture 1780–1850* (New Haven and London, Yale University Press)

Lawrance, H. (1920) 'Pocklington School Admission Register, 1626–1717' *Yorkshire Archaeological Journal* vol 25: 53–70

Lawson, J. (1959) *Primary Education in East Yorkshire* (East Yorkshire Local History Society – Local History series no 10)

Lawson, J. (1962a) *The Endowed Grammar Schools of East Yorkshire* (East Yorkshire Local History Society – Local History series no 14)

Lawson, J. (1962b) 'An Early Disciple of Locke: John Clarke (1686–1734), Educational Reformer and Moralist' *Durham Research Review* vol IV: 30–38

Lawson, J. (1963) *A Town Grammar School through six centuries. A History of Hull Grammar School against its local background* (Oxford University Press for the University of Hull)

Lawson, J. (1967) *Medieval Education and the Reformation* (Routledge and Kegan Paul) Students Library of Education

Lawson, J. and Silver, H. (1973) *A Social History of Education in England* (Methuen)

Leach, A.F. (1896) *English Schools at the Reformation 1546–8* (Westminster, Constable)

Leach, A.F. (1898, 1903) *Early Yorkshire Schools* vols I, II (Yorkshire Archaeological Society Record series vols XXVII, XXXIII)

Leach, A.F. (1907) 'Schools' *Victoria County History, Yorkshire* vol I, Page, W. (ed.): 415–500 (Archibald Constable). See also *Victoria County History, Yorkshire*

Leach, A.F., ed. (1911) *Educational Charters and Documents 598–1909* (Cambridge, Cambridge University Press)

Leach, A.F. (1916) *The Schools of Medieval England* 2nd edn (Methuen)

Leadman, A.D.H. (1898) 'Pocklington School' *Yorkshire Archaeological Journal* vol 14: 133–46

Leeds Mercury (1769–74)

Lester, D.N.R. (n.d.) *The History of Batley Grammar School 1612–1962* (Batley, J.S. Newsome)

Lewis, A.J. (1954) 'The Moravians' in Popham (ed.) *A History of Christianity in Yorkshire* (Wallington, The Religious Education Press)

Longden, H. (1865) *The Life of ...Compiled from his own Memoirs, from his Diary and Letters and other authentic documents* 10th edn (Wesleyan Conference Office)

Looney, J. J. (1989) 'Cultural Life in the Provinces: Leeds and York 1720–1820' in Beier, A.L., Cannadine, D. and Rosenheim, J.M. (eds) *The First Modern Society. Essays in English History in Honour of Lawrence Stone* (Cambridge, Cambridge University Press)

Lowther Clarke, H. and Weech, W.N. (1925) *History of Sedbergh School 1525–1925* (Sedbergh, Jackson and Son)

Lowther Clarke, W.K. (1944) *Eighteenth Century Piety* (SPCK)

Lowther Clarke, W.K. (1959) *A History of the S.P.C.K.* (SPCK)

Lupton, J.H. (1864) *Wakefield Worthies; or, Biographical Sketches of Men of Note connected, by birth or otherwise, with the Town of Wakefield in Yorkshire* (London, Hamilton; Wakefield, R. Micklethwaite)

Mc Cann, J. and Cary-Elwes, C., eds (1952) *Ampleforth and its Origins. Essays on a Living Tradition by Members of the Ampleforth Community* (Burns, Oates and Washbourne)

McClure, E. (1888) *A Chapter in English Church History: being the Minutes of the Society for Promoting Christian Knowledge for the years 1698–1704 together with Abstracts of Correspondents' Letters during part of the same period* (SPCK)

McDermid, J. (1989) 'Conservative Feminism and female education in the eighteenth century' *History of Education* vol 18: 309–22

Mackenzie, M.H. (1971–9) 'The Early Papers of the Rotherham Feoffees' *Transactions of the Hunter Archaeological Society* vol X: 350–59

McLachlan, H. (1931) *English Education under the Test Acts* (Manchester, Manchester University Press)

McMahon, C.P. (1947) *Education in fifteenth-century England* (Baltimore, The John Hopkins Press) (The John Hopkins University Studies in Education 35)

Macmahon, K.A., ed. (1956) *Beverley Corporation Minute Books (1707–1835)* (Yorkshire Archaeological Society Record Series, vol CXXII)

McMullen, N. (1977) 'The Education of English Gentlewomen 1540–1640' *History of Education* vol 6: 87–101

Mains, B. and Tuck, A., eds (1986) *Royal Grammar School Newcastle upon Tyne. A History of the School in its Community* (Stocksfield, Oriel Press)

Marchant, R.A. (1960) *The Puritans and the Church Courts in the Diocese of York 1560–1642)* (Longman)

Marchant, R.A. (1969) *The Church under the Law. Justice, Administration and Discipline in the Diocese of York 1560–1640* (Cambridge, Cambridge University Press)

Mathews, H.F. (1949) *Methodism and the Education of the People 1791–1851* (Epworth Press)

Matthews, A.G. (1934) *Calamy Revised. Being a Revision of Edmund Calamy's Account of the Ministers and others ejected and silenced, 1660–2* (Oxford, Clarendon Press)

Matthews, W.G. (1971–9) 'The Free Writing School, Sheffield, and its Masters' *Transactions of the Hunter Archaeological Society* vol X: 280–85

Medhurst, C.E. (1914) *Life and Work of Lady Elizabeth Hastings. The great Yorkshire benefactress of the XVIIIth Century* (Leeds, Richard Jackson)

Mercer, M. (1983) 'The Hollis Educational Trust: A Nonconformist Contribution to Elementary Education' *Transactions of the Hunter Archaeological Society* vol 12: 68–81

Mercer, M. (1987) 'William Ronksley (1650–1724) Schoolmaster, Writer and Philanthropist' *Transactions of the Hunter Archaeological Society* vol 14: 11–18

Mercer, M. (1996) *Schooling the Poorer Child. Elementary Education in Sheffield 1560–1902* (Sheffield, Sheffield Academic Press)

Miller, P.J. (1972) 'Women's Education, 'Self-Improvement' and Social Mobility – a late eighteenth century debate' *British Journal of Educational Studies* vol XX: 302–14

Miner, J.N. (1962) 'Schools and Literacy in later medieval England' *British Journal of Educational Studies* vol XI: 16–27

Mitchell, P.R. and Deane, Phyllis (1962) *Abstract of British Historical Statistics* (Cambridge, Cambridge University Press)

Montmorency, J.E.G. de (1902) *State Intervention in English Education. A Short History from the earliest times down to 1833* (Cambridge, Cambridge University Press)

Moore Smith, G.C. (1929–37) 'Sheffield Grammar School' *Transactions of the Hunter Archaeological Society* vol IV: 145–60

Moran, J. A. Hoeppner (1979) *Education and Learning in the City of York 1300–1560* (University of York, Borthwick Institute of Historical Research, Borthwick Papers 55)

Moran, J. A. Hoeppner (1981) 'Literacy and Education in Northern England, 1350–1550' *Northern History* vol XVII: 1–23

Moran, J. A. Hoeppner (1985) *The Growth of English Schooling 1340–1548. Learning, Literacy and Laicization in Pre-Reformation York Diocese* (Princeton, Princeton University Press)

Morehouse, H.J. (1874) *Extracts from the Diary of the Rev. Robert Meeke, minister of the ancient chapelry of Slaithwaite near Huddersfield, and founder of the Slaithwaite Free School in 1721; to which are added notes, illustrations, and a brief sketch of his life and character. Also a continuation of the History of Slaithwaite Free School, and an account of the educational establishments in Slaithwaite-cum-Lingards* by Hulbert, C.A. (H.G. Bohn)

Morehouse, H.J. and Jackson, C., eds (1877) *Yorkshire Diaries and Autobiographies in the seventeenth and eighteenth centuries* (Surtees Society LXV)

Nash, P., ed. (1970) *History and Education. The educational uses of the past* (New York, Random House). *See* Charlton, K. (1970)

National Society for the Education of the Poor in the Principles of the Established Church 5th Annual Report: 160–67. (An abstract of the Answers of the Parochial Clergy...to certain questions...1814–15) (Church of England Record Centre, London SE16)

Notestein, W. (1938) *English Folk. A Book of Characters* (Cape)

Notestein, W. (1954) *The English People on the eve of Colonization* (Hamish Hamilton)

Notestein, W. (1955) 'The English Woman 1580–1650' in Plumb, J.H. 1955 (ed) *Studies in Social History. A Tribute to G.M. Trevelyan* (Longmans Green)

Oakley, H.H. (1920) *The First Century of Silcoates* (Cheltenham, Ed. J. Burrow)

O'Day, R. (1973) 'Church Records and the History of Education in early modern England 1558–1642: a Problem in Methodology' *History of Education* vol 2: 115–32

O'Day, R. (1976) 'The Reformation of the Ministry' in O'Day, R. and Heal, F. eds *Continuity and Change. Personnel and Administration of the Church of England 1500–1642* (Leicester, Leicester University Press)

O'Day, R. (1982) *Education and Society 1500–1800. The social foundations of education in early modern Britain* (Longman)

O'Day, R. and Heal, F., eds (1976) *Continuity and Change. Personnel and Administration of the Church of England 1500–1642* (Leicester, Leicester University Press). *See* Houlbrooke, R. (1976); O'Day, R. (1976)

Ogilvie, R.M. (1964) *Latin and Greek. A History of the influence of the Classics on English life from 1600 to 1918* (Routledge and Kegan Paul)

Oliver, Mary, I.B.V.M. (1960) *Mary Ward 1585–1645* (Sheed and Ward)

Ollard, S.L. and Walker, P.C. (1927–31) *Archbishop Herring's Visitation Returns* 5 vols (Yorkshire Archaeological Society Record Series vols LXXI (1927), LXXII (1928i), LXXV (1929ii), LXXVIII (1930ii), LXXIX (1931ii). See also 'Herring Returns'

Orme, N. (1973) *English Schools in the Middle Ages* (Methuen)

Orme, N. (1976) *Education in the West of England 1066–1548. Cornwall Devon Dorset Gloucestershire Somerset Wiltshire* (University of Exeter)

Orme, N. (1989) *Education and Society in Medieval and Renaissance England* (The Hambledon Press)

Page, W. (1894–5) *The Certificates of the Commissioners appointed to survey the Chantries, Guilds, Hospitals etc, in the County of York* Parts I and II, (Surtees Society Publications XCI, XCII)

Parker, I. (1914) *Dissenting Academies in England* (Cambridge, Cambridge University Press)

Peacock, E. (1872) *A List of the Roman Catholics in the County of York in 1604* (J.C. Hotten)

Peacock, M.H. (1892) *History of the Free Grammar School of Queen Elizabeth at Wakefield. Founded A.D. 1591* (Wakefield, W.H. Milnes)

Pinchbeck, I. and Hewitt, M. (1969) *Children in English Society* vol I *From Tudor Times to the Eighteenth Century* (Routledge and Kegan Paul)

Plumb, J.H., ed. (1955) *Studies in Social History. A Tribute to G.M. Trevelyan* (Longmans Green). *See* Notestein, W. (1955)

Plumb, J.H. (1975) 'The New World of Children in Eighteenth-Century England' *Past and Present* no 67: 64–95

Pocklington: *Parliamentary Papers* 1818 IV: 146–62. Third Report from the Select Committee on the Education of the Lower Orders – evidence on Pocklington School

Ponsonby, A. (1923) *English Diaries. A Review of English Diaries from the sixteenth to the twentieth century* 2nd edn (Methuen)

Popham, F.S., ed. (1954) *A History of Christianity in Yorkshire* (Wallington, Surrey, The Religious Education Press). *See* Allott, W. (1954); Beckwith, F. (1954); Lewis, A.J. (1954); Towlson, W.C. (1954)

Porteus, B. (1786) *Letter to the Clergy of the Diocese of Chester, concerning Sunday Schools* 2nd edn (T. Payne, J. Rivington, T. Cadell)

Price, A.C. (1919) *A History of the Leeds Grammar School from its foundation to the end of 1918* (Leeds, Richard Jackson)

Priestley, J.H. (n.d.) *The History of Rishworth School* (Halifax, F. King)

Pritchard, F.C. (1949) *Methodist Secondary Education. A History of the contribution of Methodism to Secondary Education in the United Kingdom* (Epworth Press)

Pryme, G. (1870) *Autobiographic Recollections* (edited by his daughter) (Cambridge, Deighton, Bell)

Public Record Office *Lists and Indexes* no X (1899). List of Proceedings of Commissioners of Charitable Uses, appointed pursuant to the Statutes 39

Elizabeth Cap. 6, and 43 Elizabeth, Cap. 4, preserved in the Public Record Office (H.M.S.O.)

Purvis, J.S. (1948) *Tudor Parish Documents of the Diocese of York. A Selection with introduction and notes* (Cambridge, Cambridge University Press)

Purvis, J.S. (1952) *The Archives of York Diocesan Registry* (York, St Anthony's Hall Publications, no 2)

Purvis, J.S. (1953) *An Introduction to Ecclesiastical Records* (London, St Anthony's Press)

Purvis, J.S. (1959) *Educational Records* (York, St Anthony's Press)

Raine, A. (1926) *History of St. Peter's School: York A.D. 627 to the present day* (G. Bell)

Randall, J. (1750a) *An Account of the Academy at Heath, near Wakefield, Yorkshire. Its Situation, Rise, Present State, Discipline, Terms for Boarding and Teaching; and the Particulars of the Arts and Sciences etc. Taught there. Together with the Usefulness of each Branch of Education; and the Manner of cultivating the Minds of Youth there* (London, no printer or publisher)

Randall, J. (1750b) *A Course of Lectures in the Most easy, useful, and entertaining Parts of Geography, Astronomy, Chronology, & Pneumatics; As they are deliver'd, by Way of Text, To the Youth of the Academy at Heath, near Wakefield, Yorkshire* (J. and J. Rivington)

Reresby, Sir J. (1936) *Memoirs. The Complete Text and a Selection from his Letters,* A. Browning, ed. (Glasgow, Jackson, Son & Co)

Riley, M.A. (1938) 'The Foundation of Chantries in the Counties of Nottingham and York, 1350–1400' Parts I and II *Yorkshire Archaeological Journal* vol 33: 122–65, 237–85

Roach, J. (1986a) *A History of Secondary Education in England 1800–1870* (Longman)

Roach, J. (1986b) 'Boys and girls at school, 1800–70' *History of Education* vol 15: 147–59

Robson, D. (1966) *Some Aspects of Education in Cheshire in the Eighteenth century* (Manchester, Chetham Society), (Remains Historical and Literary connected with the Palatine Counties of Lancaster and Chester, vol XIII, 3rd series)

Robson, K.J.R. (1955) 'The SPCK in action. Some Episodes from the East Riding of Yorkshire' *Church Quarterly Review* vol CLVI: 266–78

Roebuck, P. (1980) *Yorkshire Baronets 1640–1760. Families, Estates and Fortunes* (Oxford, Oxford University Press for the University of Hull)

Rogers, K.M. (1982) *Feminism in Eighteenth-Century England* (Brighton, Harvester Press)

Rogers, P.W. (1954) *A History of Ripon Grammar School* (Ripon, Wakeman Press)

Rose, C. (1993) 'The origins and the ideals of the SPCK 1699–1716' in Walsh, J. Haydon, C. and Taylor, S. eds, *The Church of England c.1689–c.1833. From Toleration to Tractarianism* (Cambridge, Cambridge University Press)

Rosenthal, J.T. (1974) 'The Yorkshire Chantry Certificates of 1546; an analysis' *Northern History* vol IX: 26–47

Ryan, L.V. (1963) *Roger Ascham* (Stanford, Ca, Stanford University Press)

Sadler, J.E. (1966) *J.A. Comenius and the concept of universal education* (George Allen and Unwin)

Salmon, N. (n.d.) *Ilkley Grammar School 1607–1957* (No publisher)

Salt, J. (1964–9) 'Early Sheffield Sunday Schools and their educational importance' *Transactions of the Hunter Archaeological Society* vol IX: 179–84

Sands, P.C. and Haworth, C.M. (?1950) *A History of Pocklington School East Yorkshire 1514–1950* (A. Brown and Sons)

Sangster, P. (1963) *Pity my Simplicity. The Evangelical Revival and the Religious Education of Children 1738–1800* (Epworth Press)

Schofield, R. (1973) 'Dimensions of Illiteracy 1750–1850' *Explorations in Economic History* vol 10.4: 437–54

Scott, B. (1983) 'Lady Elizabeth Hastings' *Yorkshire Archaeological Journal* vol 55: 95–118

Scott, B. (1989) 'Ackworth Hospital 1757–1773' *Yorkshire Archaeological Journal* vol 61: 155–72

Seaborne, M. (1971) *The English School; its architecture and organization 1370–1870* (Routledge and Kegan Paul)

(Sedbergh) (1909) *The Sedbergh School Register 1546 to 1909* (Leeds, Richard Jackson)

Seed, J. (1982) 'Manchester College, York: an early nineteenth century Dissenting Academy' *Journal of Educational Administration and History* vol XIV: 9–17

Sheahan, J.J. (?1866) *History of the Town and Port of Kingston-upon-Hull* 2nd edn (Beverley, John Green)

Sheils, W.J. (1977) *Archbishop Grindal's Visitation, 1575. Comperta et Detecta Book* (Borthwick Texts and Calendars: Records of the Northern Province 4)

Simon, B., ed. (1968) *Education in Leicestershire 1540–1940. A regional study* (Leicester, Leicester University Press). *See* Simon, J. 1968a; 1968b; 1968c

Simon, J. (1954–5, 1955–6) 'A.F. Leach on the Reformation' Parts I and II *British Journal of Educational Studies* vol III: 128–43; vol IV: 32–48

Simon, J. (1957) 'The Reformation and English Education' *Past and Present* no 11: 48–65

Simon, J. (1963–4) 'A.F. Leach: a Reply' *British Journal of Educational Studies* vol XII: 41–50

Simon, J. (1966) *Education and Society in Tudor England* (Cambridge, Cambridge University Press)

Simon, J. (1968a) 'Town Estates and Schools in the Sixteenth and Early Seventeenth Centuries' in, ed. Simon *Education in Leicestershire 1540–1940. A Regional Study* (Leicester, Leicester University Press)

Simon, J. (1968b) 'Post-Reformation Developments: Schools in the County 1660–1700' in, ed. Simon *Education in Leicestershire 1540–1940 A Regional Study* (Leicester, Leicester University Press)

Simon, J. (1968c) 'Was there a Charity School Movement? The Leicestershire Evidence' in, ed. Simon *Education in Leicestershire 1540–1940 A Regional Study* (Leicester, Leicester University Press

Simon, J. (1970) *The Social Origins of English Education* (Routledge and Kegan Paul) (Students' Library of Education)

Simon, J. (1975) 'The Charity School Movement' *Society for the Study of Labour History* Bulletin no 31: 11–14

Simon, J. (1979) 'Private Classical Schools in Eighteenth-century England: a Critique of Hans' *History of Education* vol 8: 179–91

Simon, J. (1988) 'From Charity School to Workhouse in the 1720s: The SPCK and Mr. Marriott's solution' *History of Education* vol 17: 113–29

Smith, D.M. (1973) *A Guide to the Archive Collection of the Borthwick Institute of Historical Research* (Borthwick Texts and Calendars: Records of the Northern Province 1)

Smith, D. E. (1992) 'Literacy in West Yorkshire and West Sussex' *Journal of Educational Administration and History* vol 24: 58–73

Smith, G.A. *The Development of the Grammar Schools in Sheffield 1603–1933* (Typescript, Sheffield Local Studies Library)

Smith, H.L. (1982) *Reason's Disciples. Seventeenth-century English Feminists* (Urbana, University of Illinois Press)

Statutes of the Realm printed by command of his Majesty King George the Third (1817) III, 988–93. 37° Henry VIII c.4. An act for dissolution of Colleges

Stephens, J.E. (1967) 'Investment and Intervention in Education during the Interregnum' *British Journal of Educational Studies* vol XV: 253–62

Stephens, J.E. (1971) 'Yorkshire Schoolmasters 1640–1660' *Yorkshire Archaeological Journal* vol 42: 181–6

Stephens, J.E. (1977) 'Yorkshire Schools 1660–1700' *Durham Research Review* vol VIII: 56–66

Stephens, J.E. (1983) 'Yorkshire Schoolmasters 1660–1700' *Durham and Newcastle Research Review* vol X: 90–94

Stephens, J.E. (1984) 'Schools and Chancery Controls in 17th century Yorkshire' *Aspects of Education* no 31: 4–19

Stone, L. (1964) 'The Educational Revolution in England 1560–1640' *Past and Present* no 28: 41–80

Stone, L. (1969) 'Literacy and Education in England 1640–1900' *Past and Present* no 42: 69–139

Stone, L. (1977) *The Family Sex and Marriage in England 1500–1800* (Weidenfeld and Nicolson)

Stowe, A.M. (1908) *English Grammar Schools in the Reign of Queen Elizabeth* (New York, Columbia University Teachers College)

Sylvester, D.W., ed. (1970) *Educational Documents 800–1816* (Methuen)

Talbott, J. (1707) *The Christian Schoolmaster: or, The Duty of those who are Employ'd in the Publick Instruction of Children: especially in Charity Schools. To which is added, a Collection of Prayers upon several occasions, for the Use of the Master and Scholars. Together with Directions and Instructions concerning Confirmation; and suitable Devotions Before, At and After it* (Joseph Downing)

Tate, W.E. (1952–3, 1953–4) 'Some Sources for the History of English Grammar Schools' Parts I, II, III *British Journal of Educational Studies* vol I: 164–75; vol II: 67–81, 145–65

Tate, W.E. (1955) 'Some Yorkshire Charity School References in the Archives of SPCK 1700–1774' *Researches and Studies* (University of Leeds Institute of Education) no 12: 4–17

Tate, W.E. (1956) 'The Episcopal Licensing of Schoolmasters in England' *Church Quarterly Review* vol CLVII: 426–32

Tate, W.E. (1963) *A.F. Leach as a historian of Yorkshire Education with an Index of the Yorkshire Schools (c.730–c.1770) referred to in his works, etc. and some corrigenda* (York, St Anthony's Hall Publications, no 23)

Taylor, E.G.R. (1954) *The Mathematical Practitioners of Tudor and Stuart England* (Cambridge, Cambridge University Press for the Institute of Navigation)

Taylor, E.G.R. (1966) *The Mathematical Practioners of Hanoverian England 1714–1840* (Cambridge, Cambridge University Press for the Institute of Navigation)

Thompson, H. (1879) *A History of Ackworth School during its first hundred years* (The Centenary Committee, Ackworth School)

Thoresby, R. (1816) *Ducatus Leodiensis: or, The Topography of the Ancient and Populous Town and Parish of Leedes, and Parts Adjacent...* 2nd edn by Whitaker, T.D. (Leeds: Robinson Son and Holdsworth; Wakefield: John Hurst)

Thoresby, R. (1830) *The Diary of...Author of the Topography of Leeds (1677–1724)* 2 vols (Hunter, J., ed.) (Henry Colburn and Richard Bentley)

(Thornton, Alice) (1875) *The Autobiography of Mrs. Alice Thornton of East Newton co. York* (Surtees Society vol LXII)

Tompson, R.S. (1970) 'The Leeds Grammar School Case of 1805' *Journal of Educational Administration and History* vol III: 1–6

Tompson, R.S. (1971a) *Classics or Charity? The dilemma of the 18th century grammar school* (Manchester, Manchester University Press)

Tompson, R.S. (1971b) 'The English Grammar School Curriculum in the 18th Century: A Reappraisal' *British Journal of Educational Studies* vol XIX: 32–9

Towlson, C.W. (1954) 'Methodism in Yorkshire' in Popham (ed.) *A History of Christianity in Yorkshire* (Wallington, The Religious Education Press)

Turner, W. (1813–15/1957) *The Warrington Academy* (Warrington, Library and Museum Committee, reprinted)

Unwin, R.W. (1982) 'Patronage and Preferment. A Study of James Talbot, Cambridge Fellow and Rector of Spofforth, 1664–1708' *Proceedings of the Leeds Philosophical and Literary Society. Literary and Historical Section* vol XIX.II: 9–37

Unwin, R.W. (1984) *Charity Schools and the defence of Anglicanism: James Talbot, rector of Spofforth 1700–08* (University of York, Borthwick Paper no 65)

Unwin, R.W. and Stephens, W.B., eds (1976) *Yorkshire Schools and Schooldays* (University of Leeds Institute of Education Paper no 14)

Venn, J. (1904) *Annals of a Clerical Family being some account of the family and descendants of William Venn, vicar of Otterton, Devon, 1600–1621* (Macmillan)

Venn, J. (1922–7) *Alumni Cantabrigienses. Part I. From the earliest times to 1751* 4 vols (Cambridge, Cambridge University Press)

Vickerstaff, J.J. (1990) 'Profession and preferment amongst Durham County Schoolmasters 1400–1550' *History of Education* vol 19: 273–82

Victoria County History:

(The 1959–89 volumes all published by Oxford University Press for the Institute of Historical Research)

(1907) *Yorkshire* vol I W. Page (ed.): 415–500. Leach, A.F. 'Schools' (Archibald Constable)

(1959) *Cambridge and the Isle of Ely* vol III *The City and University of Cambridge* J.P.C. Roach (ed.)

(1961) *Yorkshire. The City of York* P.M. Tillott (ed.): 207–53 'York in the 18th Century'; 440–60 'Schools and Colleges'

(1969) *Yorkshire East Riding* I, *The City of Kingston-upon-Hull* K.J. Allison (ed.): 90–173 'Hull in the 16th and 17th centuries'; 174–214 'Hull, 1700–1835'; 348–70 'Education'

(1989) *Yorkshire East Riding* VI, *The Borough and Liberties of Beverley* K.J. Allison (ed.): 112–35 'Beverley 1700–1815'; 250–61 'Education'

Vincent, W.A.L. (1950) *The State and School Education 1640–1660 in England and Wales* (SPCK)

Vincent, W.A.L. (1969) *The Grammar Schools. Their Continuing Tradition 1660–1714* (John Murray)

Walker, E.M. (1945) 'Letters of the Rev. George Plaxton, Rector of Barwick-in-Elmet' *Thoresby Miscellany II* (Thoresby Society Publications vol XXXVII): 30–104

Walker, J.W. (1966) *Wakefield Its History and People* 2 vols. (3rd edn, reprint of 2nd edn, 1939, Wakefield, S.R. Publishers)

Wallis, P.J. (1951–7) 'Thomas Smith – Benefactor of Sheffield Grammar School' *Transactions of the Hunter Archaeological Society* vol VII: 188–93

Wallis, P.J. (1952) 'The Wase School Collection. A neglected source in educational history' *Bodleian Library Record* vol IV: 78–104

Wallis, P.J. (1958) 'Worsborough Grammar School' *Yorkshire Archaeological Journal* vol 39: 147–63

Wallis, P.J. (1963–4) 'Leach – Past, Present and Future' *British Journal of Educational Studies* vol XII: 184–94

Wallis, P.J. and Tate, W.E. (1956) ' A Register of Old Yorkshire Grammar Schools' *Researches and Studies* no 13: 64–104

Walsh, J., Haydon, C. and Taylor, S., eds (1993) *The Church of England c.1689–c.1833. From Toleration to Tractarianism* (Cambridge, Cambridge University Press). *See* Rose, C. (1993); Walsh, J. and Taylor, S. (1993)

Walsh, J. and Taylor, S. (1993) 'The Church and Anglicanism in the 'long' eighteenth century' in Walsh J., Haydon, C and Taylor, S. (eds) *The Church of England c.1689–c.1833......*

Wase, C. (1678) *Considerations concerning Free Schools as settled in England* (Oxford, 'at the Theater')

Watson, F. (1900) 'The State and Education under the Commonwealth' *English Historical Review* vol XV: 58–72

Watson, F. (1908) *The English Grammar Schools to 1660: their curriculum and practice* (Cambridge, Cambridge University Press)

Watson, F. (1909/1971) *The Beginning of the Teaching of Modern Subjects in England* (Isaac Pitman, reprinted East Ardsley,S.R. Publishers)

Watson, F. (1916) *The Old Grammar Schools* (Cambridge, Cambridge University Press)

Waugh, W.T. (1909) *A History of Fulneck School* (Leeds, Richard Jackson)

Webb, S. and B. (1927) *English Local Government: English Poor Law History: Part I The Old Poor Law* (Longmans Green)

Webster, C. (1975) 'The Curriculum of the Grammar Schools and Universities 1500–1660: A Critical Review of the Literature' *History of Education vol* 4: 51–68

Wenham, L.P. (1951) 'Two Notes on the History of Richmond School, Yorkshire' *Yorkshire Archaeological Journal* vol 37: 369–75

Wenham, L.P. (1955) 'The Chantries, Guilds, Obits and Lights of Richmond, Yorkshire' Parts I, II, III *Yorkshire Archaeological Journal* vol 38: 96–111, 185–214, 310–32

Wenham, L.P. (1958) *The History of Richmond School, Yorkshire* (Arbroath, The Herald Press)

Wenham, L.P., ed. (1965) *Letters of James Tate* (Yorkshire Archaeological Society Record Series vol CXXVIII)

Wentworth Papers 1597–1628, J.P. Cooper ed. (1973) (Royal Historical Society, Camden Fourth Series 12)

Whitaker, T.D. (1823) *An History of Richmondshire, in the North Riding of the County of York; together with those parts of the Everwicschire of Domesday which form the Wapentakes of Lonsdale, Ewcross and Amunderness, in the Counties of York, Lancaster, and Westmorland* 2 vols (Longman, Hurst, Rees, Orme and Brown)

Whiting, C.E., ed. (1951) *Two Yorkshire Diaries. The Diary of Arthur Jessop and Ralph Ward's Journal* (Yorkshire Archaeological Society Record Series vol CXVII

Wigfull, J. R. (1925–8) 'An Early Sheffield School' *Transactions of the Hunter Archaeological Society* vol III: 336–43

Wigfull, J.R. (1929–37) 'Sheffield Grammar School' *Transactions of the Hunter Archaeological Society* vol IV: 283–300

Wilkinson, J. (n.d.) *Worthies, Families and Celebrities of Barnsley and the District* (Bemrose and Sons)

Wilkinson, J. (1872) *Worsborough; its historical associations and rural attractions* (Farrington)

Wilson, R. (1984) 'The Archbishop Herring Visitation Returns: A Vignette of Yorkshire Education' *Aspects of Education* no 31: 92–130

Wilson, R.G. (1971) *Gentlemen Merchants. The merchant community in Leeds 1700–1830* (Manchester, Manchester University Press/Augustus M. Kelley)

Wood, N. (1931) *The Reformation and English Education. A Study of the influence of religious uniformity on English education in the sixteenth century* (Routledge)

Wood-Legh, K.L. (1965) *Perpetual Chantries in Britain* (Cambridge, Cambridge University Press)

(Workhouses 1732) *An Account of Several Work-Houses for Employing and Maintaining the Poor; setting forth The Rules by which they are governed, their great Usefulness to the Publick, and in Particular To the Parishes where they are erected. And also of several Charity Schools for promoting Work and Labour* 2nd edn (Jos. Downing)

Wright, L.B. (1935) *Middle-Class Culture in Elizabethan England* (Chapel Hill, NC, University of North Carolina Press)

[Wroe, H. and Green, W.H.] (?1934) *Rotherham Grammar School 1483–1933. A Short History commemorating the 450th Anniversary of the Foundation* (Bradford, Percy Lund, Humphries)

Wykes, D.L. (1991) 'Manchester College at York (1803–1840); Its Intellectual and Cultural Contribution' *Yorkshire Archaeological Journal* vol 63: 207–18

Yorkshire Record Offices, A Brief Guide to (1968) (York, Borthwick Institute of Historical Research)

Zouch, T. (1820) 'The Good Schoolmaster' (1798) in *The Works of...with a Memoir of his life* 2 vols (York, Thomas Wilson)

INDEX

(Complex entries are in general listed in chronological order of their appearance in the text)

General Themes

348

349

other references 53, 75, 79, 98, 99, 220, 252–3, 254; Roman Catholic schools 56, 62, 267–9; Blue Coat and Grey Coat charity schools 206–7, 239–44; private schools 276–7, 283–4; Quaker schools 264–5; Manchester College (1803–40) 263

North Riding

Ainderby Steeple 63, 85, 86, 102, 104

Ampleforth 176, 269

Arkengarthdale 150

Bagby 53

Barningham 103

Barton Cuthberts *see* Gilling

Bedale 30, 54, 86, 102, 179, 241

Bolton-upon-Swale 86

Bowes 86, 193

Brandsby (Bransby) 266

Burneston 85, 101

Catterick 241

Cleasby 103

Cold Kirkby 224

Coverham 86

Coxwold 113–14

Crambe 55

Crathorne 276

Dalby 266

Danby Wiske 85, 150

Downholme 85

East Harlesey 75

East Witton 103

Egton 62

Eriholme *see* Gilling

Forcett 86

Gilling: 84–5, 103 (Eriholme); 85, 102 (Hartforth); 103 (Barton Cuthberts)

Goathland 224

Great Ayton 201

Great Smeaton 86

Greta Bridge 275

Grinton 85

Guisborough 120, 141, 204, 295

Hackness 64

Hartforth *see* Gilling

Helmsley 78

Hipswell 86

Hovingham 53

Whitby 78, 99

West Riding

Aberford 205, 212, 275

Acaster Malbis 83–4

Acaster Selby 15, 30, 54–5

Ackworth 264

Addingham 200

Adwick-le-Street 55

Aldborough 30, 86

Almondbury 37, 53, 132–3, 193

Armley *see* Leeds

Arncliffe 98

Aston 98

Barnsley 285

Barwick-in-Elmet 80

Batley 106–7, 133, 182–3, 262

Bingley 31, 38, 60, 186–7, 252

Birstall 222, 262

Bolton Percy 99

Bolton-upon-Dearne 30, 64

Boroughbridge 85

Bradfield 161

Bradford: grammar school 31, 37–8, 53, 60, 183; John and Abraham Sharp 158, 160–61; private schools 288

Brighouse 80, 99

Brotherton 99

Burnsall 114

Calverley 99

Catcliffe *see* Rotherham

Cawthorne 30, 64

Clapham 100, 103

Coley *see* Halifax

Collingham 205, 228

Colton 99

Crofton 30, 286–8

Darrington 224

Dent 158

Dewsbury 99, 226

Doncaster 13, 31, 162, 277–8, 280, 286

Drax 55

Drighlington 180

Ecclesfield 64, 75

MELLEN STUDIES IN EDUCATION